California Standards
Enrichment Workbook

McDOUGAL LITTELL

Creating America

A History of the United States

Beginnings through World War I

California Consultant

Neal Cates
Long Beach Unified School District
Lakewood, California

McDougal Littell
A DIVISION OF HOUGHTON MIFFLIN COMPANY

ART CREDITS

xviii *left* Steve Adams/National Geographic Image Collection; *right* The Granger Collection; **xix** *left, right* The Granger Collection; **64** The Library of Congress; **186** Courtesy of the Boston Public Library

ACKNOWLEDGMENTS

Excerpt from "The Analects of Confucius," translated by Patricia Buckley Ebrey. Reprinted with the permission of The Free Press, an imprint of Simon & Schuster Adult Publishing Group, from *Chinese Civilization: A Sourcebook*, edited by Patricia Buckley Ebrey. Copyright © 1993 by Patricia Buckley Ebrey. Copyright © 1981 by The Free Press.

Excerpt from "The Laozi," translated by Patricia Buckley Ebrey. Reprinted with the permission of The Free Press, an imprint of Simon & Schuster Adult Publishing Group, from *Chinese Civilization: A Sourcebook,* edited by Patricia Buckley Ebrey. Copyright © 1993 by Patricia Buckley Ebrey. Copyright © 1981 by The Free Press.

"On Being Demoted and Sent Away to Qizhou" by Wang Wei, from *Laughing Lost in the Mountains: Poems of Wang Wei,* translated by Tony Barnstone, Willis Barnstone, and Xu Haixin. Copyright © 1991 by University Press of New England. Used by permission of University Press of New England.

History-Social Science Content Standards for California Public Schools reproduced by permission, California Department of Education, CDE Press, 1430 N Street, Suite 3207, Sacramento, CA 95814.

ISBN-13: 978-0-618-57712-5   ISBN-10: 0-618-57712-2

Printed in the United States of America.

18 19 20 21 22 23   1421   15 14 13 12
4500355794

Contents

QUICK PREP

CA STANDARDS: REPORTING CLUSTER 1: WORLD HISTORY AND GEOGRAPHY: ANCIENT CIVILIZATIONS

CA STANDARDS: REPORTING CLUSTER 2: LATE ANTIQUITY AND THE MIDDLE AGES

CA STANDARDS: REPORTING CLUSTER 5: CIVIL WAR AND ITS AFTERMATH

How to Use This Book

The *California Standards Enrichment Workbook* is yours to mark on, to write in, and to make your own. You can use it in class and take it home. The workbook will help you master social studies curriculum, point by point.

For each specific objective or goal in the Grade 8 California Content Standards, your book contains:

- a **Review** page, to summarize the most important content—the issues, ideas, and people behind important events.

- a **Practice** page, that asks you to recall, interpret, analyze, and apply the historical knowledge.

Complete the pages in the order your teacher assigns them. Your teacher will assign pages that match material in your social studies textbook.

You can use the **Quick Prep** section (pages 1–22) to scan important historic eras, leaders, data, and dates, and to look up and learn key terms. The Quick Prep section serves as a handy reference:

- As you work on Review and Practice pages, you can look up key ideas, dates, and definitions.

- The data can help you make inferences, make connections, or answer your own questions as they arise.

- Before a big test, you might use the Quick Prep to review with a peer, a tutor or family member, or on your own.

California History-Social Science Standards

GRADE 6 History-Social Science Content Standards
Reporting Cluster 1: World History and Geography: Ancient Civilizations

6.1 Students describe what is known through archaeological studies of the early physical and cultural development of humankind from the Paleolithic era to the agricultural revolution.

1. Describe the hunter-gatherer societies, including the development of tools and the use of fire.

2. Identify the locations of human communities that populated the major regions of the world and describe how human adapted to a variety of environments.

3. Discuss the climatic changes and human modifications of the physical environment that gave rise to the domestication of plants and animals and new sources of clothing and shelter.

6.2 Students analyze the geographic, political, economic, religious, and social structures of the early civilizations of Mesopotamia, Egypt, and Kush.

1. Locate and describe the major river systems and discuss the physical settings that supported permanent settlement and early civilizations.

2. Trace the development of agricultural techniques that permitted the production of economic surplus and the emergence of cities as centers of culture and power.

3. Understand the relationship between religion and the social and political order in Mesopotamia and Egypt.

4. Know the significance of Hammurabi's Code.

5. Discuss the main features of Egyptian art and architecture.

6. Describe the role of Egyptian trade in the eastern Mediterranean and Nile valley.

7. Understand the significance of Queen Hatshepsut and Ramses the Great.

8. Identify the location of the Kush civilization and describe its political, commercial, and cultural relations with Egypt.

9. Trace the evolution of language and its written forms.

6.3 Students analyze the geographic, political, economic, religious, and social structures of the Ancient Hebrews.

1. Describe the origins and significance of Judaism as the first monotheistic religion based on the concept of one God who sets down moral laws for humanity.

2. Identify the sources of the ethical teachings and central beliefs of Judaism (the Hebrew Bible, the Commentaries): belief in God, observance of law, practice of the concepts of righteousness and justice, and importance of study; and describe how the ideas of the Hebrew traditions are reflected in the moral and ethical traditions of Western civilization.

3. Explain the significance of Abraham, Moses, Naomi, Ruth, David, and Yohanan ben Zaccai in the development of the Jewish religion.

4. Discuss the locations of the settlements and movements of Hebrew people, including the Exodus and their movement to and from Egypt, and outline the significance of the Exodus to the Jewish and other people.

5. Discuss how Judaism survived and developed despite the continuing dispersion of much of the Jewish population from Jerusalem and the rest of Israel after the destruction of the second Temple in A.D. 70.

6.4 Students analyze the geographic, political, economic, religious, and social structures of the early civilization of Ancient Greece.

1. Discuss the connections between geography and the development of city-states in the region of the Aegean Sea, including patterns of trade and commerce among Greek city-states and within the wider Mediterranean region.

2. Trace the transition from tyranny and oligarchy to early democratic forms of government and back to dictatorship in ancient Greece, including the significance of the invention of the idea of citizenship (e.g., from Pericles' Funeral Oration).

3. State the key differences between Athenian, or direct, democracy and representative democracy.

4. Explain the significance of Greek mythology to the everyday life of people in the region and how Greek literature continues to permeate our literature and language today, drawing from Greek mythology and epics, such as Homer's *Iliad* and *Odyssey,* and from Aesop's Fables.

5. Outline the founding, expansion, and political organization of the Persian Empire.

6. Compare and contrast life in Athens and Sparta, with emphasis on their roles in the Persian and Peloponnesian Wars.

7. Trace the rise of Alexander the Great and the spread of Greek culture eastward and into Egypt.

8. Describe the enduring contributions of important Greek figures in the arts and sciences (e.g., Hypatia, Socrates, Plato, Aristotle, Euclid, Thucydides).

6.5 Students analyze the geographic, political economic, religious, and social structures of the early civilizations of India.

1. Locate and describe the major river system and discuss the physical setting that supported the rise of this civilization.

2. Discuss the significance of the Aryan invasions.

3. Explain the major beliefs and practices of Brahmanism in India and how they evolved into early Hinduism.

4. Outline the social structure of the caste system.

5. Know the life and moral teachings of Buddha and how Buddhism spread in India, Ceylon, and Central Asia.

6. Describe the growth of the Maurya empire and the political and moral achievements of the emperor Asoka.

7. Discuss important aesthetic and intellectual traditions (e.g., Sanskrit literature, including the *Bhagavad Gita;* medicine; metallurgy; and mathematics, including Hindu-Arabic numerals and the zero).

6.6 Students analyze the geographic, political, economic religious, and social structures of the early civilizations of China.

1. Locate and describe the origins of Chinese civilization in the Huang-He Valley during the Shang Dynasty.

2. Explain the geographic features of China that made governance and the spread of ideas and goods difficult and served to isolate the country from the rest of the world.

3. Know about the life of Confucius and the fundamental teachings of Confucianism and Taoism.

4. Identify the political and cultural problems prevalent in the time of Confucius and how he sought to solve them.

5. List the policies and achievements of the emperor Shi Huangdi in unifying northern China under the Qin Dynasty.

6. Detail the political contributions of the Han Dynasty to the development of the imperial bureaucratic state and the expansion of the empire.

7. Cite the significance of the trans-Eurasian "silk roads" in the period of the Han Dynasty and Roman Empire and their locations.

8. Describe the diffusion of Buddhism northward to China during the Han Dynasty.

6.7 Students analyze the geographic, political, economic, religious, and social structures during the development of Rome.

1. Identify the location and describe the rise of the Roman Republic, including the importance of such mythical and historical figures as Aeneas, Romulus and Remus, Cincinnatus, Julius Caesar, and Cicero.

2. Describe the government of the Roman Republic and its significance (e.g., written constitution and tripartite government, checks and balances, civic duty).

3. Identify the location of and the political and geographic reasons for the growth of Roman territories and expansion of the empire, including how the empire fostered economic growth through the use of currency and trade routes.

4. Discuss the influence of Julius Caesar and Augustus in Rome's transition from republic to empire.

5. Trace the migration of Jews around the Mediterranean region and the effects of their conflict with the Romans, including the Romans' restrictions on their right to live in Jerusalem.

6. Note the origins of Christianity in the Jewish Messianic prophecies, the life and teachings of Jesus of Nazareth as described in the New Testament, and the contribution of St. Paul the Apostle to the definition and spread of Christian beliefs (e.g., belief in the Trinity, resurrection, salvation).

7. Describe the circumstances that led to the spread of Christianity in Europe and other Roman territories.

8. Discuss the legacies of Roman art and architecture, technology and science, literature, language, and law.

6.6 **Students analyze the geographic, political, economic religious, and social structures of the early civilizations of China.**

1. Locate and describe the origins of Chinese civilization in the Huang-He Valley during the Shang Dynasty.

2. Explain the geographic features of China that made governance and the spread of ideas and goods difficult and served to isolate the country from the rest of the world.

3. Know about the life of Confucius and the fundamental teachings of Confucianism and Taoism.

4. Identify the political and cultural problems prevalent in the time of Confucius and how he sought to solve them.

5. List the policies and achievements of the emperor Shi Huangdi in unifying northern China under the Qin Dynasty.

6. Detail the political contributions of the Han Dynasty to the development of the imperial bureaucratic state and the expansion of the empire.

7. Cite the significance of the trans-Eurasian "silk roads" in the period of the Han Dynasty and Roman Empire and their locations.

8. Describe the diffusion of Buddhism northward to China during the Han Dynasty.

6.7 **Students analyze the geographic, political, economic, religious, and social structures during the development of Rome.**

1. Identify the location and describe the rise of the Roman Republic, including the importance of such mythical and historical figures as Aeneas, Romulus and Remus, Cincinnatus, Julius Caesar, and Cicero.

2. Describe the government of the Roman Republic and its significance (e.g., written constitution and tripartite government, checks and balances, civic duty).

3. Identify the location of and the political and geographic reasons for the growth of Roman territories and expansion of the empire, including how the empire fostered economic growth through the use of currency and trade routes.

4. Discuss the influence of Julius Caesar and Augustus in Rome's transition from republic to empire.

5. Trace the migration of Jews around the Mediterranean region and the effects of their conflict with the Romans, including the Romans' restrictions on their right to live in Jerusalem.

6. Note the origins of Christianity in the Jewish Messianic prophecies, the life and teachings of Jesus of Nazareth as described in the New Testament, and the contribution of St. Paul the Apostle to the definition and spread of Christian beliefs (e.g., belief in the Trinity, resurrection, salvation).

7. Describe the circumstances that led to the spread of Christianity in Europe and other Roman territories.

8. Discuss the legacies of Roman art and architecture, technology and science, literature, language, and law.

GRADE 7 History-Social Science Content Standards
Reporting Cluster 2: Late Antiquity and the Middle Ages

7.1 **Students analyze the causes and effects of the vast expansion and ultimate disintegration of the Roman Empire.**

1. Study the early strengths and lasting contributions of Rome (e.g., significance of Roman citizenship; rights under Roman law; Roman art, architecture, engineering, and philosophy; preservation and transmission of Christianity) and its ultimate internal weaknesses (e.g., rise of autonomous military powers within the empire, undermining of citizenship by the growth of corruption and slavery, lack of education, and distribution of news).

2. Discuss the geographic borders of the empire at its height and the factors that threatened its territorial cohesion.

3. Describe the establishment by Constantine of the new capital in Constantinople and the development of the Byzantine Empire, with an emphasis on the consequences of the development of two distinct European civilizations, Eastern Orthodox and Roman Catholic, and their two distinct views on church-state relations.

7.2 **Students analyze the geographic, political, economic, religious, and social structures of the civilizations of Islam in the Middle Ages.**

1. Identify the physical features and describe the climate of the Arabian peninsula, its relationship to surrounding bodies of land and water, and nomadic and sedentary ways of life.

2. Trace the origins of Islam and the life and teachings of Muhammad, including Islamic teachings on the connection with Judaism and Christianity.

3. Explain the significance of the Qur'an and the Sunnah as the primary sources of Islamic beliefs, practice, and law, and their influence in Muslims' daily life.

4. Discuss the expansion of Muslim rule through military conquests and treaties, emphasizing the cultural blending within Muslim civilization and the spread and acceptance of Islam and the Arabic language.

5. Describe the growth of cities and the establishment of trade routes among Asia, Africa, and Europe, the products and inventions that traveled along these routes (e.g., spices, textiles, paper, steel, new crops), and the role of merchants in Arab society.

6. Understand the intellectual exchanges among Muslim scholars of Eurasia and Africa and the contributions Muslim scholars made to later civilizations in the areas of science, geography, mathematics, philosophy, medicine, art, and literature.

7.3 Students analyze the geographic, political, economic, religious, and social structures of the civilizations of China in the Middle Ages.

1. Describe the reunification of China under the Tang Dynasty and reasons for the spread of Buddhism in Tang China, Korea, and Japan.

2. Describe agricultural, technological, and commercial developments during the Tang and Sung periods.

3. Analyze the influences of Confucianism and changes in Confucian thought during the Sung and Mongol periods.

4. Understand the importance of both overland trade and maritime expeditions between China and other civilizations in the Mongol Ascendancy and Ming Dynasty.

5. Trace the historic influence of such discoveries as tea, the manufacture of paper, wood-block printing, the compass, and gunpowder.

6. Describe the development of the imperial state and the scholar-official class.

7.4 Students analyze the geographic, political, economic, religious, and social structures of the sub-Saharan civilizations of Ghana and Mali in Medieval Africa.

1. Study the Niger River and the relationship of vegetation zones of forest, savannah, and desert to trade gold, salt, food, and slaves; and the growth of the Ghana and Mali empires.

2. Analyze the importance of family, labor specialization, and regional commerce in the development of states and cities in West Africa.

3. Describe the role of the trans-Saharan caravan trade in the changing religious and cultural characteristics of West Africa and the influence of Islamic beliefs, ethics, and law.

4. Trace the growth of the Arabic language in government, trade, and Islamic scholarship in West Africa.

5. Describe the importance of written and oral traditions in the transmission of African history and culture.

7.5 Students analyze the geographic, political, economic, religious, and social structures of the civilizations of Medieval Japan.

1. Describe the significance of Japan's proximity to China and Korea and the intellectual, linguistic, religious, and philosophical influence of those countries on Japan.

2. Discuss the reign of Prince Shotoku of Japan and the characteristics of Japanese society and family life during his reign.

3. Describe the values, social customs, and traditions prescribed by the lord-vassal system consisting of shogun, daimyo, and samurai and the lasting influence of the warrior code in the twentieth century.

4. Trace the development of distinctive forms of Japanese Buddhism.

5. Study the ninth and tenth centuries' golden age of literature, art, and drama and its lasting effects on culture today, including Murasaki Shikibu's Tale of Genji.

6. Analyze the rise of a military society in the late twelfth century and the role of the samurai in that society.

7.6 Students analyze the geographic, political, economic, religious, and social structures of the civilizations of Medieval Europe.

1. Study the geography of the Europe and the Eurasian land mass, including its location, topography, waterways, vegetation, and climate and their relationship to ways of life in Medieval Europe.

2. Describe the spread of Christianity north of the Alps and the roles played by the early church and by monasteries in its diffusion after the fall of the western half of the Roman Empire.

3. Understand the development of feudalism, its role in the medieval European economy, the way in which it was influenced by physical geography (the role of the manor and the growth of towns), and how feudal relationships provided the foundation of political order.

4. Demonstrate an understanding of the conflict and cooperation between the Papacy and European monarch (e.g., Charlemagne, Gregory VII, Emperor Henry IV).

5. Know the significance of developments in medieval English legal and constitutional practices and their importance in the rise of modern democratic thought and representative institutions (e.g., Magna Carta, parliament, development of habeas corpus, and independent judiciary in England).

6. Discuss the causes and course of the religious Crusades and their effects on the Christian, Muslim, and Jewish populations in Europe, with emphasis on the increasing contact by Europeans with cultures of the Eastern Mediterranean world.

7. Map the spread of the bubonic plague from Central Asia to China, the Middle East, and Europe and describe its impact on global population.

8. Understand the importance of the Catholic church as a political, intellectual, and aesthetic institution (e.g., founding of universities, political and spiritual roles of the clergy, creation of monastic and mendicant religious orders, preservation of the Latin language and religious texts, St. Thomas Aquinas's synthesis of classical philosophy with Christian theology, and the concept of "natural law").

9. Know the history of the decline of Muslim rule in the Iberian Peninsula that culminated in the Reconquista and the rise of Spanish and Portuguese kingdoms.

7.7 Students compare and contrast the geographic, political, economic, religious, and social structures of the Meso-American and Andean civilizations.

1. Study the locations, landforms, and climates of Mexico, Central America, and South America and their effects on Mayan, Aztec, and Incan economies, trade, and development of urban societies.

2. Study the roles of people in each society, including class structures, family life, warfare, religious beliefs and practices, and slavery.

3. Explain how and where each empire arose and how the Aztec and Incan empires were defeated by the Spanish.

4. Describe the artistic and oral traditions and architecture in the three civilizations.

5. Describe the Meso-American achievements in astronomy and mathematics, including the development of the calendar and the Meso-American knowledge of seasonal changes to the civilizations' agricultural systems.

GRADE 7 History-Social Science Content Standards
Reporting Cluster 2: Renaissance/Reformation

7.8 Students analyze the origins, accomplishments, and geographic diffusion of the Renaissance.

1. Describe the way in which the revival of classical learning and the arts fostered a new interest in humanism (i.e., a balance between intellect and religious faith).

2. Explain the importance of Florence in the early stages of the Renaissance and the growth of independent trading cities (e.g., Venice), with emphasis on the cities' importance in the spread of Renaissance ideas.

3. Understand the effects of the reopening of the ancient "Silk Road" between Europe and China, including Marco Polo's travels and the location of his routes.

4. Describe the growth and effect of new ways of disseminating information (e.g., the ability to manufacture paper, translation of the Bible in the vernacular, printing).

5. Detail advances made in literature, the arts, science, mathematics, cartography, engineering, and the understanding of human anatomy and astronomy (e.g., by Dante Alighieri, Leonardo da Vinci, Michelangelo de Buonarroti Simoni, Johann Gutenberg, William Shakespeare).

7.9 Students analyze the historical developments of the Reformation.

1. List the causes for the internal turmoil in and weakening of the Catholic church (e.g., tax policies, selling of indulgences).

2. Describe the theological, political, and economic ideas of the major figures during the Reformation (e.g., Desiderius Erasmus, Martin Luther, John Calvin, William Tyndale).

3. Explain Protestants' new practices of church self-government and the influence of those practices on the development of democratic practices and ideas of federalism.

4. Identify and locate the European regions that remained Catholic and those became Protestant and explain how the division affected the distribution of religions in the New World.

5. Analyze how the Counter-Reformation revitalized the Catholic church and the forces that fostered the movement (e.g., St. Ignatius of Loyola and the Jesuits, the Council of Trent).

6. Understand the institution and impact of missionaries on Christianity and diffusion of Christianity from Europe to other parts of the word in the medieval and early modern periods; locate missions on a world map.

7. Describe the Golden Age of cooperation between Jews and Muslims in medieval Spain that promoted creativity in art, literature, and science, including how that cooperation was terminated by the religious persecution of individuals and groups (e.g., the Spanish Inquisition and the expulsion of Jews and Muslims from Spain in 1492).

7.10 **Students analyze the historical developments of the Scientific Revolution and its lasting effect on religious, political, and cultural institutions.**

1. Discuss the roots of the Scientific Revolution (e.g., Greek rationalism; Jewish, Christian, and Muslim science; Renaissance humanism; new knowledge from global exploration).

2. Understand the significance of the new scientific theories (e.g., those of Copernicus, Galileo, Kepler, Newton) and the significance of new inventions (e.g., the telescope, microscope, thermometer, barometer).

3. Understand the scientific method advanced by Bacon and Descartes, the influence of new scientific rationalism on the growth of democratic ideas, and the coexistence of science with traditional religious beliefs.

7.11 **Students analyze political and economic change in the sixteenth, seventeenth, and eighteenth centuries (the Age of Exploration, the Enlightenment, and the Age of Reason).**

1. Know the great voyages of discovery, the locations of the routes, and the influence of cartography in the development of a new European worldview.

2. Discuss the exchanges of plants, animals, technology, culture, and ideas among Europe, Africa, Asia, and the Americas in the fifteenth and sixteenth centuries and the major economic and social effects on each continent.

3. Examine the origins of modern capitalism; the influence of mercantilism and cottage industry; the elements and importance of a market economy in seventeenth-century Europe; the changing international trading and marketing patterns, including their locations on a world map; and the influence of explorers and map makers.

4. Explain how the main ideas of the Enlightenment can be traced back to such movement as the Renaissance, the Reformation, and the Scientific Revolution and to the Greeks, Romans, and Christianity.

5. Describe how democratic thought and institutions were influenced by Enlightenment thinkers (e.g., John Locke, Charles-Louis Montesquieu, American founders).

6. Discuss how the principles in the Magna Carta were embodied in such documents as the English Bill of Rights and the American Declaration of Independence.

GRADE 8 History-Social Science Content Standards
Reporting Cluster 4: U.S. Constitution and the Early Republic

8.1 **Students understand the major events preceding the founding of the nation and related their significance to the development of American constitutional democracy.**

1. Describe the relationship between the moral and political ideas of the Great Awakening and the development of revolutionary fervor.

2. Analyze the philosophy of government expressed in the Declaration of Independence, with an emphasis on government as a means of securing individual rights (e.g., key phrases such as "all men are created equal, that they are endowed by their Creator with certain unalienable Rights").

3. Analyze how the American Revolution affected other nations, especially France.

4. Describe the nation's blend of civic republicanism, classical liberal principles, and English parliamentary traditions.

8.2 **Students analyze the political principles underlying the U.S. Constitution and compare the enumerated and implied powers of the federal government.**

1. Discuss the significance of the Magna Carta, the English Bill of Rights, and the Mayflower Compact.

2. Analyze the Articles of Confederation and the Constitution and the success of each in implementing the ideals of the Declaration of Independence.

3. Evaluate the major debates that occurred during the development of the Constitution and their ultimate resolutions in such areas as shared power among institutions, divided state-federal power, slavery, the rights of individuals and states (later address by the addition of the Bill of Rights), and the status of American Indian nations under the commerce clause.

4. Describe the political philosophy underpinning the Constitution as specified in the Federalist Papers (authored by James Madison, Alexander Hamilton, and John Jay) and the role of such leaders as Madison, George Washington, Roger Sherman, Gouverneur Morris, and James Wilson in the writing and ratification of the Constitution.

5. Understand the significance of Jefferson's Statue for Religious Freedom as a forerunner of the First Amendment and the origins, purpose, and differing views of the founding father on the issue of the separation of church and state.

6. Enumerate the powers of government set forth in the Constitution and the fundamental liberties ensured by the Bill of Rights.

7. Describe the principles of federalism, dual sovereignty, separation of powers, checks and balances, the nature and purpose of majority rule, and the ways in which the American idea of constitutionalism preserves individual rights.

8.3 Students understand the foundation of the American political system and the ways in which citizens participate in it.

1. Analyze the principles and contexts codified in state constitutions between 1777 and 1781 that created the context out of which American political institutions and ideas developed.

2. Explain how the ordinances of 1785 and 1878 privatized national resources and transferred federally owned lands into private holdings, townships, and states.

3. Enumerate the advantages of a common market among the states as foreseen in and protected by the Constitution's clauses on interstate commerce, common coinage, and full-faith credit.

4. Understand how the conflicts between Thomas Jefferson and Alexander Hamilton resulted in the emergence of two political parties (e.g., view of foreign policy, Alien and Sedition Acts, economic policy, National Bank, funding and assumption of the revolutionary debt).

5. Know the significance of domestic resistance movements and ways in which the central government responded to such movements (e.g., Shay's Rebellion, the Whiskey Rebellion).

6. Describe the basic law-making process and how the Constitution provides numerous opportunities for citizens to participate in the political process and to monitor and influence government (e.g., function of elections, political parties, interest groups).

7. Understand the functions and responsibilities of a free press.

8.4 Students analyze the aspirations and ideals of the people of a new nation.

1. Describe the country's physical landscapes, political divisions, and territorial expansion during the terms of the first four presidents.

2. Explain the policy significance of famous speeches (e.g., Washington's Farewell Address, Jefferson's 1801 Inaugural Address, John Q. Adams's Fourth of July 1821 Address).

3. Analyze the rise of capitalism and the economic problems and conflicts that accompanied it (e.g., Jackson's opposition to the National Bank; early decisions of the U.S. Supreme Court that reinforced the sanctity of contracts and a capitalistic economic system of law).

4. Discuss daily life, including traditions in art, music and literature, of early national American (e.g., through writings by Washington Irving, James Fenimore Cooper).

8.5 Students analyze U.S. foreign policy in the early Republic.

1. Understand the political and economic causes and consequences of the War of 1812 and know the major battles, leaders, and events that led to a final peace.

2. Know the changing boundaries of the United States and describe the relationships the country had with its neighbors (current Mexico and Canada) and Europe, including the influence of the Monroe Doctrine, and how those relationships influenced westward expansion and the Mexican-American War.

3. Outline the major treaties with American Indian nations during the administrations of the first four presidents and the varying outcomes of those treaties.

8.6 Students analyze the divergent paths of the American people from 1800 to the mid-1800's and the challenges they faced, with emphasis on the Northeast.

1. Discuss the influence of industrialization and technological developments on the region, including human modification of the landscape and how physical geography shaped human actions (e.g., growth of cities, deforestation, farming, mineral extraction).

2. Outline the physical obstacles to and the economic and political factors involved in building a network of roads, canals, and railroads (e.g., Henry Clay's American System).

3. List the reasons for the wave of immigration from Northern Europe to the United States and describe the growth in the number, size, and spatial arrangements of cities (e.g., Irish immigrants and the Great Irish Famine).

4. Study the lives of black American who gained freedom in the North and founded schools and churches to advance their rights and communities.

5. Trace the development of the American education system from its earliest roots, including the roles of religious and private schools and Horace Mann's campaign for free public education and its assimilating role in the American culture.

6. Examine the women's suffrage movement (e.g., biographies writings, and speeches of Elizabeth Cady Stanton, Margaret Fuller, Lucretia Mott, Susan B. Anthony).

7. Identify common themes in American art as well as transcendentalism and individualism (e.g., writings about and by Ralph Waldo Emerson, Henry David Thoreau, Herman Melville, Louisa May Alcott, Nathaniel Hawthorne, Henry Wadsworth Longfellow).

8.7 **Students analyze the divergent paths of the American people in the South from 1800 to the mid-1800s and the challenges they faced.**

1. Describe the development of the agrarian economy in the South, identify the locations of the cotton-producing states, and discuss the significance of cotton and the cotton gin.

2. Trace the origins and development of slavery; its effects on black Americans and on the region's political, social, religious, economic, and cultural development; and identify the strategies that were tried to both overturn and preserve it (e.g., through the writings and historical documents on Nat Turner, Denmark Vesey).

3. Examine the characteristics white Southern society and how the physical environment influenced events and conditions prior to the Civil War.

4. Compare the lives of and opportunities for free blacks in the North with those of free blacks in the South.

8.8 **Students analyze the divergent paths of the American people in the West from 1800 to the mid-1800s and the challenges they faced.**

1. Discuss the election of Andrew Jackson as president in 1828, the importance of Jacksonian democracy, and his actions as president (e.g., the spoils system, veto of the National Bank, policy of Indian removal, opposition to the Supreme Court).

2. Describe the purpose, challenges, and economic incentives associated with westward expansion, including the concept of Manifest Destiny (e.g., the Lewis and Clark expedition, accounts of the removal of Indians, the Cherokees' "Trail of Tears," settlement of the Great Plains) and the territorial acquisitions that spanned numerous decades.

3. Describe the role of pioneer women and the new status that western women achieved (e.g., Laura Ingalls Wilder, Annie Bidwell; slave women gaining freedom in the West; Wyoming granting suffrage to women in 1869).

4. Examine the importance of the great rivers and the struggle over water rights.

5. Discuss Mexican settlements and their locations, cultural traditions, attitudes toward slavery, land grant system, and economies.

6. Describe the Texas War for Independence and the Mexican-American War, including territorial settlements, the aftermath of the wars, and the effect the wars had on the lives of American, including Mexican Americans today.

GRADE 8 History-Social Science Content Standards
Reporting Cluster 5: Civil War and Its Aftermath

8.9 **Students analyze the early and steady attempts to abolish slavery and to realize the ideals of the Declaration of Independence.**

1. Describe the leaders of the movement (e.g., John Quincy Adams and his proposed constitutional amendment, John Brown and the armed resistance, Harriet Tubman and the Underground Railroad, Benjamin Franklin, Theodore Weld, William Lloyd Garrison, Frederick Douglass).

2. Discuss the abolition of slavery in early state constitutions.

3. Describe the significance of the Northwest Ordinance in education and in the banning of slavery in new states north of the Ohio River.

4. Discuss the importance of the slavery issue as raised by the annexation of Texas and California's admission to the union as a free state under the Compromise of 1850.

5. Analyze the significance of the States' Right Doctrine, the Missouri Compromise (1820), the Wilmot Proviso (1846), the Compromise of 1850, Henry clay's role in the Missouri compromise and the Compromise of 1850, the Kansas-Nebraska Act (1854), the Dred Scott v. Sandford decision (1857), and the Lincoln-Douglas debates (1858).

6. Describe the lives of free blacks and the laws that limited their freedom and economic opportunities.

8.10 **Students analyze the multiple causes, key events, and complex consequences of the Civil War.**

1. Compare the conflicting interpretations of state and federal authority as emphasized in the speeches and writing of statesmen such as Daniel Webster and John C. Calhoun.

2. Trace the boundaries constituting the North and the South, the geographical differences between the two regions, and the differences between agrarians and industrialists.

3. Identify the constitutional issues posed by the doctrine of nullification and secession and the earliest origins of that doctrine.

4. Discuss Abraham Lincoln's presidency and his significant writings and speeches and their relationship to the Declaration of Independence, such as his "House Divided" speech (1858), Gettysburg Address (1863), Emancipation Proclamation (1863), and inaugural addresses (1861 and 1865).

5. Study the views and lives of leaders (e.g., Ulysses S. Grant, Jefferson Davis, Robert E. Lee) and soldiers on both sides of the war, including those of black soldiers and regiments.

6. Describe critical developments and events in the war, including the major battles, geographical advantages and obstacles, technological advances, and General Lee's surrender at Appomattox.

7. Explain how the war affected combatants, civilians, the physical environment, and future warfare.

8.11 Students analyze the character and lasting consequences of Reconstruction.

1. List the original aims of Reconstruction and describe its effects on the political and social structures of different regions.

2. Identify the push-pull factors in the movement of former slaves to the cities in the North and to the West and their differing experiences in those regions (e.g., the experiences of Buffalo Soldiers).

3. Understand the effects of the Freedmen's Bureau and the restrictions placed on the rights and opportunities of freedmen, including racial segregation and "Jim Crow" laws.

4. Trace the rise of the Ku Klux Klan and describe the Klan's effects.

5. Understand the Thirteenth, Fourteenth, and Fifteenth Amendments to the Constitution and analyze their connection to Reconstruction.

8.12 Students analyze the transformation of the American economy and the changing social and political conditions in the United States in response to the Industrial Revolution.

1. Trace patterns of agricultural and industrial development as they relate to climate, use of natural resources, markets, and trade and locate such development on a map.

2. Identify the reasons for the development of federal Indian policy and the wars with American Indians and their relationship to agricultural development and industrialization.

3. Explain how states and the federal government encouraged business expansion through tariffs, banking, land grants, and subsidies.

4. Discuss entrepreneurs, industrialists, and bankers in politics, commerce, and industry (e.g., Andrew Carnegie, John D. Rockefeller, Leland Stanford).

5. Examine the location and effects of urbanization, renewed immigration, and industrialization (e.g., the effects on social fabric of cities, wealth and economic opportunity, the conservation movement).

6. Discuss child labor, working conditions, and laissez-faire policies toward big business and examine the labor movement, including its leaders (e.g., Samuel Gompers), its demand for collective bargaining, and its strikes and protests over labor conditions.

7. Identify the new sources of large-scale immigration and the contributions of immigrants to the building of cities and the economy; explain the ways in which new social and economic patterns encouraged assimilation of newcomers into the mainstream amidst growing cultural diversity.

8. Identify the characteristics and impact of Grangerism and Populism.

9. Name the significant inventors and their inventions and identify how they improved the quality of life (e.g., Thomas Edison, Alexander Graham Bell, Orville and Wilbur Wright).

California History-Social Science Analysis Skills (Grades 6–8)

Chronological and Spatial Thinking

CST 1   Students explain how major events are related to one another in time.

CST 2   Students construct various time lines of key events, people, and periods of the historical era they are studying.

CST 3   Students use a variety of maps and documents to identify physical and cultural features of neighborhoods, cities, states, and countries and to explain the historical migration of people, expansion and disintegration of empires, and the growth of economic systems.

Research, Evidence, and Point of View

REP 1   Students frame questions that can be answered by historical study and research.

REP 2   Students distinguish fact from opinion in historical narratives and stories.

REP 3   Students distinguish relevant from irrelevant information, essential from incidental information, and verifiable from unverifiable information in historical narratives and stories.

REP 4   Students assess the credibility of primary and secondary sources and draw sound conclusions about them.

REP 5   Students detect the different historical points of view on historical events and determine the context in which the historical statements were made (the question asked, sources used, author's perspectives).

Historical Interpretation

HI 1   Students explain the central issues and problems from the past, placing people and events in a matrix of time and place.

HI 2   Students understand and distinguish cause, effect, sequence, and correlation in historical events, including the long-and short-term causal relations.

HI 3   Students explain the sources of historical continuity and how the combination of ideas and events explains the emergence of new patterns.

HI 4   Students recognize the role of chance, oversight, and error in history.

HI 5   Students recognize that interpretations of history are subject to change as new information is uncovered.

HI 6   Students interpret basic indicators or economic performance and conduct cost-benefit analyses of economic and political issues.

Quick Prep

This Quick Prep section provides a handy reference to key facts on a variety of topics in American history.

Major Eras in World History

The term era, or age, refers to a broad period of time characterized by a shared pattern of life. Eras and ages typically do not have exact starting and ending points. Because the historical development of different regions of the world is varied, no single listing of eras applies to all of world history. This chart applies primarily to Western civilization.

Era and Dates	Description
Stone Age (2.5 million–3000 B.C.)	This long prehistoric period is often divided into two parts: the Old Stone Age, or Paleolithic Age, and the New Stone Age, or Neolithic Age. The Paleolithic Age lasted from about 2.5 million to 8000 B.C. During this time, hominids made and used stone tools and learned to control fire. The Neolithic Age began about 8000 B.C., and ended about 3000 B.C., in some areas. In this period, people learned to polish stone tools, make pottery, grow crops, and raise animals. The introduction of agriculture, a major turning point in human history, is called the Neolithic Revolution.
Bronze Age (3000–1200 B.C.)	People began using bronze, rather than stone and copper, to make tools and weapons. The Bronze Age began in Sumer about 3000 B.C., when Sumerian metalworkers found that they could melt together certain amounts of copper and tin to make bronze. The first civilizations emerged during the Bronze Age.
Iron Age (1500–1000 B.C. to the present day)	The use of iron to make tools and weapons became widespread. The Iron Age is the last technological stage in the Stone-Bronze-Iron ages sequence.
Classical Greece (2000–300 B.C.)	Greek culture developed, rose to new heights, and spread to other lands. The Greek city-states established the first democratic governments. Greek scientists made advances in mathematics, medicine, and other fields. The Greeks produced great works of drama, poetry, sculpture, architecture, and philosophy that still influence people today.
Roman Empire (500 B.C.–A.D. 500)	At its height, the Roman Empire united much of Europe, the north coast of Africa, and a large part of the Middle East. The Romans admired Greek art, literature, architecture, and science, and so they adopted and preserved much of Greek culture. The Romans also created their own legacy with outstanding achievements in engineering, architecture, the arts, and law. The Romans spread Christianity throughout Europe, and their official language—Latin—gave rise to French, Italian, Spanish, and other Romance languages. Western civilization has its roots in Greco-Roman culture.
Middle Ages (500–1200)	The West Roman Empire fell to Germanic conquerors who formed kingdoms out of former Roman provinces. A new political and military system called feudalism became established. Nobles were granted the use of lands that belonged to their king in exchange for their loyalty, military service, and protection of the peasants who worked the land. Western Europe became divided into feudal states. The Middle Ages was the time of castles and knights.
Renaissance and Reformation (1300–1600)	The Renaissance was a period of rebirth of learning and the arts based on a revival of classical study. The study of Greek classics gave rise to an intellectual movement called humanism, which emphasized human potential and achievements rather than religious concerns. The works of the Italian artists Leonardo da Vinci and Michelangelo and the English dramatist William Shakespeare represent the cultural height of the Renaissance. The Reformation was a movement for religious reform that led to the founding of Protestant churches. These churches rejected the authority of the pope. The power of the Roman Catholic Church declined.
Exploration and Colonization (1400–1800)	The monarchs of Europe financed voyages around the world, motivated by the desire for riches and the hope of spreading Christianity. Seeking spices and converts, European explorers made long sea journeys to the East. Searching for a shorter sea route to Asia, Christopher Columbus landed in the Caribbean islands and opened up the New World to European colonization. The establishment of colonies and trading networks led to worldwide cultural exchange, but also to the devastation of Native American cultures in the New World, and the enslavement of millions of Africans.
Revolution and Independence (1700–1900)	Movements toward democracy and nationalism affected most countries in the Western world. These movements sparked the Revolutionary War in America, which resulted in the independence of the British colonies and the birth of the United States. They also sparked the ten-year French Revolution. Many Latin American nations fought colonial rule and gained their independence. In Europe, great empires fell and a system of nation-states became established.

Major Empires

Name and Dates	Location	Achievements
Akkadian (c. 2350–2150 B.C.)	Mesopotamia	Became the world's first empire
Alexandrian (336–322 B.C.)	Greece, Persia, Egypt, northwest India	Spread Greek culture
Assyrian (c. 850–612 B.C.)	Southwest Asia, Egypt	Built one of the ancient world's largest libraries at Nineveh, the largest city of its day
Athenian	Greece	Developed democratic principles and classical culture
Austro-Hungarian (late 1600s–1918)	Central Europe	Became known for its cultural life, especially its great composers
Aztec (1325–1521)	Mesoamerica	Built pyramids and developed a pictorial written language
British (1600s–1980s)	United Kingdom, Americas, Africa, Asia	Held one-fourth of the world's land and spread British culture to one-fourth of the world's people
Byzantine (395–1453)	Parts of southern and eastern Europe, northern Africa, and the Middle East	Preserved Greek culture, Roman customs, and Christianity and built the Hagia Sophia
Egyptian (2780–1075 B.C.)	Egypt, Nubia, parts of Syria and Palestine	Built magnificent palaces, temples, and pyramids
Ghana (800–1076)	West Africa	Became a center of the gold-salt trade
Han (201 B.C.–A.D. 220)	China	Established a centralized, bureaucratic government and unified Chinese culture
Holy Roman (962–1806)	Western and central Europe	Was the strongest state in Europe until about 1100
Inca (1400–1532)	South America	Built a vast empire linked by an extensive road system
Mali (1200–1400)	West Africa	Became wealthy on the gold-salt trade and created an efficient government
Maya (250–900)	Mesoamerica	Built pyramids and developed the most advanced writing system in the ancient Americas
Mongol (about 1200–1294)	Europe, Asia	Created the largest unified land empire in history
Mughal (1526–1700s)	India	Built unique architecture, including the Taj Mahal
Muslim (661–1171)	Southwest Asia, North Africa	Spread scholarship and written culture
Old Babylonian (about 2000–1550 B.C.)	Mesopotamia	Compiled the Code of Hammurabi
Ottoman (about 1300–1922)	Turkey, North Africa, Southwest Asia, Southeast Europe	Became the world's most powerful empire in the 1500s and 1600s and built architectural masterpieces
Persian (about 550–330 B.C.)	Fertile Crescent, Anatolia, Egypt, India	Established a judicious, thoughtful, and tolerant government
Roman (27 B.C.–A.D. 476)	Europe, Mesopotamia, North Africa	Spread Greek and Roman culture, which became the basis of Western civilization
Songhai (1460s–1591)	West Africa	Gained control of trans-Saharan trade routes and built a thriving empire

Major Religions

	Buddhism	Christianity	Hinduism	Islam	Judaism	Confucianism
Followers worldwide (estimated 2003 figures)	364 million	2 billion	828 million	1.2 billion	14.5 million	6.3 million
Name of god	no god	God	Brahman	Allah	God	no god
Founder	the Buddha	Jesus	no founder	no founder but spread by Muhammad	Abraham	Confucius
Holy book	many sacred books, including the Dhammapada	Bible, including Old Testament and New Testament	many sacred texts, including the Upanishads	Qur'an	Hebrew Bible, including the Torah	*Analects*
Clergy	Buddhist monks	priests, ministers, monks, and nuns	Brahmin priests, monks, and gurus	no clergy but a scholar class, called the ulama, and imams, who may lead prayers	rabbis	no clergy
Basic beliefs	• Followers can achieve enlightenment by understanding the Four Noble Truths and by following the Noble Eightfold Path of right opinions, right desires, right speech, right action, right jobs, right effort, right concentration, and right meditation.	• There is only one God, who watches over and cares for his people. • Jesus is the Son of God. He died to save humanity. His death and resurrection made eternal life possible for others.	• The soul never dies but is continually reborn until it becomes divinely enlightened. • Persons achieve happiness and divine enlightenment after they free themselves from their earthly desires. • Freedom from earthly desires comes from many lifetimes of worship, knowledge, and virtuous acts.	• Persons achieve salvation by following the Five Pillars of Islam and living a just life. The pillars are faith, prayer, charity, fasting, and pilgrimage to Mecca.	• There is only one God, who watches over and cares for his people. • God loves and protects his people but also holds people accountable for their sins and shortcomings. • Persons serve God by studying the Torah and living by its teachings.	• Social order, harmony, and good government should be based on strong family relationships. • Respect for parents and elders is important to a well-ordered society. • Education is important for the welfare of both the individual and society.

Source: *World Almanac 2004*

Government and Economic Systems

Government Systems		
System	**Definition**	**Example**
aristocracy	Power is in the hands of a hereditary ruling class or nobility.	Medieval Europe
autocracy	A single person rules with unlimited power. Autocracy is also called dictatorship and despotism.	Pharaohs of ancient Egypt
democracy	Citizens hold political power either directly or through representatives. In a direct democracy, citizens directly make political decisions. In a representative democracy, the citizens rule through elected representatives.	ancient Athens (direct democracy) United States since the 1700s (representative democracy)
federalism	Powers are divided among the federal, or national, government and a number of state governments.	United States since the 1700s
feudalism	A king allows nobles to use his land in exchange for their loyalty, military service, and protection of the people who live on the land.	Medieval Europe
military state	Military leaders rule, supported by the power of the armed forces.	Assyrian Empire
monarchy	A ruling family headed by a king or queen holds political power and may or may not share the power with citizen bodies. In an absolute monarchy, the ruling family has all the power. In a limited or constitutional monarchy, the ruler's power is limited by the constitution or laws of the nation.	reign of King Louis XIV of France (absolute monarchy) United Kingdom (constitutional monarchy)
oligarchy	A few persons or a small group rule.	most ancient Greek city-states
parliamentary	Legislative and executive functions are combined in a legislature called a parliament.	United Kingdom since the 1200s
presidential	The chief officer is a president who is elected independently of the legislature.	United States since the 1700s
republic	Citizens elect representatives to rule on their behalf.	Roman Republic
theocracy	Religious leaders control the government, relying on religious law and consultation with religious scholars. In early theocracies, the ruler was considered divine.	Aztec Empire
totalitarianism	The government controls every aspect of public and private life and all opposition is suppressed.	Soviet Union under Joseph Stalin

Economic Systems		
System	**Definition**	**Example**
command	The production of goods and services is determined by a central government, which usually owns the means of production. Also called a planned economy.	former Soviet Union
communism	All means of production—land, mines, factories, railroads, and businesses—are owned by the people, private property does not exist, and all goods and services are shared equally.	former Soviet Union
free enterprise	Businesses are privately owned and operate competitively for profit, with minimal government interference. Also called capitalism.	United States
manorialism	A lord gives serfs land, shelter, and protection in exchange for work, and almost everything needed for daily life is produced on the manor, or lord's estate.	Medieval Europe
market	The production of goods and services is determined by the demand from consumers. Also called a demand economy.	United States
mixed	A combination of command and market economies is designed to provide goods and services so that all people will benefit.	present-day Israel
socialism	The means of production are owned by the public and operate for the welfare of all.	In many present-day countries, including Denmark and Sweden, the government owns some industries and operates them for the public good.
traditional	Goods and services are exchanged without the use of money; also called barter.	many ancient civilizations and tribal societies

Major Events in World History

Time and Place	Event	Significance
40,000 B.C. **Europe**	Cro-Magnons appear.	Ancestors of modern humans
8000 B.C. **Africa, Asia**	Agriculture begins.	One of the great breakthroughs in human history, setting the stage for the development of civilizations
3100 B.C. **Egypt**	Upper and Lower Egypt unite.	The Kingdom of Egypt, ruled by pharaohs, began a 3,000-year period of unity and cultural continuity.
3000 B.C. **Mesopotamia**	Civilization emerges in Sumer.	One of the world's first civilizations
2500 B.C. **Indus Valley**	Planned cities arise.	Beginning of the Indus Valley civilization; many features of modern Indian culture can be traced to this early civilization.
2350 B.C. **Mesopotamia**	Sargon of Akkad builds an empire.	World's first empire, which extended from the Mediterranean coast in the west to present-day Iran in the east
1700 B.C. **Asian steppes**	Indo-Europeans begin migrations.	The Indo-Europeans moved into Europe, the Middle East, and India, spreading their languages and changing cultures.
1532 B.C. **China**	Shang Dynasty begins.	The first Chinese civilization, which arose along the Huang He river
1200 B.C. **Mexico**	Olmec culture arises.	Oldest known civilization in the Americas
850 B.C. **Assyria**	Assyria builds an empire.	Using military force to conquer and rule, the Assyrians established an empire that included most of the old centers of power in Southwest Asia and Egypt.
800 B.C. **Greece**	Greek city-states arise.	Led to the development of several political systems, including democracy
550 B.C. **Persia**	Cyrus builds the Persian Empire.	Characterized by tolerance and wise government
500 B.C. **Rome**	Romans establish a republic.	Source of some of the most fundamental values and institutions of Western civilization
461 B.C. **Greece**	Age of Pericles begins.	Democratic principles and classical Greek culture flourished, leaving a legacy that endures to the present day.
334 B.C. **Greece**	Alexander begins to build an empire.	Conquered Persia and Egypt; extended his empire to the Indus River in India; resulted in a blending of Greek, Egyptian, and Eastern customs
321 B.C. **India**	Mauryan Empire is established.	United north India politically for the first time
202 B.C. **China**	Han Dynasty replaces Qin dynasty.	Expanded China's borders; developed a system of government that lasted for centuries
27 B.C. **Rome**	Octavian rules Roman Empire.	Took the title of Augustus and ruled the mightiest empire of the ancient world; began the Pax Romana, a 200-year period of peace and prosperity; Roman way of life spread throughout the empire.
A.D. 29 **Jerusalem**	Jesus is crucified.	Christianity spread throughout the Roman Empire.
A.D. 100 **South America**	Moche civilization emerges.	Built an advanced society in Peru
A.D. 100s **Africa**	Bantu migrations begin.	Bantu speakers spread their language and culture throughout southern Africa.
A.D. 320 **India**	Gupta Empire begins.	A great flowering of Indian civilization, especially Hindu culture
A.D. 527 **Constantinople**	Justinian I becomes Byzantine emperor.	Recovered and ruled almost all the former territory of the Roman Empire; created a body of civil laws called Justinian's Code; built beautiful churches

Time and Place	Event	Significance
618 China	Tang dynasty begins.	Created a powerful empire, improved trade and agriculture, and restored the civil service bureaucracy
000 Central America	Maya civilization thrives.	Built spectacular cities and developed the most advanced writing system in the ancient Americas
800 North America	Anasazi civilization develops.	Ancestors of the Pueblo peoples
800s–900s West Africa	Empire of Ghana thrives.	Built its wealth on the trans-Saharan gold-salt trade
814 Western Europe	Charlemagne unites much of Europe.	Established the Carolingian Empire
960 China	Song Dynasty begins.	China became the most populous and advanced country in the world.
1095 France	Pope Urban II issues call for First Crusade.	Stimulated trade, weakened the power of the pope and feudal nobles, and left a legacy of distrust between Christians and Muslims
1192 Japan	Kamakura Shogunate begins.	First shogunate, which set the pattern for military dictators, called shoguns, to rule Japan until 1868
1200s Mexico	Aztec civilization begins.	Built the greatest empire in Mesoamerica
1200s Peru	Inca Empire begins.	The largest empire in the Americas
1209 Mongolia	Genghis Khan begins Mongol conquests.	Built the largest unified land empire in world history
1215 England	King John agrees to Magna Carta.	The Magna Carta contributed to modern concepts of jury trials and legal rights.
1235 Africa	Sundiata founds Mali Empire.	Became a powerful center of commerce and trade in West Africa
1279 China	Kublai Khan conquers Song Dynasty.	Completed the conquest of China and encouraged trade; Chinese ideas then began to influence Western civilization.
1300 Italy	Renaissance begins.	Revival of classical studies revolutionized art, literature, and society
1337 France	Hundred Years' War begins.	Ended the Middle Ages
1347 Italy	Bubonic plague spreads to Europe.	Killed nearly one-third of Europe's population and disrupted medieval society
1368 China	Ming Dynasty begins.	Ended Mongol rule of China and made China the dominant power in the region
1453 Turkey	Constantinople falls to Turks.	One of the most influential cities of the 15th century, Constantinople became part of the Ottoman Empire, and its name was changed to Istanbul.
1492 Americas	Columbus sails to Hispaniola.	Opened the way for European settlement of the Americas
1517 Germany	Martin Luther begins Reformation.	Led to the founding of Protestant churches
1526 India	Babur founds Mughal Empire.	Brought Turks, Persians, and Indians together in a vast empire
1529 Anatolia	Suleiman the Magnificent rules Ottoman Empire.	The Ottoman Empire reached its greatest size and grandeur.
1603 Japan	Tokugawa Shogunate begins.	Unified Japan and began a 200-year period of isolation and prosperity
1607 North America	English settle at Jamestown.	England's first permanent settlement in North America

Major Geographic Features

United States and Canada

Climate		Vegetation		Land Forms and Bodies of Water	
Arctic	Semi-arid	Tundra	Mediterranean	Great Lakes	Rocky Mountains
Sub-arctic	Sub-tropical	Coniferous forest	scrub	Gulf of Mexico	Mississippi River
Temperate	Tropical	Broadleaf forest	Semi-desert	Appalachian	
Arid		Grassland	Desert	Mountains	

Latin America

Climate		Vegetation		Land Forms and Bodies of Water	
Tropical	Temperate	Savannah	Tropical rainforest	Orinoco River	Sierra Madre
Sub-tropical	Arid	Semi-desert	Monsoon forest	Andes Mountains	Amazon River
Desert	Semi-arid	Desert	Broadleaf forest		
		Dry tropical scrub			

Europe, Russia, and the Independent Republics

Climate		Vegetation		Land Forms and Bodies of Water	
Sub-arctic	Temperate	Tundra	Grassland	Baltic Sea	Volga River
Steppe	Mediterranean	Coniferous forest	Mediterranean	Mediterranean Sea	Alps Mountains
Tundra	Alpine	Broadleaf forest	scrub	North Sea	Pyrenees
Humid continental				Lake Baikal	Mountains
				Danube River	Ural Mountains
				Rhine River	

North Africa and Southwest Asia

Climate		Vegetation		Land Forms and Bodies of Water	
Desert	Temperate	Semi-desert	Monsoon forest	Red Sea	Sahara Desert
Sub-tropical	Arid	Desert	Dry tropical scrub	Persian Gulf	Nile River
Tropical	Semi-arid			Black Sea	Tigris River
Tropical monsoon				Dead Sea	Euphrates River

Africa South of the Sahara

Climate		Vegetation		Land Forms and Bodies of Water	
Tropical	Semi-arid	Savannah	Dry tropical scrub	Mount Kilimanjaro	Congo River
Sub-tropical	Desert	Semi-desert	Tropical rainforest	Kalahari Desert	Niger River
Arid		Desert	Monsoon forest	Victoria Falls	Zambezi River
				Nile River	

Southern Asia

Climate		Vegetation		Land Forms and Bodies of Water	
Tropical	Sub-tropical	Monsoon forest	Sub-tropical forest	Himalayan	Mekong River
Monsoon	Moderate	Tropical rainforest		Mountains	Arabian Sea
				Mount Everest	South China Sea
				Indus River	Bay of Bengal
				Ganges River	Malay Archipelago

East Asia, Australia, and the Pacific Islands

Climate		Vegetation		Land Forms and Bodies of Water	
Temperate	Sub-tropical	Savannah	Dry tropical scrub	Mount Fuji	Huang He
Arid	Tropical	Semi-desert	Tropical rainforest	Southern Alps	(Yellow River)
Semi-arid		Desert	Monsoon forest	Gobi Desert	Chang Jiang
				Great Barrier Reef	(Yangtze River)

Major Events in American History

Date	Event	Significance
1492	Columbus lands in America	Europe begins to colonize the Americas
1607	Jamestown founded	First permanent English settlement in the Americas
1620	Mayflower Compact	Helps establish idea of self-government and majority rule
1675–1676	King Philip's War	War between New England colonists and Native Americans allows settlers to expand further into Indian lands
1676	Bacon's Rebellion	Earliest rebellion of colonists against English colonial control
1754–1763	French and Indian War	British defeat the French and gain control of most of the northern and eastern parts of North America
1774	First Continental Congress	First colonial effort to act together to protest English policies; precedent for the first American government
1775	Battles of Lexington and Concord	First battles of the American Revolution
1776	Declaration of Independence signed	Colonists break away from England
1781	Articles of Confederation ratified	Becomes the first American government
1783	Treaty of Paris signed	Ends American Revolution
1786–1787	Shays's Rebellion	Makes politicians realize that they need a stronger national government
1788	Constitution ratified	Becomes blueprint for American government
1793	Cotton gin invented	Makes producing cotton much cheaper
1794	Whiskey Rebellion	National government proves that it has the power to enforce the laws

Date	Event	Significance
1803	Louisiana Purchase	More than doubles the size of the country
1804	Lewis and Clark Expedition	Expedition explores America's new territories
1812–1815	War of 1812	America proves it can defend itself
1820	Missouri Compromise	Preserves balance between free and slave states
1823	Monroe Doctrine	States that Europe should stay out of the Americas
1828	Tariff of Abominations	Leads Southerners to create the doctrine of nullification, an extreme states' rights position
1831	Nat Turner's Rebellion	Causes Southern states to pass stricter slave laws
1836	Texas Independence	Texas revolts against Mexico
1838	Trail of Tears	Cherokees forced to move to the West
1846–1848	War with Mexico	America acquires much of the Southwest
1849	California gold rush	Many Americans settle the West Coast
1857	*Dred Scott* decision	Increases tension between North and South
1860	Lincoln becomes president	Causes southern states to secede
1861	Shots fired at Fort Sumter	Beginning of the Civil War
1863	Emancipation Proclamation	Freed the slaves in Confederate states
1865	Lee surrenders at Appomattox Court House	Ends the Civil War
1877	Reconstruction ends	White Southerners regain control of their state governments

Key People in American History

Abigail Adams (1744–1818) Wife of President John Adams; mother of John Quincy Adams
Samuel Adams (1722–1803) Important leader in American Revolution
Richard Allen (1760–1831) Founder of first African-American church in United States
Susan B. Anthony (1820–1906) Leader of movement to give women the right to vote
Benedict Arnold (1741–1801) Leader during American Revolution, he switched sides and became traitor
Crispus Attucks (1723?–1770) American hero and martyr of the Boston Massacre
John James Audubon (1785-1851) Naturalist, famous for his paintings of American birds

Nathaniel Bacon (1647–1676) Virginia planter and leader of Bacon's Rebellion
Annie Bidwell (1839–1918) Founded Chico, protected Mechoopda Maidu Indians
Daniel Boone (1734–1820) Frontiersman who found trail through the Cumberland Gap
John Wilkes Booth (1838–1865) Southerner who assassinated President Lincoln after the Civil War
Joseph Brant (1742–1807) Mohawk Indian chief who fought with Americans in American Revolution
John Breckinridge (1821–1875) Politician who supported a states' rights view in early republic
John Brown (1800–1859) Militant abolitionist who led raid at Harpers Ferry
Ambrose Burnside (1824–1881) Union general in Civil War; fought at battle of Antietam

John C. Calhoun (1782–1850) Vice-president of United States; created doctrine of nullification
Mary Chesnut (1823-1886) Southern diarist who described life during the Civil War
William Clark (1770–1838) Explorer of Lewis and Clark expedition
Henry Clay (1777–1852) Politician known as "The Great Compromiser"; architect of "American System"
Christopher Columbus (1451–1506) Italian explorer of the New World
James Fenimore Cooper (1789-1851) First major novelist, wrote about the frontier
Charles Cornwallis (1738–1805) British general defeated at Yorktown during American Revolution

Jefferson Davis (1808–1889) President of Confederate States of America during Civil War
Dorothea Dix (1802–1887) Reformer who fought to improve the care of the mentally ill
Stephen A. Douglas (1813–1861) Politician who participated in Lincoln-Douglas debates in 1860
Frederick Douglass (1818?–1895) Former slave and important abolitionist

Jonathan Edwards (1703–1758) Theologian and Puritan who sparked The Great Awakening
Ralph Waldo Emerson (1803–1882) Writer and poet; popularized idea of transcendentalism
Olaudah Equiano (1750–1797) Former slave and abolitionist; wrote his autobiography

Benjamin Franklin (1706–1790) Author, publisher, inventor, and diplomat
Robert Fulton (1765–1815) Ran first commercial steamboat

Thomas Gage (1721–1787) British military governor of Massachusetts at time of American Revolution
William Lloyd Garrison (1805–1879) Printer of the abolitionist newspaper, *The Liberator*
Horatio Gates (1728?–1806) General during American Revolution who defeated British at Battle of Saratoga
George III (1738–1820) British king during American Revolution
Angelina (1805–1879) and **Sarah (1792–1873) Grimke** Abolitionist sisters

Alexander Hamilton (1755–1804) Author of many of the Federalist Papers; first Secretary of the Treasury
John Hancock (1737–1793) Important leader of American Revolution; first signer of Declaration of Independence
Nathaniel Hawthorne (1804–1864) One of the first professional fiction writers in American literature
Patrick Henry (1736–1799) Important leader in American Revolution; said "Give me liberty or give me death"
Sam Houston (1793–1863) Important leader of Texas Revolution
Ann Hutchinson (1591–1643) Banished from Massachusetts colony; one of founders of Rhode Island

Thomas "Stonewall" Jackson (1824–1863) Confederate general; fought in First Battle of Bull Run
John Jay (1745–1829) First chief justice of the Supreme Court; negotiated Jay's Treaty
John Paul Jones (1747–1792) Naval hero during American Revolution

Marquis de Lafayette (1757–1834) French hero of the American Revolution
Robert E. Lee (1807–1870) Famous Confederate general during the Civil War
Meriwether Lewis (1774–1809) Explorer of Lewis and Clark expedition
John Locke (1632–1704) English philosopher; ideas influenced American ideas about government
Henry W. Longfellow (1807–1882) Popular American poet of the 19th century

Horace Mann (1796–1859) "Father of American Education"; established Massachusetts Board of Education
John Marshall (1755–1835) Chief justice of the Supreme Court; one of most important in history
George Mason (1725–1792) Insisted on protection of individual rights in the Constitution
Increase Mather (1639–1723) Important and influential Puritan minister
Samuel Morse (1791–1872) Invented a telegraph system; developed Morse Code
Lucretia Mott (1793–1880) Helped found the women's rights movement

James Oglethorpe (1696–1785) Founded colony of Georgia

William Penn (1644–1718) Quaker; founded colony of Pennsylvania
George Pickett (1825–1875) Confederate officer; important in battle of Gettysburg
Thomas Pinckney (1750–1828) Politician; negotiated Treaty with Spanish
Tom Paine (1737–1809) Influential writer during American Revolution
Pocahontas (1595?–1617) Helped maintain peace between early colonists and Indians

Paul Revere (1735–1818) Made famous ride during American Revolution to warn of a British attack
Betsy Ross (1752–1836) Seamstress Patriot who may have created first American flag

Sacagawea (c.1786–c.1812) Indian woman; guide on the Lewis and Clark expedition
Dred Scott Slave who sued for his freedom in famous Supreme Court case
Winfield Scott (1786–1866) General in War of 1812, Mexican War, and Civil War
William Tecumseh Sherman (1820–1891) Union general; waged total war on the South
Elizabeth Cady Stanton (1815–1902) Leader of movement to give women the right to vote

Roger Taney (1777–1864) Supreme Court chief justice; wrote Dred Scott decision
Tecumseh (1768?–1813) Indian chief who fought with British in War of 1812
Henry David Thoreau (1817–1862) Author; believed in transcendentalism and civil rights
Alexis de Tocqueville (1805–1859) French author who described life in 19th century America
Sojourner Truth (1797?–1883) Former slave; leading abolitionist and defender of women's rights
Harriet Tubman (1820?–1913) Former slave; abolitionist and organized Underground Railroad
Nat Turner (1800–1831) Slave who led famous and bloody slave rebellion

David Walker (1785–1830) Black abolitionist; wrote famous pamphlet urging slaves to rebel
Daniel Webster (1782–1852) Important politician; attacked idea of states' rights
Noah Webster (1758–1843) Created first American dictionary
Walt Whitman (1819–1892) Author, poet, journalist
Eli Whitney (1765–1825) Inventor of the cotton gin
Laura Ingalls Wilder (1867–1957) Wrote a series of books about frontier life
John Winthrop (1588–1649) Important Puritan; first governor of Massachusetts Bay Colony

Brigham Young (1801–1877) Led Mormons west to escape religious persecution

John Peter Zenger (1697–1746) Journalist; his trial helped establish idea of freedom of the press

Presidents of the United States

President	Years in Office	Birth State	Political Party	Key Events During Term in Office
George Washington (1732–1799)	1789–1797	VA	none	Bill of Rights Whiskey Rebellion cotton gin invented
John Adams (1735–1826)	1797–1801	MA	Federalist	XYZ Affair Alien and Sedition Acts
Thomas Jefferson (1743–1826)	1801–1809	VA	Democratic-Republican	*Marbury* v. *Madison* Louisiana Purchase Embargo of 1807
James Madison (1751–1836)	1809–1817	VA	Democratic-Republican	War of 1812 American System
James Monroe (1758–1831)	1817–1825	VA	Democratic-Republican	industrialization Missouri Compromise Monroe Doctrine
John Quincy Adams (1767–1848)	1825–1829	MA	Democratic-Republican	Erie Canal Tariff of Abominations
Andrew Jackson (1767–1845)	1829–1837	SC	Democrat	Nullification and bank war Jacksonian Democracy Indian Removal Act
Martin Van Buren (1782–1862)	1837–1841	NY	Democrat	Trail of Tears Panic of 1837
William H. Harrison (1773–1841)	1841	VA	Whig	1st President to die in office
John Tyler (1790–1862)	1841–1845	VA	Whig	Irish and German immigrants Oregon Trail
James K. Polk (1795–1849)	1845–1849	NC	Democrat	Texas annexation and Mexican War Gold Rush Seneca Falls Convention
Zachary Taylor (1784–1850)	1849–1850	VA	Whig	Fugitive Slave Act
Millard Filmore (1800–1874)	1850–1853	NY	Whig	Compromise of 1850 *Uncle Tom's Cabin*
Franklin Pierce (1804–1869)	1853–1857	NH	Democrat	Bleeding Kansas Gadsden Purchase
James Buchanan (1791–1868)	1857–1861	PA	Democrat	*Dred Scott* Harpers Ferry raid
Abraham Lincoln (1809–1865)	1861–1865	KY	Republican	Secession and Civil War Emancipation Proclamation first President assassinated
Andrew Johnson (1808–1875)	1865–1869	NC	Democrat	13th and 14th amendments Radical Reconstruction impeachment trial sharecropping in the South
Ulysses S. Grant (1822–1885)	1869–1877	OH	Republican	15th amendment transcontinental railroad Panic of 1873 Battle of Little Big Horn
Rutherford B. Hayes (1822–1893)	1877–1881	OH	Republican	Compromise of 1877 labor unions and strikes
James A. Garfield (1831–1881)	1881	OH	Republican	assassinated
Chester A. Arthur (1829–1886)	1881–1885	VT	Republican	Standard Oil trust created Edison lights up New York City

President	Years in Office	Birth State	Political Party	Key Events During Term in Office
Grover Cleveland (1837–1908)	1885–1889	NJ	Democrat	Dawes Act Samuel Gompers and AFL
Benjamin Harrison (1833–1901)	1889–1893	OH	Republican	Wounded Knee Massacre Sherman Anti-Trust Act Populism and Hull House founded
Grover Cleveland (1837–1908)	1893–1897	NJ	Democrat	*Plessy* v. *Ferguson* Pullman strike Tammany Hall
William McKinley (1843–1901)	1897–1901	OH	Republican	new immigrants Spanish-American War Open Door policy
Theodore Roosevelt (1858–1919)	1901–1909	NY	Republican	Progressivism Square Deal and Big Stick Diplomacy
William H. Taft (1857–1930)	1909–1913	OH	Republican	Dollar diplomacy NAACP founded
Woodrow Wilson (1856–1924)	1913–1921	VA	Democrat	WWI and League of Nations 18th and 19th amendments
Warren G. Harding (1865–1923)	1921–1923	OH	Republican	Tea Pot Dome scandal cars and planes alter America
Calvin Coolidge (1872–1933)	1923–1929	VT	Republican	Jazz Age Harlem Renaissance
Herbert C. Hoover (1874–1964)	1929–1933	IA	Republican	Stock Market Crash Depression and Dust Bowl
Franklin D. Roosevelt (1882–1945)	1933–1945	NY	Democrat	1st and 2nd New Deal WWII and Holocaust Japanese Internment
Harry S Truman (1884–1972)	1945–1953	MO	Democrat	A-bomb and Marshall Plan Cold War begins and Korean War United Nations created
Dwight D. Eisenhower (1890–1969)	1953–1961	TX	Republican	McCarthyism; *Brown* v. *Board of Education* Highway Act and suburbs rock 'n' roll and youth culture
John F. Kennedy (1917–1963)	1961–1963	MA	Democrat	Camelot & March on Washington Cuban Missile Crisis; assassination
Lyndon B. Johnson (1908–1973)	1963–1969	TX	Democrat	Civil and Voting Rights acts M.L. King assassinated escalation in Vietnam anti-war and counter culture Great Society
Richard M. Nixon (1913–1994)	1969–1974	CA	Republican	feminism; environmentalism U.S. pulls out of Vietnam China visit; Watergate; resigns
Gerald R. Ford (1913–)	1974–1977	NE	Republican	pardons Nixon
James E. Carter, Jr. (1924–)	1977–1981	GA	Democrat	stagflation / energy crisis hostages in Iran
Ronald W. Reagan (1911–2004)	1981–1989	IL	Republican	rise of conservatism Cold War ends
George H. W. Bush (1924–)	1989–1993	MA	Republican	Persian Gulf War
William J. Clinton (1946–)	1993–2001	AR	Democrat	NAFTA impeachment
George W. Bush (1946–)	2001–	CT	Republican	war on terrorism Patriot Act; Iraq War

Important Documents in American History

Magna Carta (1215) English agreement that guaranteed certain rights to all Englishmen; influenced the American Bill of Rights' protections of individual rights
English Bill of Rights (1689) English agreement that guaranteed certain rights to all Englishmen; influenced the American Bill of Rights' protections of individual rights
Mayflower Compact (1620) Signed by many Pilgrims on their way to New World; they agreed to create a new government and follow its laws; helped establish the idea of self-government
Common Sense (1776) Influential pamphlet written by Thomas Paine; it urged Americans to declare their independence
Declaration of Independence (July 4, 1776) Written by Thomas Jefferson; announced the separation of the colonies from England
Articles of Confederation (1781–1789) First U.S. government; it was eventually a failure because it created a national government that was too weak
Constitution (written in 1787) Blueprint for the American government
The Federalist Papers (1787–1788) Series of essays about the nature of government by Alexander Hamilton, James Madison, and John Jay; written to help get the Constitution ratified
Bill of Rights (adopted in 1791) First 10 amendments of the Constitution; guarantees individual rights
George Washington's Farewell Address (1796) Given at his retirement from public life; he urged America to always remain neutral toward other countries
Monroe Doctrine (1823) Presidential message that said that Europe should not interfere in the affairs of Latin America and the United States would not interfere in European affairs
South Carolina Exposition and Protest (1829) Written by John C. Calhoun; outlined the doctrine of nullification, which was a strong statement for states' rights
Appeal... to the Colored People of the World (1829) Written by David Walker who was a black abolitionist; known as "David Walker's Appeal"; urged slaves to revolt; radical document that made Southerners furious
The Liberator **(1831–1865)** Newspaper printed by William Lloyd Garrison; most influential antislavery periodical in United States history; it increased sectionalism between the North and South
Lincoln's First Inaugural (1861) Lincoln said North would defend federal property in the South
Emancipation Proclamation (Jan. 1, 1863) Executive order given by Abraham Lincoln; it freed the slaves in the Confederacy
Gettysburg Address (1863) Famous speech given by Abraham Lincoln; it said that the Union was worth fighting for at any cost
Lincoln's Second Inaugural (1865) Lincoln said Civil War was about slavery and that the Union was fighting to end slavery

Important Laws in American History

English Acts Passed During the Colonial Era:
Navigation Acts (1651) laws passed to make sure that England controlled American trade according to the idea of mercantilism
Proclamation of 1763 British law at end of French and Indian War; said that Americans were not allowed to settle west of the Appalachian Mountains
Sugar Act (1764) fees placed on sugar imported into the colonies
Quartering Act (1765) required colonists to feed and shelter British troops
Stamp Act (1765) all official documents had to carry a stamp
Townshend Acts (1767) four laws that, among other things, charged new fees on goods imported into the colonies
Tea Act (1773) charged a fee on all tea imported into the colonies
Intolerable Acts (1774) four laws passed to punish colonists for the Boston Tea Party including closing the port of Boston

Laws Passed By Congress:
Land Ordinance (1785) organized the Northwest Territory on a grid system
Northwest Ordinance (1787) established a government for the Northwest Territory and described rules that a territory would follow in order to become a state
Alien and Sedition Act (1798) placed restrictions on immigrants in the country and restricted freedom of speech and freedom of the press
Embargo Act (1807) restricted American trade with other countries
Missouri Compromise (1820) preserved balance in Congress between slave and free states by admitting Missouri as a slave state and Maine as a free state; prohibited slavery north of Missouri
Indian Removal Act (1830) Indians east of the Mississippi River were to be moved to new lands in the West
Compromise of 1850 preserved balance between free and slave states and said that Congress would not regulate slavery in the territories
Fugitive Slave Act (1850) fugitive slaves in the North had to be returned to their owners; they could not testify in court or have a trial by jury; and there were heavy penalties for anyone who helped an escaped slave
Kansas-Nebraska Act (1854) repealed Missouri Compromise and allowed Kansas and Nebraska to decide for themselves whether they would allow slavery; this was the new idea of popular sovereignty
Civil Rights Act (1866) said that everyone born in the United States was a citizen and entitled to equal rights regardless of race
Reconstruction Acts (1867) known as Radical Reconstruction; imposed military control of southern states and said that they had to ratify the 14th Amendment and allow former slaves to vote

Important Supreme Court Cases

Marbury v. Madison (1803) said that Supreme Court had right to review all laws made by Congress; established the idea of Judicial Review; made Supreme Court more powerful
McCulloch v. Maryland (1819) said that a state could not tax a national bank; increased power of national government
Gibbons v. Ogden (1824) said that federal government (not the state governments) had the power to regulate trade between the states; increased power of national government
Dred Scott v. Sandford (1857) said that African Americans were not citizens of the United States and said that Missouri Compromise unconstitutional; increased sectionalism
United States v. Cruikshank (1876) said that national government could not punish someone for violating the civil rights of individuals; only the states had that power; violence against African Americans increased in the South during Reconstruction
United States v. Reese (1876) said that 15th amendment did automatically protect the right of African Americans to vote; only listed the ways that states were not allowed to prevent them from voting; southern states found other ways to prevent African Americans from voting during Reconstruction

Selected Cases Post-1877
Schenck v. United States (1919) said that free speech could be restricted under certain circumstances, including during wartime; government allowed to prevent people from criticizing the government or holding controversial opinions
Plessy v. Ferguson (1896) said that the idea of "separate but equal" was allowed by the Constitution; segregation spreads in the South
Brown v. Board of Education (1954) said that the idea of "separate but equal" was unconstitutional; made segregation in schools illegal

Important Treaties in American History

Treaty of Paris (1763) ended the French and Indian War between England and France
Treaty of Paris (1783) ended the American Revolution with England
Jay's Treaty (1794) British agreed to leave the forts they occupied on the American frontier
Pinckney's Treaty (1795) Spain allowed Americans to travel freely along the Mississippi River and settled boundary disputes between the United States and Spain
Treaty of Greenville (1795) ended the Battle of Fallen Timbers; 12 Indian tribes agreed to give up their land that consisted of most of present-day Ohio and Indiana to the U.S. government
Louisiana Purchase (1803) America acquired Louisiana territory from France; doubled size of country
Treaty of Ghent (1814) ended the War of 1812 with England
Adams-Onís Treaty (1819) Spain gave Florida to the United States
Treaty of Guadalupe Hidalgo (1848) ended the war with Mexico; United States acquired the Mexican Cession
Gadsden Purchase (1853) gave the United States more land that had been northern Mexico; completed the acquisition of land that makes up the present-day borders of the continental United States

Important Works of American Literature

James Fenimore Cooper *The Last of the Mohicans*, 1826, novel that describes life on the frontier during the French and Indian War; part of a series
Nathaniel Hawthorne *The Scarlet Letter*, 1850, novel about Puritan New England that painted a grim picture of human nature and life in the 17th century
Washington Irving "Rip Van Winkle" and "The Legend of Sleepy Hollow," 1820, humorous legends for the new country
Herman Melville *Moby Dick*, 1851, classic sea adventure
Harriet Beecher Stowe *Uncle Tom's Cabin*, 1852, novel that depicts the cruelties of slavery; it increased antislavery sentiment in the north
Henry David Thoreau *Walden*, 1854, book that celebrate nature and wilderness as well as American individualism
Walt Whitman *Leaves of Grass*, 1855, book of poetry that celebrates nature and the individual

Important Culture and Technology

Artillery—large guns and cannon, played key role in the American Revolution
Brady's photography—Matthew Brady's Civil War photographs were the start of photojournalism
Canals—man-made water routes, built in the early 1800s, enabled trade and travel
Columbian Exchange—the movement of plants, goods, and diseases between the New World and Europe
Cotton gin —1795 invention by Eli Whitney that made processing cotton much easier
Elevators—invented in late 1800s, made skyscrapers possible, contributed to urbanization
Hudson River School— group of artists living in the Hudson River valley who painted lush landscapes
Ironclads—warships covered with iron, introduced in Civil War
Railroads—developed in the early 1800s, tied the nation together and sped industrial growth
Spirituals—religious folk songs sung by African Americans, sometimes containing coded messages
Transcendentalism—19th-century philosophy emphasizing spiritual world and intuition

Key Terms in American History

Abolitionism—movement to end slavery

amend—the process of changing the Constitution

American System—1815 plan to make United States economically self-sufficient

Anti-Federalists—people who opposed ratification of the Constitution

Appomattox Courthouse—where the South finally surrendered during the Civil War

assimilation—the process of blending into society

Bacon's Rebellion—1676 revolt against colonial authority

balance of power—the distribution of power between the three branches of government

Bank War—1829–1830 attack by President Jackson on national bank

Battle of the Alamo—1836 battle between Texans and Mexican army

Battle of Fallen Timbers—1794 conflict between Indians and colonists over control of the Northwest Territory

Battle of Gettysburg—1863, ended the South's hopes of winning a battle in the North

Battles of Lexington and Concord—1775, first battles of the American Revolution

Battle of Vicksburg—1863, South lost control of Mississippi River

Battle of Yorktown—1781, last major campaign of the American Revolution

Battles of Saratoga—1777, turning point of the American Revolution

Bleeding Kansas—conflict between pro-slavery and anti-slavery people in Kansas, 1854–1859

blockade—when goods are prevented from going into or out of an area

Boston Massacre—1770, conflict between British and colonists

Boston Tea Party—1773, protest by colonists in which they dumped tea into Boston Harbor

boycott—a refusal to buy certain goods

California Gold Rush—1849, migration of people to the area after gold was discovered

cash crop—a crop grown to be sold rather than used by the farmer

charter—a contract given to someone to establish a colony

checks and balances—each of the three branches of government limits the power of the others

Columbian Exchange—the movement of plants, goods, and diseases between the New World and Europe

Compromise of 1877—ended Reconstruction

Confederacy—the southern states who seceded

Confederation Congress—first U.S. government

constituents—the people who vote for a member of government

Constitutional Convention—1787, the meeting of people that agreed on the Constitution

Continental Army—military of the colonists

Continental Congress—the group of leaders that governed the colonies during the American Revolution

cotton gin—1795 invention by Eli Whitney that made processing cotton much easier

Crittenden Plan—1861 plan that might have prevented secession

Cumberland Gap—was the principal route through the Appalachian Mountains

Democratic-Republicans—political party formed by Jefferson and Madison

doctrine of nullification—idea that states had the right to reject any law passed by Congress

due process of law—everyone is entitled to be treated equally under the law

electoral college—a group of voters chosen by each state to elect the President and Vice-President

embargo—prevents ships from entering or leaving a port

Erie Canal—1825 waterway connected Great Lakes to New York City

executive branch—the President and his cabinet

factory system—method of building goods that included many workers and machines working in one place

federalism—a system of sharing power between the states and the national government

Federalists—supported ratification of the Constitution

foreign policy—relations with governments of other countries

Fort Sumter—beginning of the Civil War

Freedman's Bureau—federal agency set up to help former slaves in the South

free enterprise system—an economic system that has few government restrictions

Free-Soil Party—political party formed in 1846 to stop the spread of slavery

French and Indian War—1754–1763, world-wide war between France and England

Fundamental Orders of Connecticut—Puritan plan of government in Connecticut in 1639

Great Awakening—religious revival, 1730–1740

Great Compromise—agreement reached during the constitutional convention that created the American system of government

habeas corpus—no one can be held by the government without cause

Harpers Ferry—1859 slave revolt

impeachment—the process of accusing a government official of wrongdoing

indentured servant—someone who agreed to work for an employer in exchange for passage to the New World

individual rights—personal liberties guaranteed by the Bill of Rights

industrialization—an economy begins to be based on factories instead of farming

Jacksonian Democracy—the idea that as many people as possible should be able to vote

Jamestown—first permanent English settlement in the New World in 1607

judicial branch—the Supreme Court

judicial review—the idea that the Supreme Court has the right to review all laws made by Congress

King Philip's War—war between Puritan settlers and Wampanoags along with other Native peoples, 1675–1676

legislative branch—the House of Representatives and the Senate; the branch that makes the laws

Lewis and Clark expedition—group that explored the lands of the Louisiana Purchase

limited government—everyone, even elected officials, must obey the laws

Louisiana Purchase—treaty with France in 1803 that allowed the United States to acquire vast extent of land

Lowell mills—textile mills founded 1826

Loyalist—someone loyal to England during American Revolution

manifest destiny—idea that America had a right to all of the land between the east and west coasts

Mayflower Compact—1620 agreement between Pilgrims to establish a government in the New World

melting pot—idea that American culture is a blend of many different cultures

mercantilism—economic system in which an empire, such as Britain, controlled the trade of its colonies

Mexican Cession—land in Southwest given up by Mexico in 1848 after the Mexican war

Mexican War—war between United States and Mexico, 1846–1848

middle passage—journey of captured Africans to the New World to be sold as slaves

militia—armed civilians who are supposed to defend their communities

Mormons—group of people who moved west to avoid religious persecution

neutral—refusal to become allies with any country

New Jersey Plan—plan of government that the Constitutional Convention considered

Northwest Territory—land that formed the states of Ohio, Indiana, Michigan, and Illinois

Oregon Trail—trail from Missouri to Oregon

Patriot—someone who supported the American Revolution

Pilgrims—founded the Plymouth colony

plantation—large farm that raises cash crops

political party—group of people that supports a candidate running for a government position

popular sovereignty—government in which the people have the power

Puritans—settled the Massachusetts Bay Colony

Radical Republicans—wanted to use the federal government to impose a new order on the South and wanted to grant citizenship rights to former slaves

ratification—the process of approving the Constitution

Reconstruction—process of re-admitting southern states into the Union

representative government—system of government in which officials are elected in order to represent the interests of the voters

republicanism—the idea that government should be based on the consent of the governed

Republican Party—political party formed in 1854

royal colony—a colony ruled by governors appointed by the king

salutary neglect—English policy of not interfering in the colonies

Santa Fe Trail—a trail from Missouri to New Mexico

secession—withdrawal of southern states from the Union

Second Great Awakening—religious revival, 1790–1800

Sectionalism—tension between North and South as each region placed their own interests above those of the country as a whole

Seneca Falls Convention—1848 women's rights meeting

separation of powers—the division of government into three branches

Shays's Rebellion—1787 uprising of farmers

slave codes—laws that regulated how slaves could be treated

slavery—a person was owned by another person in order to control their labor

Sons of Liberty—secret society that opposed British policies

states' rights—idea that the power of the states should not be trampled on by the national government

Stono Rebellion—1739 uprising of slaves

suffrage—the right to vote

tariff / tax—fees charged on an economic activity

Tariff of Abominations—1828 tariff that made Southerners angry

temperance movement—people who thought that drinking alcohol was wrong

Texas Revolution—1836, Texas declared its independence from Mexico

Three-Fifths Compromise—agreement made at the constitutional convention that allowed slaves to be counted as 3/5th of a white person

total war—Union strategy to attack not just enemy troops, but anything that helped the enemy: buildings, crops and rail lines

Trail of Tears—enforced journey by Cherokee Indians in 1838–1839 from their lands in the east to the west

transcendentalism—philosophy that believed in the goodness of humans and which valued experience and intuition above reason and logic

triangular trade—system of trade in which goods were exchanged between Europe, Africa, and the New World colonies

unalienable right—right that the government cannot take away

unconstitutional—law that is forbidden by the Constitution

Underground Railroad—series of escape routes for runaway slaves

urbanization—growth of cities

Virginia House of Burgesses—1619, first representative government in the colonies

Virginia Plan—plan of government that the constitutional convention considered

War of 1812—1812–1815 conflict between England and the United States

Whig Party—political party formed in 1834

Whiskey Rebellion—1794 protest by farmers

Wilmot Proviso—1846 proposal that would have banned slavery in any territory acquired from Mexico

women's rights movement—people who thought that women should have the same rights as men

XYZ Affair—1797 incident in which French officials demanded a bribe from U.S. diplomats

REVIEW

The Ancient Hebrews

Overall Objective: Analyze the geographic, political, economic, religious, and social structures of the Ancient Hebrews.

Read the information below to answer questions on the next page.

c. 1800 B.C.

- According to tradition, Abraham made a **covenant**, or agreement, with God in which he promised to obey God in return for God's protection of the Hebrews.
- Abraham's agreement marked beginning of **monotheism**, belief in a single God.
- Monotheism contrasted sharply with beliefs of others at the time who believed in many gods.
- Hebrews believed that God watched over all peoples everywhere.

c. 1700 B.C.

During a severe drought, Hebrews went to Egypt.

c. 1250 B.C.

- According to tradition, Moses led the Hebrews out of Egypt (an event called the Exodus) and received the **Ten Commandments** from God.
- The Ten Commandments became basis for civil and religious laws of Judaism.
- The Ten Commandments and other laws emphasized equality and the need to live a good life.
- The Ten Commandments had lasting influence on later belief systems.

c. 1020 B.C.

Saul united the Hebrews and became the first king of a new kingdom—Israel.

c. 962 B.C.

King Solomon became king of Israel and built a great temple in Jerusalem.

586 B.C.

- Babylonians captured Jerusalem and destroyed the temple.
- Jews were forced into exile.
- Prophets helped to keep Judaism alive.

515 B.C.

- The second temple in Jerusalem was completed.

63 B.C.

- Judea was conquered by Romans.

A.D. 70

- Romans destroyed the second temple.
- The **Diaspora,** the forced movement of Jews out of their homeland, intensified.
- To keep Judaism alive, Jews built synagogues (places for prayer and worship) and schools wherever they went.

Sacred Writings of Judaism

Hebrew Bible

- **Torah:** first five books of the Hebrew Bible. Tells the origins of humanity and Judaism.
- **Prophets:** stories about and writings by Jewish prophets.
- **Writings:** collection of poetry, history, stories, and writings.

Talmud

- **Mishnah:** written versions of Jewish oral (or spoken) law.
- **Gemara:** includes explanations and interpretations of the Mishnah.

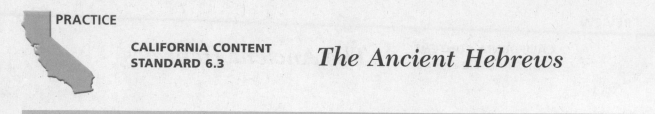

PRACTICE

CALIFORNIA CONTENT STANDARD 6.3

The Ancient Hebrews

Directions: Choose the letter of the *best* answer.

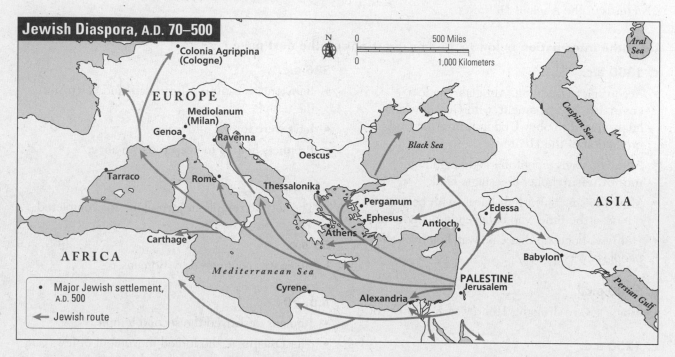

1 **An important way that early Judaism differed from other religions at the time was that Jews alone**

   A built intricate temples in which to worship and pray.

   B practiced monotheism—belief in one God.

   C believed in an afterlife, or life after death.

   D worshiped the gods of nature.

2 **Jewish civil and religious law evolved from the**

   A covenant between Abraham and God.

   B Mishnah.

   C Ten Commandments.

   D Torah.

3 **Which event was the cause of the movement shown on the map?**

   A the capture of Jerusalem by Babylonians

   B the exodus from Egypt

   C the death of Solomon and split in the Hebrew kingdom

   D the destruction of the second temple by the Romans

4 **Which of the following was a result of the Diaspora or spreading out of the Jewish people?**

   A The Jewish religion died out for hundreds of years.

   B Many Jews converted to Christianity.

   C Jews formed communities across Europe.

   D Jews settled primarily in regions throughout Asia.

REVIEW

CALIFORNIA CONTENT STANDARD 6.4

Ancient Greece

Overall Objective: Analyze the geographic, political, economic, religious, and social structures of the early civilization of Ancient Greece.

Read the summary below to answer questions on the next page.

Geography of Ancient Greece

- Rocky land divided by high mountains and deep valleys.
- The geography led to the rise of separate **city-states** rather than one united country.
- Aegean and Ionian Seas were links that united ancient Greeks for trade.

Greek City-States (700 B.C.–338 B.C.)

- City-states shared language and beliefs but had different forms of government.
- By 700 B.C., many were ruled by an **aristocracy**, or group of nobles, rather than by a single monarch.
- Some were controlled by **oligarchies**, in which a group of powerful people ruled.
- Strong individuals called **tyrants** sometimes seized control, supported by common people.

Athens—A Limited Democracy

- **Solon** outlawed debt slavery and opened the assembly to all Athenian citizens.
- **Cleisthenes** allowed all citizens to submit laws to the assembly for debate.
- **Pericles** paid public officials so that both rich and poor men could take the positions if elected.
- Limited democracy was established in which all free adult male landowners were citizens.
- All citizens participated directly in the government rather than electing representatives.

Sparta—A Military State

- Boys trained to be soldiers. Male citizens entered the army at age 20 and served until they were 60.
- Enslaved people did labor to allow male citizens to be full-time soldiers.
- Two kings ruled.
- All citizens were part of the assembly.

Persian Wars, 480 B.C.

Sparta, Athens, and other city-states united against a common foe—the Persians.

Peloponnesian War, 431 B.C.

Under Pericles, Athens began to take over neighboring city-states. Sparta declared war on Athens. Athens surrendered 27 years later.

Age of Alexander (338 B.C.–330 B.C.)

- Philip of Macedon conquered the Greek city-states.
- Philip's son, Alexander, expanded conquests east as far away as India and Egypt.
- Alexander's armies spread Greek culture wherever they went.
- Greek culture blended with those of Persia, Egypt, and India to form the Hellenistic culture.

Literature of Ancient Greece

- Greek **mythology** explained the world around them and told stories about Greek gods and goddesses.
- Greeks composed **epic poems**, such as the *Iliad* and the *Odyssey*, about their heroes.
- **Aesop** and others wrote fables, stories involving animals that teach a moral lesson.

PRACTICE

**CALIFORNIA CONTENT
STANDARD 6.4**

Ancient Greece

Directions: Choose the letter of the *best* answer.

1 Based on your knowledge of ancient Greece, what was *one* direct result of the geography of Greece on early Greek civilization?

A Tyrants were able to gain control.

B An oligarchy developed.

C A unified national state rose up.

D Separate city-states developed.

"When it is a question of putting one person before another in positions of public responsibility, what counts is not membership in a particular class, but the actual ability which the man possesses."

—Pericles, "The Funeral Oration," from Thucydides, *The Peloponnesian War*

---

2 Which factor made Athens's direct democracy different from representative democracy?

A Citizens elected representatives, who made the laws for them.

B Citizens directly made the laws themselves.

C There was a council to solve problems and an assembly to make policy.

D Political power was divided into three parts.

4 How did Pericles translate into reality the vision of citizenship he expresses in the quotation?

A He had families pass along public positions of power.

B He allowed lower classes to serve in the police force.

C He distributed all land and wealth evenly.

D He began the practice of paying public officials.

3 Why did the ancient Greeks most likely develop myths?

A to teach children useful skills and life lessons

B to explain and glorify natural and human events

C to document day-to-day activities and events

D to entertain society with dramatic stories

5 Which of the following describes a similarity between Athens and Sparta?

A They were both democracies.

B They were both military states.

C They were both on the same side in the Peloponnesian War.

D They both courageously resisted Persian advances into Greece.

Name _____ Date _____

Early Civilizations of India

Overall Objective: Analyze the geographic, political, economic, religious, and social structures of the early civilizations of India.

Read the chart below to answer questions on the next page.

Indian Civilization

The Aryans
- Migrated to India in 1500 B.C.
- May have belonged to a larger group known as the Indo-Aryans.
- Had a class system composed of three main groups: warriors, priests, and commoners.

The Caste System
- Regulated contact with non-Aryans.
- Was more complex than the original class system.
- Determined how people interacted and the kinds of jobs they held.
- People were born into caste for life.

Achievements
- The literature of **Sanskrit**, an ancient language of India, includes *Bhagavad Gita*, a sacred text that tells the story of the warrior Prince Arjuna.
- Indian architectural and artistic styles are seen in portrayals of Buddha.
- Indian mathematicians
  —invented the Hindu-Arabic numeral system
  —invented the decimal system and zero (also invented independently by the Maya)
  —identified the value of pi, the circumference of a circle divided by its diameter
- Physicians promoted health by using diet, exercise, and other methods to maintain physical energy.
- Artisans advanced metallurgy, or metal-working.

The Rise of Buddhism (528 B.C.)
Siddhartha Gautama, a Hindu prince, spent several years searching for a way to escape suffering in life. Finally, he meditated for 49 days under a tree and received insight. He became **the Buddha**, enlightened one.

The Buddha's Four Noble Truths
1. People suffer because their minds are not at ease.
2. Suffering comes from wanting what one doesn't have.
3. People can stop suffering by not wanting.
4. People can stop wanting by following the **Eightfold Path**, a path that outlines the right way to live, leading to **nirvana**, or the end of suffering.

The Buddha's Teachings
- Nonviolence.
- **Reincarnation**, a belief shared by followers of Hinduism, India's major religion.
- Rejection of the caste system and worship of Hindu deities.

After the Buddha's Death
- Buddhism spread throughout India, supported by Buddhist rulers.
- In the 7th century, Buddhism in India almost disappeared.
- Buddhism remained strong in other countries of Asia, where it was brought by traders and missionaries.

PRACTICE

CALIFORNIA CONTENT
STANDARD 6.5

Early Civilization of India

Directions: Choose the letter of the *best* answer.

Use the diagram to answer questions 1 and 2.

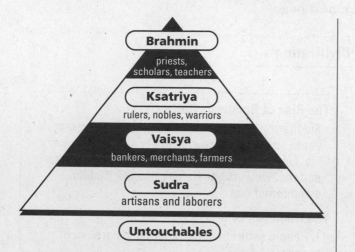

1 Why are the Untouchables placed where they are on the pyramid diagram?

A They are considered too low to be part of the caste system.

B They are foreigners who do not belong to the caste system.

C They belong to another caste system.

D They are Indians who have rebelled against the caste system.

2 Which conclusion is supported by the diagram?

A Only the bankers, merchants, and farmers had any wealth.

B The Aryans put those with knowledge at the top of the system.

C To the Aryans, trade was the highest position.

D Military skill was most highly prized in Aryan society.

3 In ancient India, Hindus and Buddhists both believe in

A the need for a caste system.

B many deities.

C nirvana.

D reincarnation.

4 According to the Four Noble Truths, people's suffering will end when they

A accept the caste system.

B take untouchables into their families.

C stop desiring what they cannot have.

D accept the Hindu deities.

5 Which of the following is an achievement associated with the Indian civilization?

A the decimal system

B representative government

C birth of democracy

D the Bible

REVIEW

CALIFORNIA CONTENT
STANDARD 6.6

Early Civilizations of China

Overall Objective: Analyze the geographic, political, economic, religious, and social structures of the early civilizations of China.

Read the chart below to answer questions on the next page.

551 B.C. Birth of Confucius	**Confucius** • Taught a code of proper conduct. • Identified five important relationships: ruler/subject; father/son; husband/wife; brothers; friends. • Believed social order, harmony, and good government should be based on family relationships.	• Taught that rulers and subjects should respect each other and that people should respect their parents and elders. • Stressed the importance of education. • Set clear family and social roles to help avoid conflict.

551 B.C. Birth of Confucius	**Confucius** • Taught a code of proper conduct. • Identified five important relationships: ruler/subject; father/son; husband/wife; brothers; friends. • Believed social order, harmony, and good government should be based on family relationships.	• Taught that rulers and subjects should respect each other and that people should respect their parents and elders. • Stressed the importance of education. • Set clear family and social roles to help avoid conflict.
c. 500s B.C. Life of Laozi	**Laozi** • Taught that a universal force called the *Dao* guides all things. • Searched for knowledge and understanding through nature. • Believed natural order is more important than social order.	• Stressed the importance of living simply and in harmony with nature. • Led to many advances in astronomy, alchemy, and medicine.
221 B.C. Beginning of Qin Dynasty under Shi Huangdi	**Shi Huangdi** • Unified and expanded China during Qin Dynasty. • Ruled harshly. • Used peasant labor to build roads to keep empire unified.	• Instituted government standards for weights, measures, coins, and writing. • Began the Great Wall to keep out northern invaders
202 B.C. Beginning of Han Dynasty	**The Han** • Developed a large government bureaucracy. • Instituted a state exam, testing knowledge of Confucianism, for government positions. • Expanded China's borders to include northern Vietnam, northern Korea, and southern provinces.	• Sent paper, silk, and pottery to the west along the Silk Roads in exchange for sesame seeds, oil, metals, and precious stones. • Was influenced by ideas, such as Buddhism, through interaction along the Silk Roads. • Invented paper from old rags, mulberry bark, and hemp fibers.

PRACTICE

CALIFORNIA CONTENT
STANDARD 6.6

Early Civilizations of China

Directions: Choose the letter of the *best* answer.

"Zigong inquired about governing.
The Master said, 'Make food supplies
sufficient, provide an adequate army,
and give the people reason to have
faith.'"

—from *Analects* by Confucius

1 Based on the quotation, what would *most likely* be Confucius's advice for rulers who want their people to have faith?

A Promise the people great wealth as a reward.

B Enforce a strict set of religious beliefs.

C Treat the people with respect and rule wisely.

D Draft everyone into the army for a period of time.

2 How did Shi Huangdi unify China?

A He built roads and set up a uniform currency and writing system.

B He surrounded himself with high-ranking nobles.

C He promoted Confucianism.

D He banned taxes.

"Do not honor the worthy,
And the people will not compete.
Do not value rare treasures,
And the people will not steal.
Do not display what others want,
And the people will not have their
hearts confused."

—from Laozi

3 Which statement *best* paraphrases Laozi's ideals expressed in the quotation?

A Misery results when when you value material possessions and status.

B People should invest in rare treasures for their family's future.

C Competition in a society leads to greater productivity and wealth.

D Most people cannot help but spend their lives in a state of confusion.

4 Which statement is *true* about China under the Han?

A China rejected Buddhism.

B China raised taxes.

C China refused to trade with others

D China expanded beyond its borders.

REVIEW

CALIFORNIA CONTENT STANDARD 6.7

The Roman Republic

Overall Objective: Analyze the geographic, political, economic, religious, and social structures during the development of Rome.

Read the summary below to answer questions on the next page.

The Founding of Rome, 753 B.C.

According to legend, Romulus, a descendant of the Trojan hero Aeneas, killed his brother in an argument over where to establish a city. He then founded Rome near the Tiber River. The early Romans were ruled by Etruscan kings. In 509 B.C., the Romans overthrew the Etruscan rule and founded a republic.

The Roman Republic

The new republic had two classes of citizens, the powerful **patricians**, or nobles, and the **plebeians**, or common people. In time, the plebeians won the right to elect representatives called tribunes. They also had their own assembly. The **Twelve Tables**, the law code written down in 451 B.C. and displayed in the Forum, helped to protect the rights of all citizens. Later laws were based on this code.

Three Branches of Government

Executive

- Two **consuls** were elected by the assembly for one year. They were chief executives of the government and commanders-in-chief of the military.

Legislative

- A **senate** of 300 members was chosen from the aristocracy.

Judicial

- Eight judges, or praetors, were chosen for one year.

End of the Republic, 46 B.C.

During a civil war, **Julius Caesar**, a Roman general, won great popularity among the people. He ended the war and two years later, he was named **dictator** for life. He was an absolute ruler but had many ideas for reform. He expanded the senate, enforced laws against crime, and created jobs for the poor before he was assassinated by senators who feared his growing power.

The Roman Empire, 27 B.C.

In 27 B.C., Caesar's great nephew, **Augustus**, became Rome's first emperor. Augustus had absolute power but retained the senate, consuls, and tribunes. Under his rule, Rome expanded and enjoyed a period of peace and prosperity.

The Roots of Christianity, A.D. 6

The Romans took over the Jewish kingdom of Judea in A.D. 6 and made it a Roman province. It was about this time that Jesus was born. He was both a Jew and a Roman subject.

Jesus preached justice and compassion, often using stories known as parables. He taught forgiveness and associated with the poor and sinful of society. Jesus's followers believed he was the messiah, or savior, whom God had promised the Jewish people. (The name **Christ** comes from the Greek word for messiah, *Christos*.)

Jesus's success made enemies of the Roman officials. As a result, he was put to death. Accounts of his **resurrection**, or rising from the dead, led to the belief that he was the son of God.

After Jesus's death, his **disciples**, or followers, continued preaching his message. Saul, who was called Paul after he came to believe in Jesus as the son of God, was the most important early Christian missionary. He converted many Gentiles, or non-Jews, to Christianity.

Name _____   Date _____

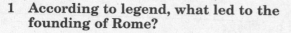
The Roman Republic

Directions: Choose the letter of the *best* answer.

1 According to legend, what led to the founding of Rome?

   A its settlement by a group of Latins

   B its settlement by a group of Etruscans

   C its colonization by Greek traders

   D the decision of Romulus to establish a city

2 In the Roman Republic, who were the consuls?

   A citizens of Rome and citizens of the provinces

   B the executive and legislative branches of the government

   C judges who interpreted Roman laws

   D the chief executives of the government

3 The Twelve Tables led to

   A protection under the law for all citizens.

   B more power for the patricians.

   C three branches of government.

   D the beginning of the Roman Empire.

4 What was Julius Caesar's contribution to Rome?

   A He was Rome's greatest judge.

   B He ended civil war and instituted reforms.

   C He fought for and preserved the ideals of the republic.

   D He wrote down the Twelve Tables.

> "The Christian Church differed from [other religious groups of that time]. . . . While the . . . [others] provided special means to salvation in the next world, they took the position of their devotees [followers] in this world for granted. The Christian Church offered a way of living in this world."
>
> —Peter Brown, *The World of Late Antiquity:* A.D. 150–750

5 According to the quotation, what was part of the unique appeal of the early Christian Church?

   A It promised life in the next world.

   B It gave followers freedom from political oppression.

   C It guided the lives of its followers.

   D It granted equality to all its members.

REVIEW

CALIFORNIA CONTENT
STANDARD 7.1

The Rise and Fall of Rome
(44 B.C.–A.D. 476)

Overall Objective: Analyze the causes and effects of the vast expansion and ultimate disintegration of the Roman Empire.

Read the chart below to answer questions on the next page.

Growth of the Roman Empire

- Strong leaders, beginning with Augustus, created a powerful government.
- A mighty army conquered lands around the Mediterranean and into northern Europe.
- Over 50,000 miles of roads allowed communication and transportation.
- A period of peace and prosperity strengthened the empire.

Decline of the Roman Empire

Internal

- Poor harvests and lack of income from new provinces
- Decrease in general level of education among citizens
- Communication breakdown within the empire
- Use of enslaved labor, less technological advances, especially in agriculture
- Political corruption
- Reduced patriotism among the people and armed forces
- Increasingly undisciplined military

External

- Invasions by Germanic tribes around the borders of the empire

Impact of the Roman Empire

- Representative government served as a model for future governments.
- Justice system, based on principles such as "equal treatment under the law" and "innocent until proven guilty," also became widespread.
- Engineering and science advanced, as in road and aqueduct construction.
- Christianity spread to become a major world religion.
- Stoic ideals, duty, and public service shaped a concept of citizenship.
- Latin became the basis for many European languages.
- Art forms, such as the mosaic, the fresco, and realistic sculpture developed.

PRACTICE

CALIFORNIA CONTENT
STANDARD 7.1

The Rise and Fall of Rome
(44 B.C.–A.D. 476)

Directions: Choose the letter of the *best* answer.

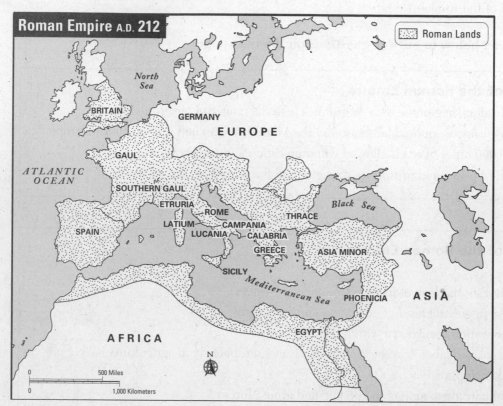

1 According to the map, by A.D. 212, Rome controlled all of

A sub-Saharan Africa.

B Asia.

C the area around the Mediterranean Sea.

D northern Europe and Scandinavia.

2 A feature of the U.S. legal system borrowed from the Romans is

A an accused person's need to prove his or her innocence.

B equality under the law for all citizens.

C the right to a speedy trial.

D no taxation without representation.

3 Which factor enabled Rome to expand and maintain order?

A aqueducts

B efficient network of roads

C enslaved labor

D Christianity

4 What was one reason Germanic tribes were able to overrun the western Roman Empire in the 400s?

A Troops were too busy conquering new territories to guard borders.

B Germanic government was more organized than that of the empire.

C Roman citizens had become overeducated and would not fight.

D The Roman military had far fewer soldiers than the tribes had.

REVIEW

CALIFORNIA CONTENT
STANDARD 7.2

Islam in the Middle Ages

Overall Objective: Analyze the geographic, political, economic, religious, and social structures of civilizations of Islam in the Middle Ages.

Read the cluster diagram below to answer questions on the next page.

Geography
The Arabian Peninsula is mostly desert and unsuitable for farming. As a result, herders developed a nomadic, or wandering, way of life. Permanent settlements were established at oases, where there was water.

Economy
• Trade grew between nomads and oasis settlements.
• Oases became major trading centers.
• Trade expanded to the Byzantine and Persian empires.

Social structure
Bedouins were nomads and belonged to clans—families of people related by blood or marriage.

Muslim Civilization

Government
• Under first the Umayyad and then the Abbasid caliphs (rulers), the empire was extended by military force and alliances.
• An extensive government, common currency, official use of Arabic, force, and a policy of inclusion, or equality among Muslims, unified the empire.
• When a rebellion broke out against the Umayyads, the family set up an Islamic kingdom in Spain.

Religion
• Muslims regard the Qur'an as the word of Allah as revealed to Muhammad. The Sunnah (Muhammad's words and deeds) and the Qur'an guide Muslims' daily lives.
• The Five Pillars of Islam, Muslims' basic religious duties, include
  — fasting at specific times
  — giving to the needy
  — making a pilgrimage to Mecca
  — praying five times a day
  — believing there is no God but Allah
• Jews and Christians received special consideration as other "people of the book," meaning their faiths were also based on holy books of teachings.
• Jews and Christians were encouraged to serve in government positions.
• Religious tolerance was extended to people of different faiths.

Culture
• Works collected from ancient Greece, India, Persia, and Egypt were translated into Arabic by Muslim scholars.
• Advances in mathematics, medicine, astronomy, and geography were made by Muslim and Jewish scholars.
• Papermaking techniques were improved.
• Calligraphy (the art of beautiful writing) and the arabesque design decorated books, tiles, mosaics, textures, and buildings.

PRACTICE

CALIFORNIA CONTENT
STANDARD 7.2

Islam in the Middle Ages

Directions: Choose the letter of the *best* answer.

1 What is *one* factor that helped spread Islam to other parts of the world?

A   military force

B   music

C   missionaries

D   agriculture

2 Jews and Christians enjoyed special privileges within the Muslim Empire because they

A   outnumbered the Muslims.

B   were more willing to convert than other groups.

C   also had holy books containing teachings.

D   were more capable of filling government positions than many of the Muslims.

3 How do the Five Pillars of Islam regulate Islamic religious life?

A   They refer to different groups of Muslims.

B   They describe the Islamic Day of Judgment.

C   They describe the most important Muslim leaders.

D   They identify Muslims' major duties.

4 Which important technology helped spread written knowledge in the Muslim Empire?

A   the invention of calligraphy

B   the invention of the abacus

C   improved papermaking techniques

D   development of an accurate calendar

"Know that the life of this world is but a sport and a pastime, a show and an empty vaunt [boast] among you, a quest for greater riches and more children. It is like the plants that flourish after rain: the husbandman [farmer] rejoices to see them grow; but then they wither and turn yellow, soon becoming worthless stubble."

—from the *Qur'an*

5 Which statement *best* expresses the central idea of the quotation from the Qur'an?

A   The activities and possessions of life do not last.

B   Nature is the source of all wisdom.

C   People should try to have as much wealth as they possibly can.

D   Life should be enjoyed to the fullest.

6 Which conclusion is accurate, based on the cultural achievements of the Muslims in the Umayyad and Abbasid empires?

A   Muslims cared little for learning.

B   Medieval Muslim scholars preserved much ancient knowledge.

C   The Muslims contributed little to Western Civilization.

D   The Muslims were the first people to make paper.

Name _____ Date _____

China in the Middle Ages

Overall Objective: Analyze the geographic, political, economic, religious, and social structures of the civilizations of China in the Middle Ages.

Read the chart and summary to answer questions on the next page.

MAJOR BELIEF SYSTEMS

Confucian Thought

- Status in society depended on the level of educational achievement.
- The right relationships maintained social order. Rulers should be virtuous and kind. Subjects should be loyal and obedient. Children should respect their elders.
- The influence of Buddhism changed the emphasis from education as the means to advancement in life to education as a way to achieve a set of ideas about what is right and wrong.

Buddhism

- Missionaries from India introduced Buddhist thought to China beginning in the first century.
- Buddhism taught that
  — unhappiness is part of life
  — people are unhappy because they are too attached to material possessions
  — people can learn to escape suffering by living a good life
- Buddhism spread after the collapse of the Han Dynasty in the 200s. It helped people to cope with their hardships during this period.

DYNASTIES IN THE MIDDLE AGES

Tang Dynasty, 618–907

- Expanded Chinese territory
- Developed an imperial state with a strong central government
- Built a network of roads and canals
- Used state exams to choose scholar-officials (educated men, mostly from the upper classes, who received government positions when they passed the exam)
- Created an elite class based on education and position in civil service
- Revived Confucianism, emphasizing the achievement of morality (living a good life) through education
- Created a law code
- Encouraged achievement in art and literature
- Became known for its horse sculptures and lively poetry

Song Dynasty, 960–1279

- Set up additional schools
- Focused the state exam on more practical matters to allow more people to pass
- Expanded trade

Yuan Dynasty (Mongols), 1279–1368

- Kept Chinese out of power
- Ended the state exam
- Encouraged foreign trade

Ming Dynasty, 1368–1644

- Sponsored Zheng He's voyages; then limited foreign trade
- Restored the state exam system
- Returned to Confucian moral standards
- Rebuilt the Great Wall of China

Tang and Song Dynasties

Oversaw techno-logical advances that would influence history.

- Papermaking spread to Europe in the 1100s.
- Gunpowder led to deadly new weapons and a change in how people waged war.
- Magnetic compass helped later European explorers travel greater distances.
- Movable type increased the availability of books.

PRACTICE

CALIFORNIA CONTENT
STANDARD 7.3

China in the Middle Ages

Directions: Choose the letter of the *best* answer.

1 Why did Buddhism spread after the collapse of the Han Dynasty in the 200s?

A   Status in society depended on the military.

B   Only Buddhists could rule the country.

C   It offered comfort in a time of uncertainty and disorder.

D   Many Buddhist missionaries from Japan came to China.

2 What is *one* factor that helped to unify China under Tang rule?

A   development of an improved system of canals and roads

B   invention of a system of writing

C   creation of a large middle class with a voice in government

D   rebuilding of the Great Wall

3 What do gunpowder, tea, and the magnetic compass have in common?

A   All three had an effect on the lives of Europeans in later centuries.

B   They were all borrowed from Japan and adapted by the Chinese.

C   Each dramatically changed the standard of living in China.

D   All were invented by the same highly educated scholar-official.

Use the quotation to answer questions 4 and 5.

"How easy for a scholar-official to offend, and now I'm demoted* and must go north. In my work I sought justice but the wise emperor disagreed."

—from the poem "On Being Demoted and Sent Away to Qizhou" by Wang Wei
*demoted: forced to take a lower-ranking job

4 What conclusion might be drawn from the poem about the position of a scholar-official in the Tang Dynasty?

A   A scholar-official risked grave consequences if he ignored the wishes of the emperor.

B   Becoming a scholar-official meant security for a lifetime.

C   Although positions were difficult to obtain, they were easy to keep.

D   Scholar-officials were pressured to continue their education even after securing their positions.

5 How might a scholar-official in the Tang Dynasty have obtained the position?

A   His family was related to the emperor.

B   He was given the job because he performed well in battle.

C   He worked his way up from a low-ranking job.

D   He showed his intelligence by performing well on a state exam.

REVIEW

CALIFORNIA CONTENT
STANDARD 7.4

Ghana and Mali

Overall Objective: Analyze the geographic, political, economic, religious, and social structures of the sub-Saharan civilizations of Ghana and Mali in Medieval Africa.

Read the sequence diagram below to answer questions on the next page.

Sahara Desert in Northern Africa

This region of Africa produced salt, which the southern part of West Africa needed. Berber traders carried this salt to trading centers in Ghana and then Mali. From Ghana, it continued its journey south. The Berbers also introduced the written Arabic language and Islam to the people in Ghana.

↓

Ghana (800–1076)

- Located between the salt-and gold-producing regions
- Supervised and taxed the trade that took place
- Grew into an empire as a result of trade wealth
- Collected tribute payments from conquered lands
- Governed by kings and members of upper classes who converted to Islam and learned to read and write Arabic
- Influenced by Islamic ethics and law

Mali (1235–1400s)

- Formed in the southern part of Ghana's empire
- Expanded beyond Ghana's borders
- Took over gold and salt trade
- Ruled by powerful Muslim kings, including Sundiata and Mansa Musa
- Established Islamic center of learning in Timbuktu

↑

Central and Southern West Africa

In the savannah or grasslands of central West Africa, people raised various crops and livestock. The southern part of West Africa was the forest region in which gold was mined. From these two areas, gold, various crops (such as millet), enslaved Africans, and livestock were sent north to Ghana and then Mali to be traded for salt.

Name _____ Date _____

Directions: Choose the letter of the *best* answer.

Africa: Vegetation

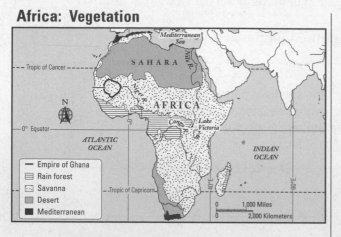

1 **According to the map, in which vegetation zone is Ghana located?**

A desert

B savannah

C rainforest

D Mediterranean

2 **Which is the correct description of the trade that took place among the regions of West Africa?**

A Gold was mined in the desert and sent south to be traded for salt taken from the banks of the Niger River.

B Crops and lumber were sent north from the rain forest to be traded for enslaved Africans and salt from the Sahara.

C Crops and gold were sent south to the rain forest from the savannah to be traded for salt and enslaved Africans.

D Salt was sent south from the desert to be traded for crops, enslaved Africans, and gold from the savannah and rain-forest regions.

3 **Which statement accurately describes the historic significance of the empire of Ghana?**

A Ghana's location allowed it to control the gold and salt trades.

B People of Ghana embraced the Christian beliefs of Berber traders.

C As Ghana expanded, it lost money caring for areas it conquered.

D Ghana was the largest empire that has existed in West Africa.

4 **The empires of Ghana and Mali were alike in that both empires**

A grew wealthy and powerful from the silk trade.

B were influenced by the laws and ethics of Islam.

C grew to be more powerful than the Roman empire.

D grew crops, such as millet, to trade with people to the south.

5 **What can be inferred from the fact that Timbuktu became an important center of Islamic scholarship under Mali's emperors?**

A The importance of trade had declined.

B A number of its people knew and could read Arabic.

C Mali rulers wanted to reinstate traditional African belief systems.

D In the 1200s, there were no other centers of Islamic scholarship in the world.

REVIEW

CALIFORNIA CONTENT STANDARD 7.5

Medieval Japan

Overall Objective: Use the following chart to analyze the geographic, political, economic, religious, and social structures of the civilizations of Medieval Japan.

Read the summary below to help you answer questions on the next page.

Major Influences on Japanese Culture

Japan is located 120 miles off the coast of East Asia. This location enabled Japan to learn and adapt aspects of both the Korean and the Chinese cultures.

Korean Influences

- **Buddhism** reached Japan from China via Korea. The Japanese combined Buddhism with their traditional Shinto rituals. Buddhism, particularly Zen Buddhism, had a major impact on the attitudes of Japanese samurai (warriors) and artists.

- The Chinese **writing system** also came to Japan through contact with Korea. The Japanese language itself is related to Korean.

Chinese Influences

- Japan adopted principles of **Confucianism** from China.

- Prince Shotoku developed the Seventeen Article Constitution, incorporating Confucian ideas, such as the importance of hard work and obedience to authority.

- The Chinese influence was also seen in **agriculture** and **the arts**. The Japanese used China's wet-field rice cultivation method. Japanese artists used Chinese themes in their landscape painting.

Feudal Japan and the Military Society

By the 1100s, a lord-vassal, or feudal system, was in place in Japan.

- The lord-vassal system developed as a result of **weak central government** and a breakdown in law and order.

- Small landowners performed military service for lords of large estates in return for protection. These lords, the **daimyo**, also hired warriors known as **samurai**.

- Samurai lived by a code of honor called **bushido**. They were required to show respect to the gods and generosity to the poor. They were to demonstrate loyalty and courage to the end. Bushido was so deeply a part of samurai culture that soldiers through the twentieth century lived by it.

- By the late 1100s, the transition to a military society occurred with the rise of the most powerful daimyo to the position of **shogun**. The shogun, the supreme military commander, ruled Japan under a figurehead **emperor**.

- Over the next four hundred years, rival daimyos vied over who would become shogun. Samurai now fought on a national level.

- In the 1500s, a series of shoguns succeeded in unifying Japan. In 1603, the **Tokugawa shogunate** began.

PRACTICE

CALIFORNIA CONTENT
STANDARD 7.5   *Medieval Japan*

Directions: Choose the letter of the *best* answer.

Use the diagram to answer questions 1 and 2.

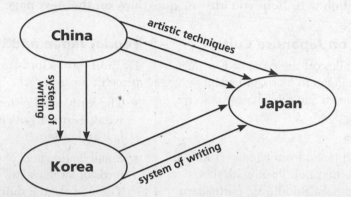

1 **In addition to the writing system, what else did Japan learn from China by way of Korea?**

A   Shintoism

B   a class system

C   the idea of samurai

D   Buddhism

2 **What are the correct labels for the two unlabeled arrows leading from China to Japan in the diagram?**

A   "Principles of Confucianism" and "Agricultural Methods"

B   "Rice-growing Techniques" and "Calligraphy"

C   "Shintoism" and "Forms of Government"

D   "Landscape Painting" and "Bushido"

3 **Which factor led to feudalism and the rise of a military society?**

A   a weak central government

B   Chinese influence

C   European influence

D   an overwhelming number of samurai

4 **Which of the following reflects the hierarchy of medieval Japan in *descending* order (greatest to least)?**

A   daimyo, shogun, samurai, emperor

B   samurai, daimyo, emperor, shogun

C   emperor, shogun, daimyo, samurai

D   shogun, emperor, daimyo, samurai

5 **According to bushido, it would be better for a samurai to**

A   retreat rather than face certain death.

B   die rather than face dishonor.

C   find another profession if he lost his fighting skills.

D   consider other options before engaging in conflict.

6 **In Japan's military society, the samurai**

A   faced massive unemployment.

B   rose to positions in the shogun's government.

C   became the major landowners.

D   became the country's army.

REVIEW

CALIFORNIA CONTENT STANDARD 7.6   *Medieval Europe*

Overall Objective: Analyze the geographic, political, economic, religious, and social structures of the civilizations of Medieval Europe.

Review the summary below to help you answer questions on the next page.

Feudalism

Feudalism developed to bring about order following the fall of the Frankish kingdom in the early 800s. To protect their property against invaders, landowners pledged their loyalty to a king. Knights became vassals of nobles, receiving land called fiefs in return for military service. Serfs worked on lords' estates, or manors. In return, serfs received protection and a share of crops. Manors were self-sufficient communities that produced almost everything people needed. Most people lived on manors in the early Middle Ages.

The Catholic Church

Powerful rulers and devoted monks helped to spread Christianity throughout Europe. The Catholic Church became a strong and unifying force in Europe, controlling the lives of common people. Frequently, popes and kings worked together toward common goals. The Church's wealth, efficient organization, and strong connections to the nobles made it a very powerful institution. It also played an important role in education, setting up universities, translating works from earlier scholars, and preserving knowledge through the work of monks and nuns. As kings grew stronger, they often clashed with the Church.

The Crusades

The Crusades, wars to win the Holy Land, began in the late 11th century. Although the Crusaders failed in their goal of winning the Holy Land, the wars broadened Europe's contact with the East and led to more trade and greater knowledge of other cultures. The increase in trade led to the growth of towns. Within these towns, guilds formed to make rules for workers in various crafts. Towns remained outside the feudal system. The Crusades also led to persecution of Jews and people of other faiths and created problems between Muslims and Christians.

Development of Democracy

Developments in England contributed to the rise of democratic thought and representative government. In 1215, King John of England signed the Magna Carta, guaranteeing certain rights to the nobles. The Model Parliament met. Independent courts of law were set up. Habeas corpus, the right not to be imprisoned unlawfully, became the law. Events in the 14th and 15th centuries weakened feudalism. The plague reduced the European population and weakened the manor system. The Hundred Years' War introduced new weapons that made castles and knights no longer necessary.

PRACTICE

CALIFORNIA CONTENT
STANDARD 7.6

Medieval Europe

Directions: Choose the letter of the *best* answer.

1 Which summary best describes feudalism?

   A a religious organization in which knights supported the pope by taking part in Crusades

   B a community in which most people farmed or raised animals such as sheep and pigs

   C a political system in which nobles pledged loyalty to the king and protected the serfs on their land

   D an economic system based heavily on trade with both neighboring and distant countries

2 Conflict grew between rulers and the Church when

   A the pope wanted to appoint bishops.

   B the Church began to set up universities.

   C kings became more powerful.

   D many knights joined the Crusades.

3 Which circumstance contributed to the growing power of the Church in the Middle Ages?

   A the Church's successful Crusades

   B the adoption of habeus corpus

   C the signing of the Magna Carta

   D the Church's ties to the ruling class

4 What was *one* effect of the Crusades?

   A Christian forces conquered Palestine.

   B Religious tolerance spread throughout Europe.

   C Europe entered into a period of isolation.

   D Demand for spices promoted trade.

5 Which event below was a step toward representative government in England?

   A the organization of the Crusades

   B the signing of the Magna Carta

   C the formation of manors

   D the creation of a kingdom

6 How did the Church promote education in the Middle Ages?

   A Monks and nuns copied ancient Latin manuscripts.

   B The Church encouraged scientific experimentation.

   C Parish churches set up village schools for children.

   D The Church distributed copies of the Bible.

REVIEW

CALIFORNIA CONTENT
STANDARD 7.7

Mesoamerican and Andean Civilizations

Overall Objective: Compare and contrast the geographic, political, economic, religious, and social structures of the Mesoamerican and Andean civilizations.

Review the information in the chart to help you answer questions on the next page.

	Maya (250–900)	Aztec (1200–1521)	Inca (1400–1532)
Geography	Mesoamerica (Mexico and Central America)	Mesoamerica (Mexico and Central America)	Andean region of South America
Social Structure	• kings • nobility: educated, wealthy; military • lower class: farmers, laborers • slaves: criminals, captives of war	• nobility: emperor, priests, officials • middle class: merchants, artisans • lower class: farmers, artisans, soldiers, enslaved captives	• nobility: emperor, priests, officials • lower class: farmers, artisans • no slaves
Religion	• over 160 gods • fasting, prayer, and sacrifice, some human • priestly duties performed by rulers	• over 1,000 gods • human sacrifice • use of complex calendar by priests to plan ceremonies	• divine emperor—son of one of the gods; priests • daily prayer, rituals, • animal sacrifices; human sacrifice rarely
Government	• independent city-states	• military empire • internal unrest under Montezuma • disease from Spanish • conquered by Cortés	• divine emperor, central government • civil war • disease from Spanish • primitive weaponry • conquered by Spanish
Economy	• agriculture: corn, beans, squash, cocoa • city-states linked by trade	• agriculture: corn, squash, chili peppers • extensive trade • huge central market • tribute (payment) from conquered areas	• agriculture: corn, potatoes, livestock • state-controlled • limited trade; no use of money
Communication	• hieroglyphics • bark-paper books (codices)	• glyph writing (pictures and symbols) • painted codices	• possibly woven writing • runner-messengers • knotted rope, quipu, accounting
Science/ Technology	• accurate calendar • base 20 numbers • invention of zero • pyramids, canals, terraced hills • observed Venus's orbit; predicted eclipses	• two calendars: farming and religious • pyramids, aqueducts, dams, irrigation systems • study of movement of stars and planets	• elaborate calendar • water management • 14,000+ miles road • terraced mountainsides

PRACTICE

CALIFORNIA CONTENT STANDARD 7.7

Mesoamerican and Andean Civilizations

Directions: Choose the letter of the *best* answer.

1 How did Inca society differ from the Aztec and Maya societies in Mesoamerica?

A The Inca nobility controlled the government.

B The Inca society had no slaves.

C The Inca noble class included farmers.

D The Inca had few skilled artisans.

2 What religious feature did all three societies have in common?

A They recorded their religious beliefs in codices.

B They prohibited the eating of certain foods.

C They had no priests so kings performed religious rituals.

D They were polytheistic, believing in many gods.

3 Which cultural achievement, called quipu, involved knots in ropes?

A the accounting system of the Inca

B the making of codices by the Maya

C the double calendar of the Aztec

D the invention of zero by the Maya

4 In the Aztec civilization, a calendar was developed to plan when to

A build stone roads.

B make bark-paper codices

C collect yearly taxes.

D perform religious ceremonies.

5 Which phrase *best* describes an achievement of the Inca Empire?

A had books called codices

B developed a system of roads

C cultivated cocoa beans

D advanced weapons technology

6 Which is *one* reason that the Spanish defeated *both* the Aztecs and the Inca?

A Many Inca and Aztec died from Spanish diseases.

B Most Incas and Aztecs had no weapons.

C Incas and Aztecs waged war with each other.

D Both the Incas and Aztecs relied on slaves as soldiers.

Name _____ Date _____

The Renaissance (1300–1600)

Overall Objective: Analyze the origins, accomplishments, and geographic diffusion of the Renaissance.

Read the outline below to answer questions on the next page.

Humanism

- The growth of trade exposed people to new ideas.
- Interest in classical learning, ideas from the ancient Greeks and Romans, grew.
- Study of these classical texts led to a movement known as **humanism,** which
  - —Focused on human potential for achievement
  - —Stressed the study of history, grammar, literature, and philosophy
  - —Promoted the importance of the individual and the need to be well-rounded
  - —Encouraged independent thought over blind acceptance of Church doctrine
  - —Balanced intellect and faith
  - —Taught that people could enjoy the good things of life

Art in the Renaissance

- Humanism led to a period of great creativity and experimentation called the Renaissance.
- Artists who were supported by wealthy patrons painted humans realistically and developed perspective, leading to a three-dimensional appearance in paintings.
  - —Leonardo da Vinci painted the *Mona Lisa* and excelled in many scientific fields.
  - —Michelangelo painted the Sistine Chapel ceiling and sculpted powerful figures.
  - —Raphael painted *The School of Athens*.
  - —Albrecht Durër created woodcuts such as *The Four Horsemen of the Apocalypse*.
  - —Jan Van Eyck painted symbolic works such as the *Annunciation*.
  - —Pieter Bruegel the Elder painted scenes of peasants dancing or children playing.
- Engineering advances led to architectural triumphs.

Literature in the Renaissance

- Writers began to write in the vernacular, their native language, instead of in Latin.
- Many writers focused on individuals and society rather than on God.
  - —Dante Alighieri wrote *The Divine Comedy*, a great poem about life after death.
  - —Machiavelli wrote *The Prince*, about how to get and hold power.
  - —William Shakespeare wrote plays showing a strong understanding of human nature.

Science and Technology in the Renaissance

- Scholars advanced the study of algebra, astronomy, and anatomy.
- Cartographers created more accurate maps.
- Johann Gutenberg invented the printing press, increasing the availability of books.

PRACTICE

CALIFORNIA CONTENT
STANDARD 7.8

The Renaissance (1300–1600)

Directions: Choose the letter of the *best* answer.

1 **Studying classical texts led humanists to focus on**

 A the philosophy of government and law.

 B art history.

 C the early Church.

 D human potential and achievements.

2 **How did the humanists approach their faith?**

 A They rejected Christian doctrine and formed independent churches.

 B They kept their faith but questioned some Church teachings.

 C They gave up worldly pleasures in order to follow their faith more strictly.

 D They followed a word-for-word interpretation of the Bible.

3 **The use of the perspective technique resulted in**

 A literature written in the vernacular.

 B paintings that appeared three-dimensional.

 C printing presses with movable type.

 D more complex buildings.

4 **Which was a result of the Renaissance?**

 A timeless works of literature exploring human nature

 B better forms of transportation

 C new emphasis on simple and pious living

 D new theories of crop rotation

5 **Why did the printing press encourage writers to use their local languages?**

 A Movable type could not be used to print Latin.

 B Books became more widely available but most people could not read Latin.

 C The Church reserved the use of Latin for the Bible and religious texts only.

 D It was not possible to write poetry in Latin.

6 **Once the Bible was available in the vernacular, more people**

 A drew their own conclusions about religious teachings.

 B turned to the clergy for religious instruction.

 C became missionaries.

 D became Catholics.

Name _____ Date _____

Overall Objective: Analyze the historical developments of the Scientific Revolution and its lasting effect on religious, political, and cultural institutions.

Read the cause-and-effect chart below to answer questions on the next page.

Roots of the Scientific Revolution
- Greek approach to learning about the world through rationalism or logical thought
- Greek ideas about science and math, such as the importance of observation in medical diagnosis, the use of dissection, and the basics of geometry
- Preservation of classical knowledge by medieval Muslim and Jewish scholars
- Scientific and mathematic advances by medieval Muslim and Jewish scholars
- Humanism-inspired interest in experimentation and exploration
- Renaissance interest in scientific learning
- Development of new technology such as the printing press
- Studies by Renaissance artists that increased knowledge of the human body
- Increase in knowledge of the world as a result of greater exploration

Spirit of questioning and access to more knowledge led to the Scientific Revolution.

The Scientific Revolution
- New scientific theories
  —Copernicus and Keppler proved that Ptolemy's earth-centered view of the universe was wrong and that the planets revolve around the sun.
  —Galileo Galilei, using the telescope he made, determined that Copernicus was right and the earth did revolve around the sun.
  —Sir Isaac Newton proved that gravity acts on all objects in the universe.
  —William Harvey discovered how blood circulates.
- New scientific inventions: The microscope, the telescope, the barometer, and the thermometer increased accuracy of data collection and led to further advances.
- New philosophies
  —René Descartes questioned beliefs until reason could prove them true or untrue.
  —Sir Francis Bacon developed the scientific method: observe, describe the problem or question, form a hypothesis, test the hypothesis, and draw a conclusion.

The Scientific Revolution changed religion and politics.

Consequences of the Scientific Revolution
- The Catholic Church weakened as people questioned traditional beliefs and thought for themselves.
- Thinkers such as John Locke applied new principles to government, which planted the seeds of democracy.

Name _____   Date _____

The Scientific Revolution (1500s–1700s)

Directions: Choose the letter of the *best* answer.

Use the chart to answer questions 1–3.

1543	Nicolaus Copernicus identifies sun as center of universe (heliocentric theory).
1609	Johannes Kepler proves that planets revolve around the sun.
1628	William Harvey describes the circulation of blood.
1643	Evangelista Torricelli invents the barometer.
1670s	Anton van Leeuwenhoek builds a microscope and observes microscopic life.
1687	Sir Isaac Newton publishes the law of gravity.
1714	Gabriel Fahrenheit invents the first mercury thermometer.

1 **What theory of the universe was held before 1543?**

   A The moon was the center of the universe.

   B The earth was the center of the universe.

   C Each planet was the center of its own universe.

   D Heaven was the center of the universe.

2 **Which statement *best* describes the historical contribution of the events on the chart?**

   A made possible further scientific discoveries

   B reinforced ancient Greek ideas

   C increased the power of the Catholic Church in Europe

   D increased the power of the kings in Europe

3 **What conclusion about the Scientific Revolution can be drawn from the chart?**

   A Most major scientific advances of the period occurred during the 1500s.

   B The 1600s were active years for scientific breakthroughs.

   C Literature and art were neglected in the 1600s.

   D Enthusiasm for discovery was fading by the mid-1600s.

4 **In what way did the medieval Muslim and Jewish scholars contribute to the Scientific Revolution?**

   A They invented the microscope used by Galileo.

   B Their humanistic ideals encouraged the spirit of inquiry.

   C Their translations made ancient texts available to European scholars.

   D They developed the principles of the scientific method.

Name _____ Date _____

The Age of Exploration and the Enlightenment (1500s–1700s)

Overall Objective: Analyze the political and economic change in the sixteenth, seventeenth, and eighteenth centuries (the Age of Exploration, the enlightenment, and the Age of Reason).

Read the summary charts below to answer questions on the next page.

Age of Exploration
• Better ships, instruments such as the magnetic compass and astrolabe, and more accurate maps led to explorers' being able to make longer voyages more easily.
• European desire for spices and silks led to efforts to find shorter routes to Asia. —Portuguese sailor **Bartolomeu Dias** first sailed around the tip of Africa. —Portuguese explorer **Vasco da Gama** sailed to Asia by going around Africa. —**Columbus** tried a western route that led him to the Americas.
• Portuguese led the trade of spices and other goods between Europe and Asia.
• Goods and ideas were exchanged across the Atlantic in a movement known as the **Columbian Exchange**.
• Disease spread by Europeans in the Americas killed over 20 million Native Americans.
• The trans-Atlantic slave trade was begun.
• European countries competed for colonies.
• Colonization brought changes to the European economy. — New wealth encouraged the growth of cottage industries and **capitalism**, private ownership of resources and the use of those resources. — Countries adopted **mercantilism**, which called for a favorable balance of trade and the discovery of rich natural resources to increase a country's wealth.
• The Europeans' worldview changed as they learned more about lands beyond the Atlantic and shifted their focus away from Asia.

The Enlightenment
• People applied the scientific approach to society.
• Political scientists and philosophers put forth new ideas about government. — **John Locke** believed that people consent to be governed in return for the protection of their natural rights. — **Voltaire** was for freedom of speech and people's right to liberty. — **Montesquieu** advised separation of powers. — **Rousseau** wanted democracy and people's right to choose their government.
• Enlightenment ideas swept across Europe.
• Salons, gatherings of intellectuals, spread enlightenment thinking.
• Enlightenment thought led women like **Mary Wollstonecraft** to call for reform.
• Democratic ideas spread to colonial America.
• Enlightened rulers, such as Frederick II of Prussia, Joseph II of Austria, and Catherine the Great of Russia, tried reforms.
• Americans declared independence and created a republic based on Enlightenment ideas.
• Democratic ideas in the English Bill of Rights became a model for the U.S. Bill of Rights.
• The *Declaration of the Rights of Man and of the Citizen* was adopted during the French Revolution.

Copyright © McDougal Littell/Houghton Mifflin Company

PRACTICE

CALIFORNIA CONTENT
STANDARD 7.11

The Age of Exploration and the Enlightenment (1500s–1700s)

Directions: Choose the letter of the *best* answer.

1 As a result of the voyages of da Gama and Dias the Portuguese

  A sent many missionaries to South America.

  B claimed large parts of South America.

  C gained control of the African route to Asia.

  D gained control of the spice trade with Asia.

The Columbian Exchange
From Americas → Europe, Africa, and Asia
• Vegetables (squash, sweet potato, potato, avocado, tomato, corn)
• Cacao beans
• Vanilla
• Quinine
• Tobacco
From Europe, Africa, and Asia → Americas
• Diseases (smallpox, influenza, measles)
• Grains (wheat, rice, barley, oats)
• Livestock (horses, cows, sheep, pigs)
• Fruit (citrus, grapes, bananas, peaches, pears)
• Sugar cane
• Coffee beans

2 From the chart, what can you infer about the effects of the Columbian Exchange?

  A exposed Europeans, but not Native Americans, to many new foods

  B enriched life in the Americas but not life in Europe

  C led to some harmful effects for people in the Americas

  D led to the raising of pigs and cows on European farms

3 Under the economic policy of mercantilism, a country's power was based on its

  A army and navy.

  B form of government.

  C natural resources.

  D method of transportation

4 Which circumstance explains the growth of capitalism during the Age of Exploration and the Enlightenment?

  A The collapse of strong kingdoms created problems in the financial markets.

  B Enlightened rulers wanted to increase trade with other countries' colonies.

  C More wealth let merchants reinvest their profits in other businesses.

  D The spread of disease led to advances in the field of medical technology.

5 U.S. citizens put John Locke's idea that people give their consent to be governed into practice by

  A exercising their right to bear arms.

  B using their free speech to criticize the government.

  C supporting their government in all circumstances.

  D voting for their representatives in government.

REVIEW

CALIFORNIA CONTENT STANDARD 8.1.1

The Great Awakening and the American Revolution

Specific Objective: Describe the relationship between the moral and political ideas of the Great Awakening and the development of revolutionary fervor in the American colonies.

Read the summary below to answer questions on the next page.

Dates

1730s and 1740s

Religious Movement

The Great Awakening, a religious revival, swept through the American colonies several decades before the American Revolution. The revival altered the way many people thought about themselves. Historians contend that these changes opened American minds to new ideas about society and politics. If the nature and practice of religion could change, maybe other traditions could too.

New Ideas

The fiery sermons of Great Awakening preachers, both in England and in the Colonies, stressed that people had their own moral choices to make. Jonathan Edwards, a minister from New Haven, Connecticut, was considered one of the great theologians and scholars. His sermon "Sinners in the Hands of an Angry God" compared sinners to spiders dangling over a pit of fire. Gilbert Tennent, a Presbyterian minister from New Jersey, also stirred up strong emotions at crowded sermons. People began to openly discuss and dwell on moral issues.

Effects of the Great Awakening

- The movement caused a rise in church membership, particularly in new denominations such as the Baptists.
- Several colleges were founded to train new ministers, including King's College, in Princeton, New Jersey.
- Some churches began to welcome women, Native Americans, and African Americans as members.
- The movement inspired colonists to help those in need, through new orphanages, schools, and mission projects.
- New ideas were hotly and openly discussed and debated—ideas about moral choices, such as what is absolutely right or absolutely wrong.
- Historians agree that such ideas and discussions shaped American culture, opening minds to later ideas of independence.

PRACTICE

CALIFORNIA CONTENT
STANDARD 8.1.1

The Great Awakening and the American Revolution

Directions: Choose the letter of the *best* answer.

1 What element, common in the sermons of the Great Awakening, may have opened minds to ideals of independence and equality?

A sermons often held outdoors

B plans for changing government

C topics addressing moral deeds

D images of dangling spiders

2 Why might the church revival movement of the 1730s and 1740s be referred to as the Great Awakening?

A Many sermons preached about overthrowing the king.

B New churches, schools, and missions attracted members.

C Before this movement, Americans had little interest in religion.

D Churches services were held at dawn.

3 Which of the following was one effect of the Great Awakening?

A Colonial church membership grew and became more diverse.

B Some churches now allowed women to become ministers.

C Colonial America began to have a public school system.

D Restrictions to separate church and state became law.

4 Historians agree that the Great Awakening influenced America's fight for independence by

A challenging people to make moral choices and to act on them.

B making people believe they were destined to go to heaven.

C inspiring the colonies to outlaw slavery and all forms of injustice.

D preaching that colonists should fight a war to break from English rule.

5 When did the Great Awakening occur in relation to the War for Independence?

A in the decade leading up to the war

B during the aftermath of the war

C a few decades prior to the war

D just as the war broke out

6 How did the Great Awakening affect women, Native Americans, and African Americans?

A It made the groups compete for political status.

B Women and minorities gained political rights.

C Some churches allowed women and non-whites to attend.

D Separate churches were started for women and minorities.

Name _____ Date _____

Specific Objective: Analyze the philosophy of government expressed in the Declaration of Independence, with an emphasis on government as a means of securing individual rights.

Read the quotation and call-outs below to answer questions on the next page.

1. People are born with individual rights that cannot be taken away from them.

2. These rights include
—the right to live
—the right to have freedom, or liberty
—the right to pursue happiness

"We hold these truths to be self-evident, that all men are created equal, that they are endowed by their Creator with *certain unalienable Rights*,[1] that among these are *Life, Liberty and the pursuit of Happiness*;[2] that *to secure these rights, Governments are instituted among Men*,[3] deriving their just powers from the consent of the governed; that *whenever any Form of Government becomes destructive of these ends, it is the Right of the People to alter or to abolish it*,[4] and to institute new Government, laying its foundation on such principles and organizing its powers in such form, as to them shall seem most likely to effect their Safety and Happiness."

—Declaration of Independence

3. The job of government is to protect these rights.

4. If a government does not protect these rights but in fact weakens them, the government should be changed or removed.

Philosophy of Government

Thomas Jefferson was the main author of the Declaration of Independence. To a large extent, he built upon the writings of the English philosopher John Locke. Locke argued that "just," or fair, governments

- are based on the consent of the people
- protect people's "natural rights" to life, liberty, and property
- should be changed or replaced if they become unfair

Instead of property, Jefferson listed the "pursuit of happiness" as one of people's natural rights.

PRACTICE

CALIFORNIA CONTENT
STANDARD 8.1.2

The Declaration of Independence

Directions: Choose the letter of the *best* answer.

Use the quotation to answer questions 1–2.

"... all men are created equal, that they are endowed by their Creator with certain unalienable Rights, that among these are Life, Liberty and the pursuit of Happiness; that to secure these rights, Governments are instituted among Men, deriving their just powers from the consent of the governed; that whenever any Form of Government becomes destructive of these ends, it is the Right of the People to alter or to abolish it. ..."

—Declaration of Independence

1 According to the Declaration of Independence, what three rights are people born with that cannot be taken away?

A free speech, the right to have opinions, and the right to own property

B the right to live, the right to be free, and the right to try to find happiness

C free elections, fair trials, and the right to alter government

D the right to be born, the right to die, and the right to be happy

2 What does the Declaration of Independence proclaim is an important right of the people when a government fails to protect their freedoms?

A write letters and petitions

B move to another country

C support or uphold the government

D change or dispose of the government

3 According to the Declaration of Independence, which reason best describes why governments are created?

A to protect people's rights or natural condition of freedom

B to help people find what they want to do in life

C to protect people from harm and make them feel secure

D to create opportunities for people and improve their lives

4 Which government challenge would arise directly from protecting individual freedoms?

A The country will have a long-term ruler who takes too much power.

B People will expect the government to provide for all their needs.

C There will be no common traditions or ideas that people share.

D The country will have to balance individual power with government power.

5 In the philosophies of John Locke and Thomas Jefferson, what must a government have in order to be considered just, or fair?

A agreement from the people living under a government's rule

B a justice system where criminals can be fairly tried

C a system of elections to determine fair and just leaders

D absolute power derived from consent of the church

REVIEW

CALIFORNIA CONTENT
STANDARD 8.1.3

Effects of the American Revolution

Specific Objective: Analyze how the American Revolution affected other countries, especially France.

Read the summary below to answer questions on the next page.

Ties Between the Colonies and France

Europe was stunned when the American colonies managed to win their freedom against the English army and navy, arguably the strongest in the world. In part, this success was due to financial and military help from France. Though France was an absolute monarchy, Louis XVI hated England and was happy to help the colonists fight against the English crown. Because France was involved in the American Revolution, there was much intermingling of ideas between French and American revolutionaries. Benjamin Franklin lived in France during the American Revolution and borrowed ideas from some French philosophers.

The Writings of Thomas Paine

Thomas Paine, a British writer and political philosopher, had come to America in 1774. In 1776 he published the famous pamphlet *Common Sense*, in which he argued for complete freedom from England. In 1791 Paine moved to France, after publishing the first part of another tract called *The Rights of Man*. In this document he argued in favor of the revolution in France. He believed that people were better off without kings and other hereditary rulers, and that they should take control of their own governments.

Effects on Other Countries

After the Revolution, America became a symbol of freedom and democracy. The Revolution was inspiring to citizens in Europe and Latin America who were organizing to fight for their own freedom. Some new democracies used the *Declaration of Independence* and the *U.S. Constitution*, along with earlier documents, such as the *English Bill of Rights*, as templates for their own documents.

Effects on France

At the time of the American Revolution, a growing middle class in France was becoming hungry for freedom and power. They saw that their counterparts in America had argued for and won freedom for the individual. Most thought they could do the same. The French Revolution began in 1789, less than a decade after the American Revolution had ended.

PRACTICE

CALIFORNIA CONTENT
STANDARD 8.1.3

Effects of the American Revolution

Directions: Choose the letter of the *best* answer.

Use the cartoon to answer questions 1 and 2.

THE HORSE AMERICA, throwing his Master.

—American Memory collections,
Library of Congress

1 The caption for this 1779 cartoon is "The Horse America, Throwing His Master." Why might an artist in 1779 use a bucking horse to represent the American colonies?

A Americans were known for raising horses.

B The cowboy was a known symbol of the American frontier.

C America had supported a ruling owner, and now rebelled.

D Horses are known to be rebellious by nature.

2 This cartoon was published in London. What do you think the artist wanted to say about the American Revolution?

A The Americans have a strong spirit and will win the war for independence.

B The British have the most weapons and troops and will continue to rule.

C The Americans will win the war, but will be worse off for it.

D The British and Americans need each other's cooperation to function.

3 What is one reason France decided to help the American colonists?

A to return the help Americans gave in the French Revolution

B to help any foe of France's old enemy, England

C to try out several forms of new weapons technology

D to prevent revolution from happening in France

4 How did the American Revolution affect the French middle classes?

A It inspired them to continue reaching for their own freedom.

B It taught them the best fighting methods to use in revolutions.

C It made them cautious about fighting against a stronger power.

D It caused them to see themselves as nobility and royalty.

5 How has the U.S. Constitution been helpful to many democratic governments around the world?

A It outlines the steps for starting a democracy.

B It gives favored trade status to democracies.

C It has been used as a model for other governments.

D It explains the philosophy of revolution.

REVIEW

CALIFORNIA CONTENT
STANDARD 8.1.4

A New Style of Government

Specific Objective: Describe the nation's blend of civic republicanism, classical liberal principles, and English parliamentary traditions.

Read the summary below to answer questions on the next page.

Before the war, Americans were angry that they did not have the same rights as English citizens. Once they declared their independence, they began to work toward a new goal—to have their own republic, a form of self-government.

Civic Republicanism

The ideas of civic republicanism originated in classical Greece, from around 500 to 300 B.C. These ancient Greeks ruled themselves using a **direct** democracy, not through representatives. For this system to work, citizens must all place the good of the community and country above their own individual interests. Citizens must all be well informed, participate actively in politics, be willing to fight for their country, and be "civic-minded" in all areas.

Classical Liberalism

The classical liberal view stressing **representative** democracy, in which citizens elect someone to represent, or look after, their interests, evolved in ancient Rome. The philosophy is different than a direct democracy where each citizen participates directly in government decisions and operations. In the classical liberal view, the best government is one that protects individual and minority rights through limits on government power. Freedom of speech, freedom of the press, free elections, and freedom of association are all important rights in this view, to ensure that the elected government is accountable to the public.

English Parliamentary Traditions

The British Parliament consisted of two chambers, or governing bodies. The House of Commons was filled with representatives elected by citizens. The House of Lords was made up of
non-elected judges, nobles, and church officials. Parliament provided a partial model for the colonists' representative government. When the time came for Americans to develop their own form of government, the idea of having two chambers developed into the Senate (modeled on ancient Rome) and the House of Representatives (based on the British Parliament).

PRACTICE

CALIFORNIA CONTENT
STANDARD 8.1.4

A New Style of Government

Directions: Choose the letter of the *best* answer.

1 **A republic is ruled by**

   A a king, queen, or emperor.

   B an elected representative group.

   C a council of priests or ministers.

   D people not accountable to citizens.

2 **Which statement *best* represents how the rights of citizens are protected in a classical liberal system?**

   A Take away most powers of government.

   B Make laws that protect the most wealthy.

   C Ensure that elections are free and fair.

   D Allow each leader to appoint an heir or successor.

3 **What is *one* example of an English parliamentary tradition that was incorporated into the U.S. system of government?**

   A a commander-in-chief elected by a majority

   B laws passed directly by a majority of citizens

   C representatives of lords and commoners

   D two law-making chambers, or houses

4 **A student council with one student representative elected from each class follows the political example of**

   A civic republicanism.

   B classical liberalism.

   C the English parliament.

   D modern liberalism.

5 **In a civic republic, citizens must**

   A make strong laws limiting the power of government.

   B honor the commands of a strong leader.

   C put what is best for the country ahead of oneself.

   D elect representatives to protect individual interests.

6 **In the English Parliament, there are elected representatives in**

   A the House of Commons.

   B the House of Lords.

   C both houses of parliament.

   D neither house of parliament.

REVIEW

CALIFORNIA CONTENT
STANDARD 8.2.1

*Influences on the
Constitution*

Specific Objective: Discuss the significance of the Magna Carta, the English Bill of Rights, and the Mayflower Compact.

Read the summary below to answer questions on the next page.

The Magna Carta, 1215

In the year 1215, a group of rebellious nobles forced King John of England to agree to the demands spelled out in a document called the Magna Carta. The Magna Carta proclaimed that

- a landowner's property could not be seized by the king or his officials
- taxes could not be imposed unless a council of prominent men agreed
- free landowners could not be put on trial without witnesses
- landholders could be legally punished only by a jury of their peers

Over time, the rights listed in the Magna Carta were granted to all English citizens, not just nobles and landholders. The Magna Carta signified the first time that the powers of the king were limited by a written document.

The English Bill of Rights, 1689

In the Glorious Revolution of 1688, King James II of England was forced to leave the throne and flee the country. He was replaced with William and Mary. The new rulers had united with Parliament to force James out and had agreed to sign a document limiting their royal authority. In 1689, the new rulers signed, as agreed, the English Bill of Rights. The document protected "the rights of Englishmen," ensuring the following:

- freedom from royal interference with the law
- freedom from taxation by royal decree, without agreement by Parliament
- freedom to petition the king
- freedom from a peace-time army, without agreement by Parliament
- freedom to bear arms for self-defense, as allowed by law
- freedom to elect members of Parliament
- the freedom of speech in Parliament
- freedom from cruel and unusual punishments
- freedom from fines and forfeits without trial

The Mayflower Compact, 1620

The men on the Mayflower signed an agreement to obey laws created for the good of the community. The Compact helped establish the principles of self-government and majority rule. It was built on the understanding that government can only be legitimate if it is founded on the consent of the governed.

PRACTICE

CALIFORNIA CONTENT
STANDARD 8.2.1

Influences on the Constitution

Directions: Choose the letter of the *best* answer.

1 What aspect of the Magna Carta has the *most* historical significance?

  A Over time, the rights listed in the document were expanded.

  B It was the first document to limit the power of the English king.

  C It was signed hundreds of years before the Constitution.

  D Rights in it applied only to landholding men, excluding others.

2 Which of the following documents influenced the writing of all the others?

  A Declaration of Independence

  B English Bill of Rights

  C Mayflower Compact

  D Magna Carta

3 The Mayflower Compact showed unique thinking because it

  A was based on the assumption that people could govern themselves.

  B promised the same individual rights later put into the Bill of Rights.

  C laid out the basic framework for the Constitution.

  D protected the same list of individual rights for women as for men.

4 What is *one* individual right the English Bill of Rights protects?

  A the right to petition the king

  B the right to keep a standing army

  C the right to privacy

  D the right to impeach the king

5 In matters of criminal justice, the English Bill of Rights demands that the accused has the right to

  A a hearing behind closed doors.

  B freedom from cruel punishments.

  C representation by a court lawyer.

  D an appeal, if he or she is found guilty.

REVIEW

CALIFORNIA CONTENT
STANDARD 8.2.2

Implementing the Ideals of the Declaration of Independence

Specific Objective: Analyze the Articles of Confederation and the Constitution and the success of each in implementing the ideals of the Declaration of Independence.

Read the summary below to answer questions on the next page.

The three documents listed below show how the founding fathers worked toward ideals of self-government.

The Declaration of Independence (1776) listed the colonists' grievances against England and stated there were certain unalienable rights that must be protected by any fair and realistic government.

- Individual rights to life, liberty, pursuit of happiness
- Ability to elect government representatives
- Local representatives able to pass laws
- Control over when government meets
- Taxation only with representation
- Speedy trial, trial by jury

The Articles of Confederation (adopted 1777, ratified 1781) contained the American colonists' ideas about how to create a new and better government. The colonists were so wary of an overly powerful central ruler (such as they had in King George), that they gave too much power to the states and too little to the federal, or central, government.

- States retain sovereignty.
- States enter into "firm league of friendship" with other states.
- States choose their delegates to Congress.
- Taxes are levied by states, not by the federal government.

The Constitution (written 1787, ratified 1789) balances power between the states and the federal, or national, government. It also balances power between branches of government. Ten amendments were added that spelled out individual rights. Together, these ten amendments were called the Bill of Rights.

- People elect their representatives to Congress and the Senate.
- Clear directives detail the balance of power between the branches.
- Congress levies taxes.
- The Bill of Rights (adopted 1789, ratified 1791) addresses the concerns of states for individual rights that were not protected in the original Constitution.

Name _____ Date _____

Implementing the Ideals of the Declaration of Independence

Directions: Choose the letter of the *best* answer.

1 Which of the following ideas are contained in the Declaration of Independence?

A how to balance power between state and federal government

B how a new American government should operate

C the colonists' grievances against the king

D the procedures for free and fair elections

2 One problem with the Articles of Confederation was that they

A gave too much power to the states.

B gave too much power to the federal government.

C were not agreed upon by every state.

D gave too many details about lawmaking.

3 How did the Constitution correct the problems of the Articles of Confederation?

A It took away state-level law making.

B It gave the states the power to collect taxes.

C It let southern states make laws for northern states.

D It moved some power from state to federal government.

4 Which statement accurately describes the Bill of Rights?

A It is the first part of the Constitution.

B It is a name for the first ten amendments to the Constitution.

C It protects the exact same set of freedoms as the English Bill of Rights.

D It protects the rights of states under the federal government.

5 The Bill of Rights was critical to ratifying the Constitution because it

A protects individual rights not mentioned in the Constitution.

B addresses the concerns of British Loyalists.

C rejects some rights mentioned in the Declaration of Independence.

D explains the thinking behind the Constitution.

REVIEW

CALIFORNIA CONTENT
STANDARD 8.2.3

Writing the Constitution

Specific Objective: Evaluate the major debates that occurred during the development of the Constitution and their ultimate resolutions.

Read the summary below to answer questions on the next page.

The Great Compromise At the constitutional convention, the founding fathers struggled, arguing about how much power different parts of the government should have. Two plans emerged about how best to balance freedom and power.

- **The Virginia plan** proposed a legislature with two houses, each filled with a number of representatives based on a state's population.

- **The New Jersey plan** was for a single house, with each state sending one delegate.

- **The Great Compromise** called for one house with equal representation (the Senate), and one with representation based on population (the House of Representatives).

Divided State and Federal Power Federalists argued for a strong executive branch, while Anti-Federalists wanted a strong legislature, or lawmaking body. Anti-Federalists feared that a strong president could become like a king. In the end, checks and balances in the Constitution balanced government powers.

- **Anti-Federalists** Patrick Henry and other Anti-Federalists opposed ratification of the Constitution. They said it would give the federal government too much power and that the states should be stronger.

- **Federalists** James Madison and other Federalists argued that the Constitution would offer states protection and keep a balance of power among them. Federalists supported the ratification of the Constitution.

- **Bill of Rights** Anti-Federalists wanted more protections for individuals and states. Some states, including North Carolina, Rhode Island, and Massachusetts insisted that there be a Bill of Rights before they ratify the Constitution.

Slavery Southern states would not have ratified the Constitution if they had been forced to give up slavery. So, some of the Constitution's framers compromised, allowing slavery but hoping it would gradually decline on its own. One compromise on slavery, known as the Three-fifths Compromise, stated that slaves would count toward a state's population only as "three-fifths" of a person.

The Commerce Clause and Indian Nations The commerce clause in Article 1, Section 8 of the Constitution gives Congress the power "to regulate commerce with foreign nations, and among the several states, and with the Indian tribes." The clause provides the legal basis for the special status of Native American groups—neither state governments nor foreign governments, they maintain some sovereignty, or self-rule as nations, under U.S. law. The sovereign status allows Native American groups to use their land for businesses subject to different laws than other businesses. Such businesses also pay different taxes than others.

PRACTICE

CALIFORNIA CONTENT
STANDARD 8.2.3

Writing the Constitution

Directions: Choose the letter of the *best* answer.

1 **What two ideas did the Constitution try to balance?**

A the rights of slaves and the needs of slave owners

B the right to know and the right to privacy

C the power of government and the rights of the individual

D the needs of government and the rights of the majority

2 **The Anti-Federalists were afraid that**

A a strong executive branch might lead to tyranny.

B state governments would have too much power.

C a Bill of Rights would guarantee too many individual freedoms.

D most voters were too uneducated to vote wisely.

3 **In the final draft of the Constitution, slavery was**

A legalized and protected for a term of 100 years.

B neither banned nor obviously protected.

C highly taxed as a business trade.

D allowed to continue but restricted to the South.

4 **States such as North Carolina opposed ratifying the Constitution because it**

A did not provide enough guarantees of individual rights.

B created a weak national government.

C solved the problems created by the Articles of Confederation.

D gave too little power to the executive branch.

5 **Which name correctly describes opponents of the original Constitution?**

A Federalists

B Republicans

C Anti-Federalists

D Whigs

6 **A small state would have been more likely to support the New Jersey Plan, because**

A representation in Congress would be based on a state's population.

B there would be two houses of Congress.

C larger states would have more power in Congress.

D it allowed each state equal representation.

REVIEW

The Federalist Papers

Specific Objective: Describe the political philosophy underpinning the Constitution as specified in the Federalist Papers and the role of leaders in the writing and ratification of the Constitution.

Read the summary and charts below to answer questions on the next page.

The Federalist Papers James Madison, Alexander Hamilton, and John Jay wrote 85 essays, published in New York newspapers in 1787 and 1788, to try to convince New York to ratify the proposed Constitution. They hoped to increase public support for the document by explaining the merits of a strong unified central government that was limited by law and was required to protect the rights of individuals. Madison, Hamilton, and Jay argued that the Constitution would offer states protection, keep a balance of power among them, and set up government in branches (judicial, executive, and legislative) that would guard or check each other.

Title	Paraphrase
"The Union as a Safeguard Against Domestic Faction and Insurrection"	A representative government must be strong to protect against internal conflicts and rebellions.
"Restrictions on the Authority of the Several States"	The states must not act as nations. They should have equal and limited power.
"The Particular Structure of the New Government and the Distribution of Power Among Its Different Parts"	With different branches of government, no one branch will have too much control.
"These Departments Should Not Be So Far Separated as to Have No Constitutional Control Over Each Other"	The different branches need to have some power over one another in order to check or guard against abuse of power.
"The Structure of the Government Must Furnish the Proper Checks and Balances Between the Different Departments"	Legislative, executive, and judicial branches should govern different areas and have certain power over one another.

Some of the People Involved in Creating the Constitution	
James Madison	known as the "Father of the Constitution" because of his influential role in shaping it
Alexander Hamilton, John Jay	defended the federalist position
Roger Sherman	helped draft the Bill of Rights, the first ten amendments
George Washington	presided over the Constitutional Convention
Gouverneur Morris	emphasized being an "American" rather than the citizen of a particular state, favored federal over state power
James Wilson	emphasized the rights of the common man

PRACTICE

**CALIFORNIA CONTENT
STANDARD 8.2.4**

The Federalist Papers

Directions: Choose the letter of the *best* answer.

1   What was the immediate goal of the Federalist Papers?

  A to provide historical background for the Constitution

  B to improve on the ideas in the Constitution and the Bill of Rights

  C to declare American strengths to the world

  D to persuade the citizens of New York to ratify the Constitution

2   What is one long-term benefit of the Federalist Papers?

  A They contain laws not stated in the Constitution.

  B They pinpoint and clarify ideas behind the Constitution.

  C Copies of the originals still exist, unlike the Constitution.

  D They detail all views expressed at the Constitutional Convention.

3   What role did George Washington play in the writing of the Constitution?

  A He was one of the authors of the Federalist Papers.

  B He authored the Bill of Rights.

  C He presided over the Constitutional Convention.

  D He crafted the style of the writing.

4   What is one view expressed by the Federalist Papers and the Constitution?

  A States should act as sovereign nations.

  B Strong centralized power can be limited by law.

  C The Constitution should not be questioned.

  D A lawmaking body should have three houses.

5   What philosophy or position did James Madison support in framing the Constitution?

  A A nation is best protected by strong centralized government.

  B Common working people are the nation's biggest strength.

  C A leader can take quick decisive action if given total power.

  D A union of states must allow each state to decide its own laws.

6   Which of the following correctly describes the relationship between the Federalist Papers and the Constitution?

  A one is a first draft for the other

  B one explains the intentions in the other

  C one expresses views not contained in the other

  D one was added to the other to help it become law

REVIEW

Religious Freedom and Separation of Church and State

Specific Objective: Understand the significance of Jefferson's Statute for Religious Freedom as a forerunner of the First Amendment and the origins, purpose, and differing views of the founding fathers on the issue of the separation of church and state.

Read the excerpt and chart below to answer questions on the next page.

Thomas Jefferson drafted the "Statute for Religious Freedom" for Virginia's constitution in 1779. James Madison finally convinced the legislature to adopt it in 1786. It remains in that state's constitution today. Jefferson and Madison helped ensure that the right of religious freedom be protected in the Bill of Rights in the Constitution as well.

> "Be it enacted by the General Assembly, That no man shall be compelled to frequent or support any religious worship, place, or ministry whatsoever, nor shall be enforced, restrained, molested, or burthened [burdened] in his body or goods, nor shall otherwise suffer on account of his religious opinions or belief; but that all men shall be free to profess, and by argument to maintain, their opinion in matters of religion, and that the same shall in no wise [in no way] diminish, enlarge, or affect their civil capacities."

—from "Statute for Religious Freedom" (1786), drafted by Thomas Jefferson

Some Founding Fathers on the Separation of Church and State		
Founding Father	**Opinion**	**Position on Church and State**
James Madison	supported religious liberty	completely separate
Rufus King	supported state aid to religion	separate, but related
Edmund Randolph	claimed government should have no power over religion	completely separate
Charles Pinckney	opposed religious tests for office	completely separate
George Mason	spoke against the establishment of a state religion	completely separate
Noah Webster	also opposed a state religion	completely separate

PRACTICE

CALIFORNIA CONTENT
STANDARD 8.2.5

Religious Freedom and Separation of Church and State

Directions: Choose the letter of the *best* answer.

Use the quotation to answer questions 1 and 2.

"Believing with you that . . . the legitimate powers of government reach actions only, and not opinions, I contemplate . . . that act of the whole American people which declared that their legislature should make no law respecting an establishment of religion. . . thus building a wall of separation between church and state."

—Thomas Jefferson, Letter to the Danbury Baptists, 1802

1 What does Jefferson mean when he says that "the legitimate powers of government reach actions only, and not opinions"?

A The power of government is very limited.

B Unjust governments cannot make people change their opinions.

C Government can tell you what to do, but not what to think.

D Government has no right to tell you what to do.

2 What does Jefferson mean by "building a wall of separation?"

A Religion and government do not function well when they are separate, or walled off.

B Americans should take care to keep church and government in separate buildings.

C The First Amendment ensures government and religion have no power over one another.

D America should pass a law banning religious words and religious people in government.

3 What important American document protects a citizen's right to freedom of religion today?

A Declaration of Independence

B Bill of Rights

C Articles of Confederation

D Federalist Papers

4 What was the most common view expressed by the founding fathers about church and state?

A Church and state have a better influence when they work together.

B Religion has a vital role to play in the governing of the country.

C Church and state should exist completely apart from each other.

D Some religious activities should be funded by government.

5 In America, under the protections guaranteed in the Constitution, citizens are free to

A go to any church they choose, as long as it is a Christian church.

B practice any religion they want, as long as they believe in God.

C decide not to go to church, as long as they believe in God.

D hold any—or no—religious beliefs, including not believing in God.

Name _____ Date _____

The Constitution and the Bill of Rights

Specific Objective: Enumerate the powers of government set forth in the Constitution and the fundamental liberties ensured by the Bill of Rights.

Read the chart and highlights below to answer questions on the next page.

Governmental Powers Set out in the Constitution		
Legislative (Congress)	**Executive (President)**	**Judicial (Courts)**
collect taxes; impose duties, imposts, and excises	act as Commander in Chief of Army and Navy	judge all cases arising from the Constitution, laws, and treaties
regulate commerce	make treaties	interpret the Constitution; determine whether laws are constitutional or not
coin money	commission officers	
secure patents for scientists and artists	take care that laws be faithfully executed	
declare war		
raise and support armies		
make laws		

Individual Rights Guaranteed in the Bill of Rights

- Freedom of speech, press, assembly, religion
- Right to bear arms
- Probable cause; no unreasonable search or seizure
- Due process (everyone gets the same sort of trial)
- Speedy and public trial; trial by jury
- No cruel or unusual punishment; no excessive fines

PRACTICE

CALIFORNIA CONTENT
STANDARD 8.2.6

The Constitution and the Bill of Rights

Directions: Choose the letter of the *best* answer.

1 What set of responsibilities does the Constitution assign to the Congress?

A appoint judges, make treaties, collect taxes, and appoint ambassadors

B declare war, make laws, collect taxes, and regulate commerce

C interpret the Constitution and decide the constitutionality of laws

D collect taxes and make treaties and agreements with other countries

---

"United States Constitution, Article 1, Section 8, Clause 1: The Congress shall have Power to lay and collect Taxes, Duties, Imposts, and Excises, . . . but all Duties, Imposts, and Excises, shall be uniform throughout the United States."

---

2 According to the excerpt, what is one limit the Constitution puts on Congress's power to collect duties or government fees?

A The president must agree to all duties or fees.

B The Supreme Court must agree to all duties or fees.

C Congress cannot borrow money from the states.

D Congress must treat every state the same way.

3 Which protection does the Bill of Rights give to people accused of crimes?

A the right to be released on bail

B funding to hire any lawyer

C the right to bargain with the accuser

D access to a trial before a fair jury

4 What can you infer is the reason the Bill of Rights guarantees "a speedy and public trial" to those accused of crimes?

A to allow the public to decide on the punishment

B to allow the government to save time and money

C to prevent unfair imprisonment of the innocent

D to prevent the accused from hiring a lawyer

5 What is one way that a branch of government checks, or keeps a watch on, another branch, under the Constitution?

A Courts can decide the constitutionality of laws made by Congress.

B The president commands the army and can declare war.

C Congress writes the laws, but the president passes them into law.

D The president decides the tax amount, and Congress collects the tax.

REVIEW

CALIFORNIA CONTENT
STANDARD 8.2.7

The Principles of the American System of Government

Specific Objective: Describe the principles of federalism, dual sovereignty, separation of powers, checks and balances, the nature and purpose of majority rule, and the ways in which the American idea of constitutionalism preserves individual rights.

Read each principle to answer questions on the next page.

The following principles are embodied in the Constitution in order to protect the two ideals of self-government and individual rights.

Federalism

The power of government is shared between state governments and a strong, representative national (federal) government.

Dual Sovereignty

- Federal and state laws have separate areas of influence and jurisdiction. While citizens are subject to both sets of laws, state laws govern many areas where federal lawmaking does not apply.
- Over time, the concept of dual sovereignty has changed with evolving interpretations of constitutional law.

Separation of Powers

Three branches of government—executive, legislative, and judicial—govern separate areas (leadership command, lawmaking, and criminal justice) in order to prevent one person or group from abusing power.

Checks and Balances

Each of the three branches of government makes sure the others are working properly. Each of the three branches exercises certain control over the others.

Majority Rule

Decisions are made by a majority. The rights of the minority are protected by a Bill of Rights, and by the accountability of elected representatives.

Constitutionalism

Government's power must be limited by a foundation of law with checks and balances.

PRACTICE

CALIFORNIA CONTENT STANDARD 8.2.7

The Principles of the American System of Government

Directions: Choose the letter of the *best* answer.

1 Federalism can be defined as a belief in a government where

  A a central government controls the states.

  B the central government has no power over the states.

  C states and a central government share power.

  D states decide what power to give the central government.

2 The concept of dual sovereignty means that

  A federal and state laws exist, and each governs separate, specific areas.

  B each person is a citizen of a state first, then a citizen of the United States.

  C U.S. citizens with ancestors in other countries, are citizens of both places.

  D people can choose whether to be tried under state or under federal law.

3 The "separation of powers" means that

  A people who work for one branch of government may not work for another.

  B three branches of government divide power so that one branch does not get too powerful.

  C the citizens can vote to impeach a president if he or she breaks the law.

  D the government cannot control the church, and the church cannot control the government.

4 Checks and balances in the federal government specify that

  A the Supreme Court can overturn laws passed by the Congress.

  B the Congress appoints Supreme Court justices.

  C the president can veto decisions of the Supreme Court.

  D the Congress can overturn laws made by the president.

5 Which statement correctly defines "majority rule"?

  A Individuals follow the agreements made by most of the group.

  B Decisions cannot be made without all voters present.

  C The Constitution applies to most of the citizens.

  D An elected leader makes most of the rules.

6 Constitutionalism can best be defined as a belief that

  A a constitution creates limits and rules for a government.

  B a constitution contains the only laws a country needs.

  C all countries should have a constitution.

  D all constitutions are basically similar.

Name _____   Date _____

REVIEW

CALIFORNIA CONTENT
STANDARD 8.3.1

Early American State Constitutions

Specific Objective: Analyze the principles and concepts codified in state constitutions between 1777 and 1781 that created the context out of which American political institutions and ideas developed.

Read the summary and chart below to answer questions on the next page.

Writing New State Constitutions

As the colonies declared themselves free, they no longer wanted to be governed by old, colonial charters. Creating a new state constitution was a chance to do away with unfair or repressive government and to try new political ideas. None of the new constitutions, however, gave rights to slaves, or allowed women to vote. Most state constitutions restricted who could vote and who could hold office.

Many of the ideas from state constitutions found their way into the United States Constitution. Protection of individual rights, for example, served as a model for the Bill of Rights.

Virginia
- Popular sovereignty
- Rotation in office
- Fair elections
- Protected fundamental rights
- Trial by jury
- Freedom of the press

Georgia
- By and for the people

New York
- Two law-making bodies: House and Senate

South Carolina
- Separation of church and state

Chart of State Constitutions

Important Events	Creation of State Constitutions
Boston Tea Party, May 10, 1773	New Hampshire: January 5, 1776 South Carolina: March 26, 1776 Virginia: June 29, 1776 New Jersey: July 2, 1776
Declaration of Independence, July 4, 1776	Delaware: September 21, 1776 Pennsylvania: September 28, 1776 Maryland: November 11, 1776 North Carolina: December 18, 1776
Treaty of Paris, September 30, 1783 Constitutional Convention, 1787	Georgia: February 5, 1777 New York: April 20, 1777 Vermont: July 8, 1777 Massachusetts: March 2, 1780

PRACTICE

CALIFORNIA CONTENT
STANDARD 8.3.1

*Early American
State Constitutions*

Directions: Choose the letter of the *best* answer.

Use the chart on page 81 to answer questions 1 and 2.

1 Looking at the dates in the chart, choose which important event happened in the same year that many states were adopting new constitutions.

   A the Boston Tea Party

   B the French and Indian War

   C the Declaration of Independence

   D the Boston Massacre

2 Which of the following states all had constitutions in place when the colonies declared their independence from England?

   A Maryland, Massachusetts, and New Hampshire

   B Delaware, New Jersey, and Vermont

   C New Hampshire, South Carolina, and Virginia

   D Massachusetts, New York, and Virginia

3 In 1776 and 1777, why did many states decide to write new state constitutions?

   A Great Britain had revoked their colonial charters.

   B They disliked the Articles of Confederation.

   C They wanted to better express new ideas about government.

   D They wanted to abolish slavery in their states.

"No minister of the gospel or public preacher of any religious persuasion, while he continues in the exercise of his pastoral function, and for two years after, shall be eligible either as governor, lieutenant-governor, a member of the senate, house of representatives, or privy council in this State."

—South Carolina constitution

4 Which principle of government is reflected in the quotation from the South Carolina constitution?

   A separation of church and state

   B legal protection of individual rights

   C government by and for the people

   D freedom of the press

5 Which of the following ideas was part of a state constitution, and later a part of the U.S. Constitution?

   A the right to hold slaves

   B the establishment of public schools

   C a legislature with two houses

   D military commanded by the president

6 In providing for voting rights, state constitutions

   A gave all white men the right to vote.

   B gave some women the right to vote.

   C strictly limited the right to vote.

   D did not address the issue of voting rights.

REVIEW

CALIFORNIA CONTENT STANDARD 8.3.2

Early Expansion in the West

Specific Objective: Explain how the ordinances of 1785 and 1787 privatized national resources and transferred federally owned lands into private holdings, townships, and states.

Read the summary below to help you answer questions on the next page.

The new Confederation Congress controlled a vast territory of western land that stretched from the Appalachian Mountains to the Mississippi River. These lands were not states, and they did not have local governments the way the states did. The Confederation Congress was worried that, as Americans settled this western territory, confusion and chaos would result if no one knew who owned indiviual plots of land. Congress passed two laws to divide and organize the western territory in an orderly manner.

Land Ordinance of 1785

This law laid the foundation for nearly 80 years of policy on dividing and selling public lands.

- It defined the basic land unit as a township, a six-mile by six-mile square, broken into 36 one-mile by one-mile square sections (640 acres each).
- Section 16 of each township was set aside for the "maintenance of public schools."
- All other sections were auctioned off to the public at a minimum starting bid of $1 an acre.
- The Ordinance was eventually modified when it became clear that most families could not afford to purchase the minimum 640-acre plot.

Land Ordinance of 1787

Also called the Great Northwest Ordinance, this law established the government for the Northwest Territory and explained how territories could become states. Giving rights to the settlers of the western territories encouraged westward migration.

- Applied to territories west of the original colonies but east of the Mississippi River and north of the Ohio River
- At least three but no more than five states to be formed from the territory
- Eligible for state status when free inhabitants numbered 60,000 or more
- Civil rights guaranteed
- Slavery prohibited— first national limit on the spread of slavery

PRACTICE

CALIFORNIA CONTENT
STANDARD 8.3.2

Early Expansion in the West

Directions: Choose the letter of the *best* answer.

1 In the Land Ordinance of 1785, a township was defined as an area made up of

  A at least 60,000 people.

  B 640 farm plots.

  C 36 lots of one square mile each.

  D a school and a courthouse.

2 Which aspect of the Land Ordinance of 1785 was *most* important to the quality of frontier communities?

  A giving a section of township for schools

  B having a starting bid of $1 per acre

  C defining a township as six miles square

  D defining a plot as 1 mile square

3 How many states did the Land Ordinance of 1787 say could be formed from the Northwest Territories?

  A three

  B between three and five

  C five

  D no specific number

4 A territory could apply to become a state

  A when the Native American population had moved out.

  B when its population reached 60,000 free inhabitants

  C after it had been a territory for 10 years.

  D when there were at least 10 farms per square mile.

5 Why was the Northwest Ordinance an important law?

  A It set aside land in the Northwest for Native Americans.

  B It encouraged the expansion of slavery into new territories.

  C It ensured that the settlement of the West would be orderly.

  D It forbade settlement west of the Mississippi River.

CALIFORNIA CONTENT STANDARD 8.3.3

Building Blocks of a Common Market

Specific Objective: Enumerate the advantages of a common market among the states as foreseen in and protected by the Constitution's clauses on interstate commerce, common coinage, and full-faith and credit.

Read the summary below to help you answer questions on the next page.

Today, we take some things for granted. We can travel from one state to another. Any store in any state will accept our money. A pound of sugar in California weighs the same as one in Colorado. But when the Constitution was written, this had not been the case. States had made their own laws about buying and selling. Often state laws conflicted, making it nearly impossible to do business with someone in another state. The framers of the Constitution gave Congress the power to make states work together.

Article 1, Section 8, Clause 3

"The Congress shall have Power to regulate Commerce
with foreign Nations, and among the several States,
and with the Indian Tribes."

Advantage: Consistency from state to state with respect to laws about prices and transportation.

Article 1, Section 8, Clause 5

"The Congress shall have Power to coin Money, regulate the
Value thereof, and of foreign Coin, and fix the Standard of
Weights and Measures."

Advantage: Every state uses the same monetary system and the same system of wieght and measurement. A dollar is worth the same amount and an inch measures the same distance in every state.

Article 4, Section 1

"Full faith and credit shall be given in each state to the public
acts, records, and judicial proceedings of every other state.
And the Congress may by general laws prescribe the manner in
which such acts, records, and proceedings shall be proved,
and the effect thereof."

Advantage: Each state respects the public acts of all the other states. You don't have to get a different driver's license for every state you drive through.

PRACTICE

CALIFORNIA CONTENT
STANDARD 8.3.3

Building Blocks of a Common Market

Directions: Choose the letter of the *best* answer.

1 **According to Article 1, Section 8, Clause 3, what does the Constitution dictate about U.S. trade with Indian Tribes, or Native American nations?**

   A Indian Tribes are only allowed to trade with one another.

   B Congress determines how trade with Indian tribes is regulated.

   C Only certain states may trade with Indian Tribes.

   D Each state can decide how it wants to trade with Indian Tribes.

2 **Without the commerce clause in Article 1, Section 8, Clause 3, which of the following activities would be difficult?**

   A manufacturing goods in one state and selling them in another

   B farming and running a store on the same piece of property

   C buying and selling goods in a single state

   D farming on Indian land

3 **Why was it beneficial for Congress to be able to regulate commerce between states?**

   A It could prevent states from trading with foreign nations.

   B Buying and selling things between states was easier and more profitable.

   C Individuals who couldn't find work in one state could get jobs in other states.

   D Native Americans were encouraged to enter the business world.

4 **What problems might arise in government without Article 1, Section 8, Clause 5?**

   A Foreigners could not bring money into the United States.

   B The dollar would be less valuable than foreign currency.

   C Each state could make its own coins and bills worth different amounts.

   D Americans would have to learn the metric system.

5 **How does having a standardized system of weights and measures help increase trade?**

   A People get better deals when they make purchases.

   B Certain sizes and weights of products are easier to sell.

   C People can trust that they are getting what they pay for.

   D There is no need to make laws about trade.

6 **What problem might arise without Article 4, Section 1, of the Constitution?**

   A A driver's license issued in one state might not be recognized in another.

   B States might refuse to issue driver's licenses.

   C People might not be allowed to move to a different state.

   D Banks might not issue credit cards in any state.

REVIEW

CALIFORNIA CONTENT
STANDARD 8.3.4

The Beginning of the Two-Party System

Specific Objective: Understand how the conflicts between Thomas Jefferson and Alexander Hamilton resulted in the emergence of two political parties (e.g., view of foreign policy, Alien and Sedition Acts, economic policy, National Bank, funding and assumption of the revolutionary debt).

Read the summary and chart below to answer questions on the next page.

Hamilton, Jefferson, and the Birth of Political Parties

Political parties emerged during the 1790s because Americans disagreed about how the new country should be run. Thomas Jefferson disagreed with the policies of Alexander Hamilton, Secretary of the Treasury. Jefferson formed the Democratic-Republicans and Hamilton formed the Federalist Party. These parties differed mainly with respect to how they saw the role of the federal government. Federalists wanted a strong federal government and less power for individuals. The Democratic-Republicans were against large government and supported the rights of states and individuals.

Issues	Alexander Hamilton Federalist Party	Thomas Jefferson Democratic-Republican Party
foreign policy	supported diplomatic ties with England based on our financial interests	supported diplomatic ties with France based on political ideals and loyalty
economic policy	envisioned an economy based on industry	envisioned an economy based on agriculture
National Bank	chartered a national bank	wanted national government finances to remain simple
funding for Revolutionary War debt	wanted federal government to assume state debts	supported independent finances for states
Alien & Sedition Acts	supported Alien and Sedition Acts of 1798	believed these acts to be unconstitutional

PRACTICE

CALIFORNIA CONTENT
STANDARD 8.3.4

The Beginning of the Two-Party System

Directions: Choose the letter of the *best* answer.

1 **When did political parties first appear in American politics?**

A   1760s

B   1790s

C   1830s

D   1860s

2 **Political parties were first formed in America because**

A   Americans disagreed with the British about how the country should be run.

B   Americans were looking for a way to fight British tyranny and oppression.

C   Americans disagreed with each other over how the country should be run.

D   Many Americans were unhappy with President Washington.

3 **Which of the following is *true* about Jefferson's foreign policy?**

A   Jefferson thought that foreign relations should be based on our national ideals.

B   Jefferson thought working with Revolutionary France might be dangerous.

C   Jefferson believed in reunion with England.

D   Jefferson thought we should support France, only if it would help us financially.

4 **Which of the following is *true* about Hamilton's financial policy?**

A   Hamilton wanted simpler national finances, with a large degree of independence for the states.

B   Hamilton wanted the U.S. government to take on states' war debts.

C   Hamilton believed the federal government should not play too strong a role in financial policy.

D   Hamilton thought states ought to pay their own debts from the Revolutionary War.

5 **What is true about Jefferson's Democratic-Republicans?**

A   They did not think that farmers were important to the economy.

B   They wanted the national government to take on state debts.

C   They supported the creation of a national bank.

D   They opposed the Alien and Sedition Acts of 1798.

6 **What is *true* about Hamilton's Federalists?**

A   They opposed the charter of a national bank.

B   They supported an economy based on industry.

C   They believed that individual states should manage their own finances.

D   They favored diplomatic ties with France.

Name _____ Date _____

CALIFORNIA CONTENT
STANDARD 8.3.5

Domestic Resistance

Specific Objective: Know the significance of domestic resistance movements and ways in which the central government responded to such movements (e.g. Shays's Rebellion, the Whiskey Rebellion).

Read the descriptions to help you answer questions on the next page.

Not long after the end of the Revolutionary War, when the country was still defining itself, there were two important rebellions. As in the war that forced America's break with England, in both domestic rebellions, citizens felt their government was treating them unfairly, and they engaged in armed resistance.

Shays's Rebellion (Fall 1786 to Spring 1787)

Shays's Rebellion is named for Captain Daniel Shays, a Revolutionary War veteran and Massachusetts farmer. He led a group of insurgents, mainly farmers, who occupied courthouses where people unable to pay their debts were being tried and sent to jail. By occupying the courts, they hoped to prevent others from being tried. Many people were in debt after the war, and the farmers were getting the worst of it. The rebellion was quelled and the leaders were sentenced to death. However, Governor John Hancock pardoned most of them.

In the summer of 1787, the Constitutional Convention was underway in Philadelphia. The delegates worked to create a stronger central government that would (quoting from the opening of the Constitution) "establish justice" and "insure domestic tranquility." The strength of the federal government helped to put the rebellion to rest. Shays's Rebellion is thought to be one reason why people rallied behind the Constituion.

The Whiskey Rebellion (1794)

Farmers also started the Whiskey Rebellion, which occurred in western Pennsylvania. The federal government was charging a 25 percent excise tax on whiskey to help pay the national debt. Whiskey allowed farmers to make money from their grain crops. It was also traded for other goods that they needed. Farmers had little cash and could not pay the tax. This problem and others that farmers blamed on the federal government led to a series of attacks by angry mobs. President Washington issued a proclamation and called up a large federal militia. At news of the army's approach, the rebels fled. This action set a precedent for the new federal government's authority, even in the affairs of individual states.

PRACTICE

CALIFORNIA CONTENT
STANDARD 8.3.5

Domestic Resistance

Directions: Choose the letter of the *best* answer.

1 Captain Daniel Shays was

   A a governor of Massachusetts, angry at the interference of the federal government.

   B a Revolutionary War veteran, angry at not getting his pension or benefits.

   C a farmer, angry that the crops had failed.

   D a farmer and veteran, angry that farmers were being sent to jail because of debts.

2 What was the outcome of Shays's Rebellion?

   A The uprising was defeated; most of the leaders were later pardoned.

   B All the farmers in the region had their debts pardoned.

   C The territory became independent from the rest of Massachusetts.

   D Shays was executed; the farmers were sent to debtor's prison.

3 How did Shays's Rebellion influence the writing of the U.S. Constitution?

   A It delayed the start of the Constitutional Convention.

   B It increased the power of common people in framing the Constitution.

   C It helped strengthen the idea of the need for a strong central government.

   D The Constitution established a permanent federal army.

4 Why had the government imposed a tax on whiskey?

   A to make people stop drinking

   B to support an army on the frontier

   C to pay off the national debt

   D to provide relief for struggling farmers

5 How did the central government respond to the Whiskey Rebellion?

   A It sent an ambassador to negotiate with the rebels.

   B It called up a massive militia to put down the rebellion.

   C It battled the rebels in court cases.

   D It agreed to let Pennsylvania deal with the problem by itself.

6 The federal government's response to the Whiskey Rebellion showed that it

   A would assist a state when the state was in trouble.

   B had the power and determination to enforce its laws.

   C was sympathetic to the problems of backcountry farmers.

   D imposed unfair taxes and was unwilling to compromise.

REVIEW

CALIFORNIA CONTENT STANDARD 8.3.6

The Laws of the Land

Specific Objective: Describe the basic law-making process. Describe how the Constitution provides numerous opportunities for citizens to participate in the political process and to monitor and influence government (e.g., function of elections, political parties, interest groups).

Read the summary below to help you answer questions on the next page.

Making Laws The Constitution created a Congress with two houses to make laws: the House of Representatives and the Senate. The citizens of each state elect members of the House and Senate. Either house can propose a new bill, but both houses have to approve it through a majority vote in order for the bill to become law. If the two houses pass different versions of the same bill, a conference committee consisting of members from both houses of Congress works out a compromise version. The bill is then sent back to both houses for final approval. Once Congress has passed a bill, the president has ten days to veto it or sign it into law. A bill that has been vetoed by the president can still become law if it receives two-thirds of the votes in both houses of Congress.

Participation One of the important foundations of the Constitution is the idea of government by the consent of the governed. Citizens participate in government by voting. They can vote in local, state, and national elections. By voting, citizens make their wishes known. Citizens can also participate by taking part in community activities, working for a political party, or running for office.

Monitoring or Watching Citizens are meant to know how their elected representatives make decisions and conduct governmental business. The Constitution includes a requirement (Article 1, Section 5) that the houses of Congress keep public records of their proceedings and their votes. A free press helps citizens monitor their government.

Opportunities to Influence

- **Voting** If an elected official does not act in accord with the will of the people, the citizens are free to elect someone who does. Citizens can also contact their lawmakers and tell them their concerns.

- **Special Interest Groups** Voters who share a concern or interest can work together to bring demands to lawmakers. They lobby, or influence, through petitions, groups of votes, and other means. Labor unions, environmental organizations, and chambers of commerce are examples of interest groups.

PRACTICE

CALIFORNIA CONTENT
STANDARD 8.3.6

The Laws of the Land

Directions: Choose the letter of the *best* answer.

1 **What happens if the House and Senate pass different versions of the same bill?**

   A Both bills become law, unless the president vetoes them.

   B One house agrees to drop its bill and accepts the version written by the other house.

   C A congressional committee works out the differences, and the Congress votes on the compromise version.

   D The president decides which bill to sign into law.

2 **A bill that is vetoed by the president can still become law if**

   A a conference committee makes a new version.

   B the bill is passed by a two-thirds vote in both houses of Congress.

   C enough citizens protest and contact their lawmakers.

   D the president's veto is not witnessed by anyone.

3 **Which of the following is *one* example of citizen participation in the political process?**

   A supporting community scouting organizations

   B voting in local elections

   C keeping their neighborhood clean

   D supporting a local sports team

4 **What is a legal way for you as a citizen to try to influence elected officials?**

   A Explain that you will pay money if they do what you ask.

   B Buy them presents or pay for their meals and vacations.

   C Write or call them to explain your views and concerns.

   D Threaten to harm them if they do not do what you ask.

5 **What role do interest groups play in American politics?**

   A They are primarily responsible for making laws.

   B They use illegal means to influence government officials.

   C They help voters with similar concerns influence government.

   D They are not part of the American political system.

"Article 1, Section 5: Each House shall keep a Journal of its Proceedings, and from time to time publish the same."

6 **According to the excerpt, what is the purpose of Article 1, Section 5 of the Constitution?**

   A It helps citizens monitor what is going on in Congress.

   B It allows members of Congress to keep their votes secret.

   C It encourages Congress to hold its meetings in private.

   D It prevents citizens from influencing the work of government.

Name _____ Date _____

CALIFORNIA CONTENT STANDARD 8.3.7

Freedom of the Press

Specific Objective: Understand the functions and responsibilities of a free press.

Read the summary below to help you answer questions on the next page.

The Importance of a Free Press

The First Amendment to the Constitution prohibits Congress from making any laws limiting freedom of speech or of the press. The founding fathers recognized the importance of conversation and debate about political matters. Thomas Jefferson said, "If it were left to me to decide whether we should have a government without newspapers or newspapers without a government, I should not hesitate a moment to prefer the latter." Abraham Lincoln also thought the press was important. He said, "Let the people know the facts, and the country will be safe."

Functions of the Press

- **Dissemination of information:** The press can educate the people about candidates, important issues, new laws, and judgments made by the courts.

- **Watchdog:** One of the key roles of the press is to serve as a watchdog for the people—keeping its eye on government and blowing the whistle when it finds evidence of wrongdoing.

Responsibilities of the Press

- **Truth:** News stories must be true and responsible. There are laws against **libel**—a printed statement or picture that unjustly damages a person's name or reputation. The press is protected from "prior restraint" (government censorship), but it must be careful not to print libel.

- **Decency:** The press may not publish obscenity—those materials that are judged obscene by prevailing community standards.

- **Objectivity:** The press should strive to present all sides of an issue. The more objective it is in its presentation of information, the more useful that information is to the citizenry.

Name _____   Date _____

Freedom of the Press

Directions: Choose the letter of the *best* answer.

1   The freedom of the press in the United States is protected by the

   A   Declaration of Independence.

   B   Constitution as first ratified.

   C   First Amendment.

   D   Fifth Amendment.

2   If a newspaper prints something damaging about a politician that it knows is not true, that crime is called

   A   error.

   B   libel.

   C   obscenity.

   D   treason.

3   "Prior restraint" occurs when

   A   a newspaper acts to prevent a politician from saying something.

   B   the government tries to censor something before it is published.

   C   a newspaper had a court order against it in the past.

   D   a newspaper censors what it writes because it was sued in the past.

4   What would be the danger to a democracy of having a government-controlled newspaper as the only source of information in a country?

   A   Journalists would be out of work.

   B   Only one side of the story would be published.

   C   The newspaper business would not be very profitable.

   D   The government would lie all the time.

5   Freedom of the press helps protect the majority of citizens by

   A   informing citizens about candidates and elected officials.

   B   working with candidates to help them get elected.

   C   influencing judges and juries.

   D   helping businesses find customers.

6   Which of the following *best* states the law of freedom of the press in the United States?

   A   War is the only event that can limit freedom of the press.

   B   The press is free to publish anything, even stories that are untrue.

   C   The press is not allowed to criticize the government too harshly.

   D   The press is free but has the responsibility to be true and fair.

REVIEW

Our Changing Landscape

Specific Objective: Describe the country's physical landscapes, political divisions, and territorial expansion during the terms of the first four presidents.

Read the summary and chart below to answer questions on the next page.

First Four Presidents of the United States

George Washington (1789–1797)
John Adams (1797–1801)
Thomas Jefferson (1801–1809)
James Madison (1809–1817)

Physical Landscapes

When George Washington was elected as the first president, the United States consisted of only 11 states, from New Hampshire to Georgia, almost all along the Atlantic Coast. Moving west meant going to the Northwest Territory, an area that included what is now Ohio. The country stopped at the Mississippi River. During Jefferson's presidency, the United States doubled in size by acquiring the Louisiana Territory from the French.

States that elected Washington	Connecticut, Delaware, Georgia, Maryland, Massachusetts, New Hampshire, New Jersey, New York, Pennsylvania, South Carolina, Virginia
New states that joined during the presidency of:	
Washington	North Carolina (1789), Rhode Island (1790), Vermont (1791), Kentucky (1792), Tennessee (1796)
Adams	none
Jefferson	Ohio (1803)
Madison	Louisiana (1812), Indiana (1816), Mississippi (1817)
Capital was located first in New York; moved to Philadelphia in 1790; moved again in 1800 to the District of Columbia, which was in the middle of the country at that time	

Political Divisions

Political parties developed from the split of opinions in Washington's cabinet. Those who favored strong central government became members of the Federalist party. Those who favored strong state governments became members of the Republican party. Later this was called the Democratic-Republican party. For a while power was divided fairly evenly. Adams was elected as a Federalist. Then Jefferson was elected as a Democratic-Republican. As time went by, the Federalists lost power until the party died out by the end of Madison's presidency.

Territorial Expansion

When the United States acquired the Louisiana Territory in 1803, it was not just doubling in size, it was adding unknown terrain. Explorers were busy for years exploring and mapping this territory.

- Pinkney's Treaty (1795)—settled boundary disputes between Spain and United States; allowed Americans to travel freely along Mississippi River
- Treaty of Greenville (1795)—12 Indian tribes gave up land to the U.S. government that constituted most of present-day Ohio and Indiana
- Louisiana Purchase (1803)—America acquired Louisiana Territory from France, doubling the size of the United States
- Lewis and Clark expedition (1804–1806)

PRACTICE

CALIFORNIA CONTENT
STANDARD 8.4.1

Our Changing Landscape

Directions: Choose the letter of the *best* answer.

United States, 1787

BRITISH TERRITORY

Disputed with
Britain

MAINE

Lake Superior

Lake Michigan

Lake Huron

L. Ontario

L. Erie

N.H.

NEW
YORK

MASS.

R.I.

CONN.

PENNSYLVANIA

NEW JERSEY

DELAWARE

MARYLAND

NORTHWEST
TERRITORY

Wabash R.

Ohio R.

Missouri R.

VIRGINIA

NORTH
CAROLINA

LOUISIANA
TERRITORY
(SPANISH)

Mississippi R.

SOUTH
CAROLINA

ATLANTIC
OCEAN

GEORGIA

N

Disputed with
Spain

SPANISH
FLORIDA

Gulf of
Mexico

0   250 Miles

0   500 Kilometers

Settled areas
Frontier areas
Disputed territory

1 According to the map, in 1787 the United States western border ended at which river?

A the Ohio River

B the Mississippi River

C the Wabash River

D the Missouri River

2 The United States doubled in size during the presidency of

A George Washington.

B John Adams.

C Thomas Jefferson.

D James Madison.

3 *One* reason the District of Columbia was chosen as the nation's new capital was that it was

A very small.

B near the middle of the country.

C the home of George Washington.

D far from New York, the first capital.

4 *One* major feature of the United States between 1789 and 1817 was

A equal rights for all people.

B race riots.

C territorial expansion.

D development of railroads.

Name _____ Date _____

The Rise of Capitalism

Specific Objective: Analyze the rise of capitalism and the economic problems and conflicts that accompanied it (e.g., Jackson's opposition to the National Bank; early decisions of the U.S. Supreme Court that reinforced the sanctity of contracts and a capitalist economic system of law).

Read the summary and chart below to answer questions on the next page.

In 1776 Scottish economist Adam Smith wrote in *The Wealth of Nations* that if governments didn't interfere with the self-interest of individuals, wealth would increase. Twenty years later, Slater's Mill in Rhode Island became the first American factory. Alexander Hamilton supported the idea of industrialization. Thomas Jefferson, who had seen the pollution caused by factories in England, had doubts. The development of the cotton gin meant increased cotton production in the South and an increased demand for slave labor. As coal and steam power gave rise to improved transportation, new markets in the western part of the country opened up and modern capitalism was in operation.

National Bank

Andrew Jackson was not a supporter of Hamilton's National Bank. He believed it corrupted democracy. He said the bank was run by "stockjobbers" who were robbing workers of their hard-won incomes. He vetoed a bill in 1832 that was meant to extend the National Bank's charter past 1836. In 1833 he forcibly removed the federal deposits from the Bank's vaults and distributed them among smaller banks. He was a fiscal conservative who valued hard cash over credit.

Supreme Court Decisions

- *Fletcher* v. *Peck* (1810)—Upheld the sanctity of contracts
- *McCulloch* v. *Maryland* (1819)—Confirmed the constitutionality of the Bank of the United States
- *Dartmouth College* v. *Woodward* (1819)—Again upheld the sanctity of contracts
- *Gibbons* v. *Ogden* (1824)—Affirmed the power of Congress over interstate commerce

Panic of 1819

Small banks folded when the National Bank started foreclosing on mortgages and tightening credit, thereby causing a panic. Congress then raised tariffs and plunged the country into six years of depression.

PRACTICE

CALIFORNIA CONTENT STANDARD 8.4.3

The Rise of Capitalism

Directions: Choose the letter of the *best* answer.

1 Adam Smith believed that wealth would increase if governments

  A raised taxes.

  B taxed only income.

  C subsidized industry.

  D left individuals alone.

2 What did Andrew Jackson do in connection with the National Bank?

  A hired stockjobbers to run it

  B vetoed a bill extending its charter

  C praised it for securing democracy

  D made large federal deposits to its vaults

3 Which of the following happened during the Panic of 1819?

  A Congress lowered tariffs.

  B Small banks tightened credit.

  C The country pulled out of depression.

  D The National Bank foreclosed on mortgages.

4 *Fletcher* v. *Peck* was one of several early Supreme Court decisions that

  A supported free speech.

  B affirmed the power of the states.

  C upheld the sanctity of contracts.

  D acknowledged the right to bear arms.

5 New transportation modes and inventions gave rise to

  A abolitionism.

  B the cotton gin.

  C modern capitalism.

  D small farming.

6 The cotton gin, which helped increase cotton production, also increased

  A pollution in cities.

  B markets in the West.

  C demand for slave labor.

  D the cost of transportation.

Name _____ Date _____

Specific Objective: Discuss daily life, including traditions in art, music, and literature, of early national America (e.g., through writings by Washington Irving, James Fenimore Cooper).

Read the summary and chart below to answer questions on the next page.

In the early 1800s, while many people lived on farms, the industrial revolution was just around the corner, and families were moving to cities. Where once a family made everything it needed, now more and more items were for sale. Some of these items were made in factories, others in homes, often by the whole family.

At that time, American art traditions were mostly borrowed from Europe, but a shift was beginning to occur and American artists were starting to think about what it was to be American and to reflect that in their artwork. Two such American artists were **Washington Irving** (1783–1859) and **James Fenimore Cooper** (1789–1851). Both authors worked to give the new country a sense of its own magic and history.

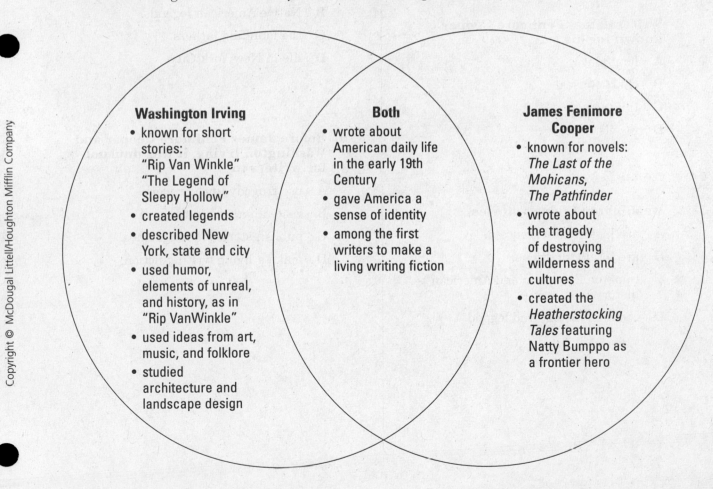

Washington Irving
- known for short stories: "Rip Van Winkle" "The Legend of Sleepy Hollow"
- created legends
- described New York, state and city
- used humor, elements of unreal, and history, as in "Rip VanWinkle"
- used ideas from art, music, and folklore
- studied architecture and landscape design

Both
- wrote about American daily life in the early 19th Century
- gave America a sense of identity
- among the first writers to make a living writing fiction

James Fenimore Cooper
- known for novels: *The Last of the Mohicans*, *The Pathfinder*
- wrote about the tragedy of destroying wilderness and cultures
- created the *Heatherstocking Tales* featuring Natty Bumppo as a frontier hero

PRACTICE

CALIFORNIA CONTENT
STANDARD 8.4.4

The Nation's Early Literature

Directions: Choose the letter of the *best* answer.

1 How was daily life changing in America around the beginning of the 19th Century?

A More people were going to Europe to study art.

B Fewer people now lived in cities.

C It was becoming more difficult to make a living as a writer.

D It was getting easier to buy things instead of making them.

2 Writer James Fenimore Cooper is known for his

A long plays.

B short stories.

C tall tales.

D novels.

3 Washington Irving's stories

A are historically accurate.

B are totally fictitious.

C combine European and American history.

D combine history and legend.

4 Washington Irving's fiction was known for its

A design.

B humor.

C religion.

D tragedy.

5 James Fenimore Cooper wrote about

A the western frontier.

B Native American legends.

C the founding fathers.

D life in New York City.

6 Before James Fenimore Cooper and Washington Irving, it was unusual for writers to

A use tragedy in their work.

B write anything but essays.

C publish stories in magazines.

D make a living writing fiction.

REVIEW

CALIFORNIA CONTENT STANDARD 8.5.1

The War of 1812

Specific Objective: Understand the political and economic causes and consequences of the War of 1812. Know the major battles, leaders, and events that led to a final peace.

Read the summary to answer the questions on the next page.

Causes of the War of 1812

Tensions grew between the United States and England for three reasons:

1. England tried to prevent America from trading with England's enemies; Americans wanted to be able to trade with everybody.

2. England impressed (or kidnapped) American sailors to work on British ships; the most famous incident occurred when the British ship *Leopard* attacked the American ship *Chesapeake*.

3. Americans were angered because they thought the British were encouraging Native American tribes to attack settlers on the frontier.

The War of 1812

1812—Americans begin to assemble a naval fleet on lake Erie, under Oliver Hazard Perry.

1813—England blockaded America's Atlantic coast.

1813—The American navy under Oliver Hazard Perry won important victories around the Great Lakes.

  —Battle of the Thames: William Henry Harrison defeated the British in Canada and killed Tecumseh.

1814—The British burned the White House and other important buildings in Washington D.C. but failed to take Baltimore.

1815—Battle of New Orleans: General Andrew Jackson's forces defeated the British.

Consequences of the War of 1812

There was no clear winner in the war—neither side gained any land or new territory. There were four consequences:

1. **Foreign Affairs**—America proved that it could defend itself from attack by a European power.

2. **Economy**—Since it was not able to trade with England, America had to make many of the manufactured goods that it normally imported; this helped the economy.

3. **Frontier**—Many Indians helped the British fight the Americans during the war. When the British withdrew, Native Americans were not able to resist American settlers moving onto their lands.

4. **Patriotism**—Many Americans felt good that America did not allow England to defeat them; this helped Americans feel more patriotic about their country.

PRACTICE

CALIFORNIA CONTENT
STANDARD 8.5.1

The War of 1812

Directions: Choose the letter of the *best* answer.

1 **Which of the following was *one* cause of the War of 1812?**

A   Native American alliances with Great Britain.

B   British companies withdrawing from American markets

C   Thomas Jefferson's 1807 trade embargo

D   George Washington's poor training of American sailors

2 **Which was a famous battle of the War of 1812?**

A   Lexington and Concord

B   New Orleans

C   Carthage

D   Antietam

3 **Who won the War of 1812?**

A   Americans

B   British

C   French

D   There was no clear winner.

4 **What was an economic result of the War of 1812?**

A   The British economy boomed.

B   American manufacturing increased.

C   The American economy weakened.

D   American products were boycotted.

5 **Whom did many Native Americans support during the war?**

A   Americans

B   British

C   Canadians

D   French

6 **What was *one* consequence for the United States of the War of 1812?**

A   lesser tariffs, or fees on imports

B   increased manufacturing

C   an end to the slave trade

D   stronger Native American forces

Name _____   Date _____

American Foreign Policy and Territorial Expansion

Specific Objective: Know the changing boundaries of the United States. Describe the relationships the country had with its neighbors (current Mexico and Canada) and Europe, including the influence of the Monroe Doctrine. Describe how those relationships influenced westward expansion and the Mexican-American War.

Read the summary and the map to answer questions on the next page.

The Monroe Doctrine and Expansion

When European countries were thinking about fighting to regain colonies in Latin America, some citizens of the United States thought this was a danger to the United States. The **Monroe Doctrine** of 1823 said the United States would not allow any European country to try to create new colonies anywhere in North or South America. In return, the United States would not get involved in any European political affairs.

During the first seventy years after the Revolutionary War, the boundaries of the United States kept expanding, through negotiations, purchases, and wars.

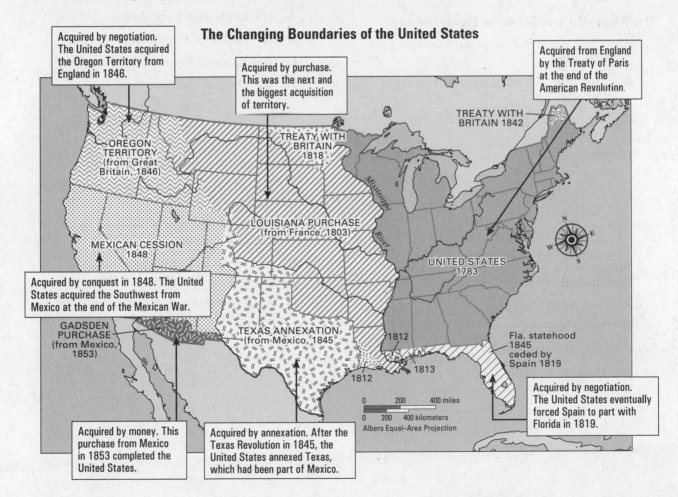

The Changing Boundaries of the United States

Acquired by negotiation. The United States acquired the Oregon Territory from England in 1846.

Acquired by purchase. This was the next and the biggest acquisition of territory.

Acquired from England by the Treaty of Paris at the end of the American Revolution.

TREATY WITH BRITAIN 1842

OREGON TERRITORY (from Great Britain, 1846)

TREATY WITH BRITAIN 1818

LOUISIANA PURCHASE (from France, 1803)

MEXICAN CESSION 1848

Acquired by conquest in 1848. The United States acquired the Southwest from Mexico at the end of the Mexican War.

UNITED STATES 1783

GADSDEN PURCHASE (from Mexico, 1853)

TEXAS ANNEXATION (from Mexico, 1845)

1812

1812

1813

Fla. statehood 1845 ceded by Spain 1819

Acquired by money. This purchase from Mexico in 1853 completed the United States.

Acquired by annexation. After the Texas Revolution in 1845, the United States annexed Texas, which had been part of Mexico.

0   200   400 miles
0   200   400 kilometers
Albers Equal–Area Projection

Acquired by negotiation. The United States eventually forced Spain to part with Florida in 1819.

PRACTICE

CALIFORNIA CONTENT
STANDARD 8.5.2

*American Foreign Policy
and Territorial Expansion*

Directions: Choose the letter of the *best* answer.

1 **What motivated President Monroe to announce the Monroe Doctrine?**

A He worried about conflicts in Latin America.

B He wanted to acquire territory in Europe.

C He tried to show Canada that the U.S. was superior.

D He hoped to push Native Americans onto reservations.

2 **What did the Monroe Doctrine say?**

A The United States should become part of Europe.

B The United States should conquer Canada.

C Europe should stay out of Latin America.

D The United States would always have free trade.

3 **The event that gave the United States *most* of its territory in the Southwest was the**

A Louisiana Purchase.

B Texas Annexation.

C Gadsden Purchase.

D Mexican Cession.

4 **The United States acquired Florida through negotiation with**

A France.

B Great Britain.

C Mexico.

D Spain.

5 **Which was the first major acquisition of territory by the United States in the 19th century?**

A the Louisiana Purchase

B the Gadsden Purchase

C the Mexican Cession

D the Oregon Territory

6 **To what does *annexation* refer?**

A the addition of territory to an existing country or state

B the application of a territory to become a state

C the secession, or withdrawal, of a state from the United States

D the negotiation of a treaty between two countries

REVIEW

CALIFORNIA CONTENT
STANDARD 8.5.3

Treaties with American Indian Nations

Specific Objective: Outline the major treaties with American Indian nations during the administrations of the first four presidents and the varying outcomes of those treaties.

Read the summary below to answer the questions on the next page.

Pressure on Native Americans

- Settlers wanted more and more land on the frontier.
- Native Americans suffered from the effects of diseases and alcohol.
- Shrinking territory led to increased competition for hunting grounds and conflicts between tribes.
- Individual Indian nations found it difficult to match up against U.S. firepower.
- Many chiefs and tribal leaders felt they had to agree to the treaties offered.
- More than 75 treaties were made with Native Americans, 1789–1817.

General Terms of the Treaties

- Native American groups gave up rights to live on and hunt in certain areas of land.
- Native American groups received money and trade goods in payment for land.
- Native American groups received a specified area of land that was set aside for their use.
- U.S. negotiators promised not to seek further land for settlement.

The Treaty of Greenville

- The treaty was signed in 1795, a year after the U.S. victory in the Battle of Fallen Timbers.
- Twelve tribes gave the United States much of present-day Ohio and Indiana and the area that would someday become the city of Chicago.

Shawnee Chief Tecumseh's Challenge

- He believed that the land belonged to all Native Americans collectively.
- He felt that no tribe or group of tribes had the right to give away collective land.
- He refused to sign the Treaty of Greenville.
- He called for tribes to unite to fight against the whites and preserve Native American land and culture.

PRACTICE

CALIFORNIA CONTENT
STANDARD 8.5.3

Treaties with American Indian Nations

Directions: Choose the letter of the *best* answer.

1 The main purpose of most of the treaties made with Native Americans between 1789 and 1817 was to

  A negotiate trade terms.

  B acquire more land for white settlers.

  C prevent warfare among the tribes.

  D protect the rights of native people.

2 What did Native Americans receive as a result of treaties with the United States government in this period?

  A more land for hunting

  B a free education

  C money and trade goods

  D the right to vote

3 The Treaty of Greenville was signed by

  A representatives of twelve tribes.

  B representatives of the Sioux.

  C Tecumseh and his followers.

  D representatives of the Cherokee.

4 The land ceded to the United States in the Treaty of Greenville was most of present-day

  A Illinois and Iowa.

  B Ohio and Illinois.

  C Indiana and Illinois.

  D Ohio and Indiana.

Use the quotation to answer questions 5 and 6.

"The way, and the only way, to check and to stop this evil, is for all the red men to unite in claiming a common and equal right in the land, as it was at first, and should be yet; for it never was divided, but belongs to all for the use of each. For no part has a right to sell, even to each other, much less to strangers—those who want all, and will not do with less."

—Chief Tecumseh in speech to Governor William Henry Harrison in council at Vincennes, August 12, 1810

5 The "evil" that Tecumseh hopes to stop refers to what historical event?

  A warfare among Native American nations

  B the spread of smallpox among Native Americans

  C the sale of land by Native Americans to settlers

  D the breaking of treaties by Native Americans

6 According to the quotation, what does Tecumseh believe the U.S. government wants?

  A to be able to use some Native American lands

  B to own all the land where Native Americans live

  C to settle who owns which lands

  D to make treaties with Native

Name _____   Date _____

Industrialization and Urbanization in the Northeast

Specific Objective: Discuss the influence of industrialization and technological developments on the region, including human modification of the landscape and how physical geography shaped human actions (e.g., growth of cities, deforestation, farming, mineral extraction).

Read the summary to answer the questions on the next page.

Factors that Led to Industrialization

- The War of 1812 reduced trade with England and increased American manufacturing.
- Businessmen invested in factories to meet demand for manufactured goods.
- Inventions like the steam engine meant factories could produce goods more efficiently.
- Improved transportation made it easy to get manufactured goods to consumers.

Main Features of Industrialization

- Industrialization occurred first in the Northeast.
- Machines began to do the work that people used to do.
- Large factories were a part of industrialization.
- Factory work became more common than farm work in the Northeast.
- Unskilled workers replaced skilled workers, lowering the cost of production.
- More people worked; women and children began to work in mills and factories.

Factors that Led to Urbanization

- Factories were built in towns and cities where there were more potential workers and often better transportation and communication links.
- Once the factories were built, more people moved to towns and cities in search of work.

Push Factors and Pull Factors in Urbanization

- Push factor: lack of good farmland in the Northeast pushed people to the cities.
- Pull factor: new factory jobs pulled people, especially new immigrants, to the cities.

Other By-Products of Industrialization

- Demand for fuel led to large-scale coal mining operations in the Northeast. Experienced immigrants came from Great Britain to do this dangerous work.
- Deforestation occurred as land was cleared for bigger cities and farms, and as the demand for wood as fuel and raw material increased.

Name _____ Date _____

Industrialization and Urbanization in the Northeast

Directions: Choose the letter of the _best_ answer.

1 The War of 1812 led to Northern industrialization by creating demand for

A more food for the United States army.

B slaves to run machines in the Northeast.

C manufactured goods that used to be imported.

D weapons to ship to England and France.

"In Lowell live between seven and eight thousand young women, who are generally daughters of farmers of the different states of New England. Some of them are members of families that were rich in the generation before. . . ."

—*The Harbinger*, "Female Workers of Lowell"

---

2 The newspaper account makes it clear that factory workers in Lowell, Massachusetts were mainly

A farm owners.

B immigrants.

C experienced men.

D young women.

3 Many people in the Northeast in the 1820s were attracted to factory work because

A factories paid high wages.

B the quality of local farmland was poor.

C factory work led to better jobs.

D factories offered free medical care.

4 A by-product of industrialization is

A deforestation.

B educated workers.

C less immigration.

D rich topsoil.

5 Industrialization led to urbanization by moving the demand for labor to

A cities.

B farms.

C small towns.

D the frontier.

6 What was one "pull" factor in urbanization?

A Poor soil "pulled" workers off the farms.

B Deforestation "pulled" workers out of the woods.

C New factory jobs "pulled" workers into the cities.

D Boats "pulled" new workers to America.

REVIEW

CALIFORNIA CONTENT STANDARD 8.6.2

An American Transportation System

Specific Objective: Outline the physical obstacles to and the economic and political factors involved in building a network of roads, canals, and railroads (e.g., Henry Clay's American System).

Read the summary below to answer the questions on the next page.

In the first years of the new United States, getting from place to place generally meant traveling by water or following one of many Native American trails. Almost all settlements were on rivers or on the coast. The government did not maintain the trails, and they often became impassable. Moreover, the Allegheny Mountains interfered with river travel westward. New canals, railroads, and the National Road improved transportation.

Canals and Railroads

- Canals in the Northeast linked farming areas with cities.
- Erie Canal—363 miles long, completed in 1825; linked Lake Erie with the Hudson River; reduced travel times by half and shipping costs by 90 percent; powerful effect on westward migration; increased the importance of New York City as a trading hub.
- Steam-powered railroads—began in the 1830s; by the 1850s and 1860s, a large railroad network connected most of the settled part of the country; strategic resource and military target during the Civil War.
- The first transcontinental railroad line was completed in 1869.

National Road

- Part of Henry Clay's "American System," it was meant to connect New England with Northwest Territory
- Ran from Cumberland, Maryland to Wheeling, West Virginia by 1818; extended to Vandalia, Illinois, by 1841
- First federal highway, used state-of-the-art technology
- Growth of railroads dampened interest in its completion.
- Political obstacles: Easterners did not see the need to travel west; Southerners were focused on states' rights; President Monroe vetoed a bill to establish tolls; President Jackson gave control of the road to the states.

Henry Clay

- Senator from Kentucky
- Proposed American System in 1815, a plan designed to make the United States economically self-sufficient. The American System proposed a National Bank, tariffs promoting industry, and federal support for a National Road.

CALIFORNIA CONTENT STANDARD 8.6.2

An American Transportation System

Directions: Choose the letter of the *best* answer.

1 *Most* settlements in the early United States were

  A west of the Mississippi River.

  B very densely populated.

  C south of the Ohio River.

  D built on rivers or along the coast.

2 The Erie Canal linked

  A Erie, Pennsylvania with Hartford, Connecticut.

  B Lake Erie with the Hudson River.

  C Lake Erie with Lake Ontario.

  D Cumberland, Maryland with Wheeling, West Virginia.

3 One of the strongest advocates for a federally maintained interstate road was

  A Abraham Lincoln.

  B Andrew Jackson.

  C Henry Clay.

  D James Monroe.

4 The National Road was the first highway to

  A charge a toll to users.

  B be federally funded.

  C run from Maine to Florida.

  D cross the Mississippi River.

5 By 1841, the National Road

  A had reached its goal of the Northwest Territory.

  B stretched as far as Vandalia, Illinois.

  C never got beyond Cumberland, Maryland.

  D was declared unconstitutional.

6 Railroads were an important mode of transportation

  A during the American Revolution.

  B during the Civil War.

  C when Washington was president.

  D for the early Native Americans.

Name _____ Date _____

The Growth of Immigration

Specific Objective: List the reasons for the wave of immigration from Northern Europe to the United States and describe the growth in the number, size, and spatial arrangements of cities (e.g., Irish immigrants and the Great Irish Famine).

Read the summary to answer the questions on the next page.

Who Immigrated in the First Half of the 1800s

- British, Irish, German, Scandinavians, Chinese
- Most immigrants from Northern Europe
- 4 million immigrants in 1790; 32 million immigrants in 1860

Why They Immigrated

Push Factors in Europe

- Population growth after 1750 led to overcrowding.
- The growth of large farms forced tenants off the land.
- Crop failures left farmers in debt and people hungry, as in the Irish Potato Famine of 1845–1854.
- The Industrial Revolution put artisans out of work.
- Religious and political turmoil caused people to flee, as in the failed German revolution of 1848.

Pull Factors in the United States

- Religious and political freedom
- Greater economic opportunity
- Abundant and relatively cheap land

Changes in Cities

- The Industrial Revolution caused existing cities to grow and new Northern cities to be formed.
- Most immigrants settled in the Northeast and Midwest, especially in growing cities.
- Poor Irish fleeing the famine concentrated in port cities—Boston, New York, Philadelphia, Baltimore.
- Cities like New York, St. Louis, and Cincinnati experienced huge, rapid population growth.
- Cities experienced overcrowding, sanitation, and crime problems.
- Tension grew between native-born Americans and recent immigrants.

Name _____ Date _____

The Growth of Immigration

Directions: Choose the letter of the *best* answer.

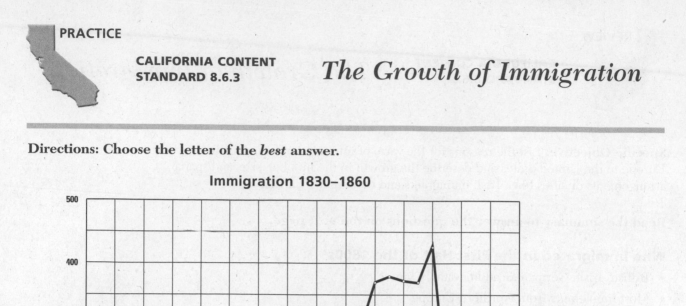

Immigration 1830–1860

Total Immigration by Decades		
1831–1840	**1841–1850**	**1851–1860**
599,125	1,713,251	2,598,214

Use the graph to answer questions 1 and 2.

1 **German immigration to the United States between 1847 and 1852 was generally**

A the same as Irish immigration.

B lower than Irish immigration.

C slightly higher than Irish immigration.

D much higher than Irish immigration.

2 **What pattern of Irish immigration is shown after the beginning of the Potato Famine in 1845?**

A It peaked in the first two years.

B It increased steadily through 1851.

C It increased steadily through 1854.

D It was not affected by the famine.

3 **Immigration after the Great Irish Famine is an example of immigration caused by**

A the Industrial Revolution.

B a trend to larger farms.

C failure of a major crop.

D population increase.

4 **How did immigration affect the growth of cities in the United States?**

A Growth was limited to eastern ports.

B Cities grew in the Northeast and Midwest.

C Older cities declined as new cities grew.

D Most immigrants lived on farms

REVIEW

CALIFORNIA CONTENT STANDARD 8.6.4

Advocates for Freedom and Equality

Specific Objective: Study the lives of black Americans who gained freedom in the North and founded schools and churches to advance their rights and communities.

Read the summary to answer the questions on the next page.

Richard Allen

- Born a slave in Philadelphia (1760)
- Converted, along with his master, to Methodism
- Bought his freedom and taught himself to read and write
- Became an assistant minister in a mixed-race Methodist church
- Formed the Free African Society to help slaves achieve freedom
- Founded the African Methodist Episcopal Church and was its first bishop (1794)
- Opened a day school (1795)
- Founded the Society of Free People of Colour for Promoting the Instruction and School Education of Children of African Descent (1795)
- Schools for African Americans in Philadelphia by 1811

Frederick Douglass

- Born a slave (1817), raised in Baltimore
- Taught to read and write by his master's wife
- Escaped to Massachusetts (1838)
- Began an abolitionist crusade across the North
- Wrote his autobiography *Narrative of the Life of Frederick Douglass, an American Slave, Written by Himself* (1845)
- Founded the journal *North Star,* dedicated to abolition and ending racial discrimination
- Convinced Abraham Lincoln to make the end of slavery a goal of the Civil War

Sojourner Truth

- Born Isabella Baumfree to slaves in New York (1797)
- Raised speaking Dutch, taught herself English, never lost her Dutch accent
- Mistreated by three different masters and forced to marry an older slave
- Freed in 1828 when New York abolished slavery
- After a spiritual revelation, changed her name to Sojourner Truth
- Walked through New England preaching
- Joined the Northampton Association for Education and Industry, a utopian community in Massachusetts
- Supported abolition and the right of women to vote
- Dictated her memoirs *The Narrative of Sojourner Truth: A Northern Slave* (1850)

PRACTICE

CALIFORNIA CONTENT
STANDARD 8.6.4

Advocates for Freedom and Equality

Directions: Choose the letter of the *best* answer.

1 **Richard Allen, Frederick Douglass, and Sojourner Truth were all**

A born in slavery.

B escaped slaves.

C ministers.

D school teachers.

"We solemnly dedicate the North Star to the cause of our long oppressed and plundered fellow countrymen . . . It shall fearlessly assert your rights, faithfully proclaim your wrongs, and earnestly demand for you instant and even-handed justice."

—Frederick Douglass, first edition, *North Star* (1847)

2 **The "countrymen" Douglass is referring to in the quotation are**

A African Americans.

B Native Americans.

C abolitionists.

D tenant farmers.

3 **Many of Richard Allen's accomplishments were concerned with**

A politics.

B journalism.

C education.

D the right of women to vote.

4 **Sojourner Truth**

A bought her freedom.

B escaped from slavery.

C ran the Underground Railroad.

D taught herself English.

"I have as much muscle as any man, and can do as much work as any man. I have plowed and reaped and husked and chopped and mowed, and can any man do more than that?… can carry as much as any man, and can eat as much too, if I can get it. I am as strong as any man that is now."

—Sojourner Truth, 1851

5 **In the quotation, Sojourner Truth is speaking out for**

A educational reform.

B women's rights.

C labor reform.

D abolition.

6 **Frederick Douglass influenced which president?**

A George Washington

B Thomas Jefferson

C Andrew Jackson

D Abraham Lincoln

Name _____ Date _____

REVIEW

CALIFORNIA CONTENT
STANDARD 8.6.5

American Education

Specific Objective: Trace the development of the American education system from its earliest roots, including the roles of religious and private schools and Horace Mann's campaign for free public education and its assimilating role in American culture.

Read the summaries of events affecting U.S. education. Then answer the questions on the next page.

1600s

1635   Boston Latin School founded in Massachusetts; run by Puritans

1636   Harvard founded; first American college; originally to train ministers

1642   Massachusetts law—all free children (boys and girls) must learn to read, know religious principles, and know the laws of the commonwealth

1647   Massachusetts law—all towns of 50 families or more must hire a schoolmaster to teach reading and writing

1690   New England Primer published; combined alphabet and religious instruction; 5 million copies sold; in use for over 100 years

---

1700s

- School terms could be as short as two months a year.
- Slaves could not be taught to read or write.
- Thomas Jefferson proposed a system of free, tax-supported elementary schools for all children (except slaves). His bill was defeated.
- Benjamin Rush proposed a much more extensive system of education that would replace Greek and Latin with scientific study and educate girls.
- The Land Ordinances of 1785 and 1787 set aside plots of land in every township for a public school. School was not required, but encouraged.

1800s

1827   Massachusetts passed a law establishing high schools.

1833   Oberlin College was founded. It was first to admit students regardless of gender or race.

1837   Horace Mann, the "Father of American Education," headed the Massachusetts Board of Education, the first in the country. He also established training schools for teachers, lengthened the school term to six months (from three), and secured more funding for salaries, books, and facilities. He argued for common schools—children of all levels of society would learn together.

1850   Many Northern states had public elementary schools; most barred African Americans.

PRACTICE

CALIFORNIA CONTENT
STANDARD 8.6.5

American Education

Directions: Choose the letter of the *best* answer.

1 The first formal school in the colonies was opened in the

A 1500s.

B 1600s.

C 1700s.

D 1800s.

2 The Land Ordinances of 1785 and 1787

A required daily school attendance.

B lengthened the school term.

C made grants for teacher's colleges.

D set aside land for public education.

3 The "Father of American Education" was

A Thomas Jefferson.

B Benjamin Rush.

C Horace Mann.

D George Washington.

4 Even progressive thinkers in the early 1800s rarely argued for the education of

A African Americans.

B girls.

C poor people.

D teachers.

"The tax which will be paid [to support free public education] is not more than the thousandth part of what will be paid to kings, priests and nobles who will rise up among us if we leave the people in ignorance."

—Thomas Jefferson to George Wythe, 1786.

5 According to the quotation, which of the following best explains what Jefferson thought about taxes and public education?

A Taxing everyone to pay for public education is unfair and too expensive.

B Kings, priests, and nobles are bad leaders who often impose heavy taxes.

C Taxes to pay for public education are a good investment.

D Only people who will become leaders should receive free education.

6 Which state played a key role in the first 100 years of public education in the United States?

A Massachusetts

B New York

C Pennsylvania

D Virginia

REVIEW

CALIFORNIA CONTENT
STANDARD 8.6.6

Champions of Women's Rights

Specific Objective: Examine the women's suffrage movement (e.g., biographies, writings, and speeches of Elizabeth Cady Stanton, Margaret Fuller, Lucretia Mott, Susan B. Anthony).

Read the summary to answer the questions on the next page.

Many women worked tirelessly throughout the 19th century to secure equal rights for women, including suffrage or the right to vote. Many of these women also fought against slavery, and later, for the rights of African Americans to vote.

Elizabeth Cady Stanton (1815–1902)

- Best known advocate for women's equality in the 19th century
- Married to Henry Stanton, a well-known abolitionist; mother of seven
- Organized the 1848 Seneca Falls Convention, first national convention for women's rights, where she drafted a "Declaration of Sentiments," modeled on the Declaration of Independence
- Began to work with Susan B. Anthony in 1851; wrote many of her speeches
- President of the National Woman Suffrage Association
- Wrote the *History of Woman Suffrage* (1881–1885)

Susan B. Anthony (1820–1906)

- Main organizer of the woman suffrage movement
- Quaker-educated, taught school for ten years
- Activist for abolition and temperance before meeting Stanton
- Founded International and National Councils of Women
- President of National American Woman Suffrage Association until she was 80
- Arrested in 1872 for voting illegally

Margaret Fuller (1810–1850)

- According to Stanton and Anthony, "possessed more influence on the thought of American women than any woman previous to her time"
- Member of Ralph Waldo Emerson's Transcendentalist circle
- Brilliant and accomplished; worked as translator, editor, author, critic
- Published *Woman in the Nineteenth Century* (1845); groundbreaking study

Lucretia Mott (1793–1880)

- Quaker minister and organizer for abolition and women's rights
- Delegate to the World's Anti-Slavery Convention in London in 1840
- Helped her friend Elizabeth Stanton organize the Seneca Falls Convention and draft the "Declaration of Sentiments"
- First president of the American Equal Rights Convention, which argued for the voting rights of women and freed black men

PRACTICE

CALIFORNIA CONTENT
STANDARD 8.6.6

Champions of Women's Rights

Directions: Choose the letter of the *best* answer.

1 Susan B. Anthony's role in the woman suffrage movement was to

A write an important book about women's rights.

B help organize the Seneca Falls Convention.

C run a school to educate girls about their rights.

D organize the movement and give speeches.

"We hold these truths to be self-evident: that all men and women are created equal; that they are endowed by their Creator with certain inalienable rights."

—Elizabeth Cady Stanton, The Seneca Falls "Declaration of Sentiments" (1848)

2 From the quotation, you can determine that Stanton purposefully modeled the "Declaration of Sentiments" on which important document?

A the Bill of Rights

B the Declaration of Independence

C the Mayflower Compact

D the Preamble to the Constitution

3 Susan B. Anthony was arrested for

A leading a protest march.

B voting in an election.

C refusing to pay taxes.

D hiding escaped slaves.

"It is twenty-eight years ago to-day since the first woman's rights convention. . . . Could we have foreseen, when we called that convention, the ridicule, persecution, and misrepresentation that the demand for woman's political, religious and social equality would involve . . ."

—Elizabeth Cady Stanton, from letter to Lucretia Mott, 1876

4 You can infer from the quotation that the fight for woman suffrage

A had the support of the clergy, or church.

B quickly succeeded.

C was more difficult than expected.

D caused more damage than help to women.

5 A "suffragist" is a person who

A organizes unions for workers' rights.

B fights for women's right to vote.

C supports education reform.

D works to ban the sale of alcohol.

6 In the middle of the 19th century, many of the women involved in the struggle for women's rights were also

A abolitionists.

B novelists.

C ministers.

D recent immigrants.

Name _____ Date _____

American Art and Literature

Specific Objective: Identify common themes in American art as well as transcendentalism and individualism (e.g., writings about and by Ralph Waldo Emerson, Henry David Thoreau, Herman Melville, Louisa May Alcott, Nathaniel Hawthorne, Henry Wadsworth Longfellow).

Read the summary to answer the questions on the next page.

Emerging American Culture
- Source of pride to Americans in the 1840s and 1850s
- Sought independence from Europe but influenced by romanticism, a European intellectual movement that emphasized emotion, imagination, and personal and artistic freedom
- Stressed individualism; each person should learn about life from self-examination and nature

19th-century American Art
- Celebrated the American landscape, birds, and animals

19th-century American Literature
- Celebrated the American character, history, and landscape

Key Painters

Hudson River School
- Painted wilderness areas in New York and the West

Thomas Cole (1801–1848)
- leader of the school

Key Writers

The Transcendentalists

To transcend is to look beyond the material world to find spiritual truth within self and nature

- Intellectual movement centered in New England, led by Ralph Waldo Emerson

Ralph Waldo Emerson (1803–1882)
- Essays: Nature, "Self Reliance," "The Oversoul"
- Lecture: "The American Scholar"

Henry David Thoreau (1817–1862)
- Writings: "Civil Disobedience," *Walden*

Other Key American Writers

Louisa May Alcott (1832–1888)
- Novels: *Little Women, Little Men*

Nathaniel Hawthorne (1804–1864)
- Novels: *The Scarlet Letter, The House of the Seven Gables*

Herman Melville (1819–1891)
- Novels: *Moby Dick, Billy Budd*

Henry Wadsworth Longfellow (1807–1882)
- Poems: "Paul Revere's Ride," *Evangeline*

PRACTICE

CALIFORNIA CONTENT
STANDARD 8.6.7

American Art and Literature

Directions: Choose the letter of the *best* answer.

1 An important influence on American culture in the 1840s and 1850s was

  A Romanticism.

  B materialism.

  C American politics.

  D religion.

2 An important belief in American culture in the 1840s and 1850s was that one could learn about life from

  A newspapers.

  B self-examination.

  C politics.

  D religion.

3 A common theme among many 19th-century American artists was

  A history.

  B immigration.

  C materialism.

  D nature.

4 The leader of the Transcendentalist movement was

  A Alcott.

  B Emerson.

  C Longfellow.

  D Thoreau.

5 Transcendentalism emphasized

  A the importance of order in society.

  B the importance of the spiritual world.

  C belonging to the right church.

  D improving working conditions.

6 An important Transcendentalist writer was

  A Thoreau.

  B Alcott.

  C Longfellow.

  D Hawthorne.

REVIEW

CALIFORNIA CONTENT
STANDARD 8.7.1

Cotton and the Economy of the South

Specific Objective: Describe the development of the agrarian economy in the South. Identify the locations of the cotton-producing states. Discuss the significance of cotton and the cotton gin.

Read the summary and the map to answer questions on the next page.

The Agrarian Economy of the South

The economy of the South was agrarian (based on agriculture). The warm climate meant a long growing season. Farms and large plantations produced agricultural products such as cotton, tobacco, corn, sugar, and rice. The economy depended on slave labor to produce these products cheaply. The South was mostly rural, with few large cities.

Cotton and the Cotton Gin

- English textile mills had created a huge demand for cotton, but cotton took a lot of time and workers to grow and harvest. The most time-consuming task was cleaning the cotton—separating the seeds from the cotton fibers.

- In 1793 Eli Whitney invented a machine called the cotton gin (short for "engine") that cleaned cotton much more quickly and efficiently. One worker could clean 1 pound a day by hand, but 50 pounds a day with the gin.

- This invention changed life in the South dramatically in the following ways:

  1. Planters grew more cotton, and cotton exports increased.

  2. Slavery expanded to meet the growing demand for cotton production.

  3. Cotton growing spread further south and west, eventually reaching Texas. More American Indian groups were driven off their land as it was taken over for cotton plantations.

The Cotton Kingdom, 1840

Name _____   Date _____

CALIFORNIA CONTENT
STANDARD 8.7.1

Cotton and the Economy of the South

Directions: Choose the letter of the *best* answer.

1 What was the cotton gin?

A   a machine that cleaned cotton

B   a machine that harvested cotton

C   a type of alcohol made from cotton

D   a machine that planted cotton

2 Who was the inventor of the cotton gin?

A   Benjamin Franklin

B   Robert Fulton

C   Thomas Jefferson

D   Eli Whitney

3 Why was the cotton gin important to Southern agriculture?

A   It transformed the way that clothing was produced.

B   It made it much cheaper to produce cotton.

C   It made slaves unnecessary on cotton plantations.

D   It made it possible for cotton to be grown in colder climates.

4 What effect did the cotton gin have on slavery?

A   It made slavery less popular in the South.

B   It eliminated the need for slave labor.

C   It sped up the spread of slavery.

D   Slaves acquired more rights.

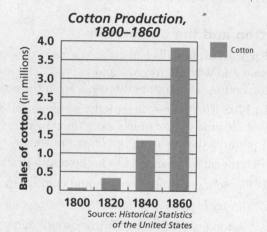

Cotton Production, 1800–1860

Source: *Historical Statistics of the United States*

5 According to the graph, which of the following statements is *true*?

A   From 1820 to 1840, cotton production increased slightly.

B   In 1820, more than a million bales of cotton were produced.

C   Cotton production in 1840 was less than one million bales.

D   From 1840 to 1860, cotton production more than doubled.

REVIEW

CALIFORNIA CONTENT
STANDARD 8.7.2

Slavery in the United States

Specific Objective: Trace the origins and development of slavery. Trace its effects on black Americans and on the South's political, social, religious, economic, and cultural development. Identify the strategies that were tried to both overturn and preserve it.

Read the summary to answer the questions on the next page.

Origins and Development of Slavery

The Spanish and Portuguese first brought African slaves to the Americas in the 1400s and 1500s. The slaves worked mainly in the Caribbean sugar plantations. Slavery on the sugar plantations was particularly brutal. The first slaves came to the American South in 1619. The slave trade, which brought slaves from West Africa to the Americas, increased dramatically in the 1700s.

Slavery's Effects on Black Americans

Life under slavery in the American South was harsh and unforgiving. Enslaved African Americans endured wretched living conditions, hard labor, and brutal punishments. Families were broken up when owners sold off children or separated husbands and wives. Despite all this, the enslaved people managed to forge a new African-American culture that offered them comfort, hope, and the courage to resist. Religion, music, and family were important parts of this culture.

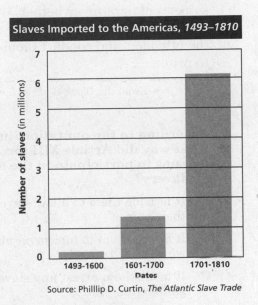

Slaves Imported to the Americas, *1493–1810*

Source: Phillip D. Curtin, *The Atlantic Slave Trade*

Slavery's Effects of the Development of the South

Slavery affected all aspects of Southern culture and society, including economics, politics, and religion. The South depended on unpaid labor to grow cotton, tobacco, and rice. Slavery made it possible for a few people to become extremely rich. Most Southerners did not own slaves but supported the system.

Efforts to Do Away With Slavery and Efforts to Preserve It

- Slaves resisted their condition by working slowly, damaging goods, or running away. Armed slave rebellions were rare but spread fear among the white population. In 1822, Denmark Vesey planned a revolt in Charleston, South Carolina. Nat Turner led the most famous revolt, in Virginia in 1831. Both leaders were hanged. White and black abolitionists, working mainly in the North, spoke out against slavery.

- Slaveholders fought to protect slavery through harsh slave codes. These laws promised severe punishments to slaves who tried to run away or resist. The South also pushed through national laws that made it illegal to help run-away slaves.

PRACTICE

CALIFORNIA CONTENT
STANDARD 8.7.2

Slavery in the United States

Directions: Choose the letter of the *best* answer.

"ARTICLE XIII forbids slaves belonging to different masters to assemble in crowds, by day or by night. . . . It also commands all subjects of the King, whether officers or not, to seize and arrest the offenders and conduct them to prison. . . ."

—From the *Black Code of Louisiana,*
March, 1724

1 According to the quotation, in what way did Article XIII force free persons to participate in the system of slavery?

A It forbade them to allow slaves in their homes.

B It forced them to inform on blacks who acted strangely.

C It made them arrest any slaves gathered in groups.

D It required them to beat their slaves.

2 One *unplanned* effect of Nat Turner's rebellion was that

A slaveholders made laws restricting free African Americans.

B slaves on many plantations were liberated.

C more people began to argue for emancipation of slaves.

D Turner led more than 50 followers to attack plantations.

"The state of Ohio is separated from Kentucky by just one river; on either side of it the soil is equally fertile, and the situation equally favorable, and yet everything is different. Here [on the Ohio side] a population devoured by feverish activity, trying every means to make its fortune. . . There [on the Kentucky side] are people who make others work for them and show little compassion. . . These differences cannot be attributed to any other cause but slavery."

—Alexis de Tocqueville, *Journey to America*

3 The writer of the quotation views slave owners as

A unlucky.

B lazy and cruel.

C eager to succeed.

D intelligent.

4 Slavery in the South was harsh in that it

A lasted for a brief period.

B broke up families.

C spread religion.

D was not profitable.

5 What *two* aspects of culture became most important to enslaved African Americans?

A social clubs and family ties

B music and books

C religion and higher education

D family ties and religion

REVIEW

CALIFORNIA CONTENT
STANDARD 8.7.3

Society in the South before the Civil War

Specific Objective: Examine the characteristics of white Southern society and how the physical environment influenced events and conditions prior to the Civil War.

Read the summary to answer the questions on the next page.

Life in the South

The fertile soil and long growing season in the South supported the focus on a rural way of life. Geography led to the growth of isolated, self-sufficient plantations rather than cities. As the North experienced the beginnings of the Industrial Revolution in the first half of the 19th century, the South lagged behind. To some extent, the very revolution that was taking place in the North led the South to become more set in its ways.

King Cotton

The demand for cotton for textile mills in England and in the Northeast increased as the Industrial Revolution took hold. The invention of the cotton gin made it easier to make a profit from cotton and the economy became more dependent on cotton. This trend called for more slaves to work the fields and support life on the plantations. The region became even more dependent on the right to own slaves.

A Two-Tiered Society

- Most of Southern society was controlled by a handful of wealthy plantation owners. They made large profits from the labor of slaves and from exports to other countries. They felt no incentive to invest in industry.
  - Only one third of white families owned slaves in 1840.
  - One tenth of these had 20 or more slaves (fewer than 4 in 100 white families).
- Most of the whites in the South were poor farmers. They didn't own slaves but they hoped to one day.

A Working Plantation

A large plantation was like a small town. It produced nearly everything it needed. What little it couldn't produce it would acquire through local trade. Plantations were likely to grow tobacco, cotton, rice, or sugar cane for profit, but they also produced, for their own use

- a variety of grains, fruits, and vegetables
- meat and eggs
- yarn and cloth
- clothing, shoes, and leather goods
- furniture, tools, and bricks

PRACTICE

CALIFORNIA CONTENT
STANDARD 8.7.3

Society in the South Before the Civil War

Directions: Choose the letter of the *best* answer.

1 Most plantations were self-sufficient. What they could not produce themselves, they

  A got along without.

  B traded for locally.

  C bought at the store.

  D ordered from a catalog.

"We have seen that there were joyous breaks in the days of labor, which made [the slaves'] plantation, not only an abode of much comfort but a scene of marked beauty. . . ."

—From *The Old Plantation* by James Battle Avirett

---

2 According to the quotation, the author believes that

  A slaves on plantations had time for leisure activities.

  B plantations were worked by paid servants.

  C plantations were not a successful form of farming.

  D the plantation owner's children liked to play games.

3 Before the Civil War, approximately what percentage of white families owned slaves?

  A one fourth

  B one third

  C one half

  D three fourths

4 Most free southerners were

  A rich merchants.

  B factory workers.

  C slave owners.

  D poor farmers.

5 How did the Industrial Revolution affect the South?

  A It polluted the rivers and hurt farming.

  B It increased demand for cotton.

  C It lowered wages for southern workers.

  D It moved slaves from farms to factories.

Name _____ Date _____

Free Blacks in the North and South

Specific Objective: Compare the lives of and opportunities for free blacks in the North with those of free blacks in the South.

Read the summary to answer the questions on the next page.

Before the Civil war, there was a sizeable population of free blacks in the North, and in the South as well. Conditions for free blacks in the North and the South were certainly very different, but both groups faced discrimination, unequal treatment, and restrictions on their activities.

Free Blacks in the North

- Fought with the patriots against the British in the American Revolution
- Worked in mills and other factories, in shipyards and on ships, as merchants and carpenters, and at many other jobs and trades
- Gained prominence in fields such as poetry (Phillis Wheatley), mathematics (Benjamin Banneker), and business (Paul Cuffe)
- By the early 1800s, slavery was outlawed in most Northern states.
- In 1827, the first black newspaper, *Freedom's Journal*, aimed at the almost 500,000 free blacks in the country.
- Blacks were still considered inferior by most whites and treated accordingly. They were refused service in many public places; most states did not allow blacks to vote; they were taught in inferior schools, and barred from white churches. They faced restrictions on their activities and movements. For example, they were not allowed to carry weapons or meet with slaves. In the end, freedom did not mean equality, dignity, or any guarantee of basic civil rights.

Free Blacks in the South

- Fought with the patriots against the British in the American Revolution
- In 1840, 8 percent of African Americans in the South were free. They had either been born free, been freed by an owner, or had purchased their own freedom.
- A significant number were skilled workers and made a good living. Some became planters and owned slaves themselves. Many lived in Baltimore, Washington, D.C., and other cities.
- Some states made blacks leave once they gained freedom. Some states did not permit them to vote or receive an education.
- Whites worried that free blacks would inspire slaves to revolt, so they were forced to live in segregated communities.
- The most terrifying threat was the possibility of being captured and sold into slavery. Free blacks had to carry around their papers at all times showing that they were free. Without the documents, they could be sold into slavery at any time.

PRACTICE

CALIFORNIA CONTENT
STANDARD 8.7.4

Free Blacks in the North and South

Directions: Choose the letter of the *best* answer.

Use the quotation to answer questions 1 and 2.

"Where was I? What was the meaning
of these chains? . . . I felt of my
pockets, so far as the fetters would
allow—far enough, indeed, to [see]
that I had not only been robbed of
liberty, but that my money and free
papers were also gone!"

—From *Twelve Years a Slave* by
Solomon Northup

---

1 **Why might it be especially alarming to Solomon Northup that his "free papers" have been taken?**

A He could be fined for traveling without his papers.

B Another person might try to take over his identity.

C Without them he could be sold into slavery.

D Those kinds of documents were hard to replace.

2 **What is *most* likely to happen next to Solomon Northrup in this scene?**

A Northup might realize he was foolish for carrying his papers with him.

B Northup will likely be rescued by police and given a fair hearing.

C Now that they have his money, Northup's captors might let him go.

D Northup's captors might sell him back into slavery.

3 **What was the importance of *Freedom's Journal*?**

A It was an abolitionist newspaper produced by Frederick Douglass.

B It was the leading newspaper produced by white abolitionists.

C It was the first autobiography about the life of a free black.

D It was an important newspaper produced by and for free blacks.

4 **Free African Americans in the North compared to free African Americans in the South**

A faced many similar problems.

B were allowed to vote and attend most schools.

C faced very little discrimination.

D were free to live however they wanted.

5 **About what percent of African Americans in the South were free before the Civil War?**

A less than 10 percent

B about 20 percent

C about one third

D more than half

6 **Which of the following was a well-known free African-American poet of early America?**

A Benjamin Banneker

B Paul Cuffe

C Simon Northup

D Phillis Wheatley

REVIEW

The Jackson Years

Specific Objective: Discuss the election of Andrew Jackson as president in 1828, the importance of Jacksonian democracy, and his actions as president (e.g., the spoils system, veto of the National Bank, policy of Indian removal, opposition to the Supreme Court).

Read the summary below to answer questions on the next page.

The Election of 1828

- The 1828 campaign was bitter. Andrew Jackson and John Quincy Adams were again opponents as they had been in 1824, when Jackson lost.
- Jackson's appeal to the common people helped him win in 1828. He was the first president from the West. He was also a war hero.
- Jackson's election ended the idea of government elected by wealthy, well-educated people. His belief that all white men should have the right to vote and have a say in government, thus ensuring majority rule, was called **Jacksonian democracy.**

Conflicts During the Jackson Presidency

Indian Removal	National Bank	Spoils System
White settlers wanted native lands; Jackson proposed the Indian Removal Act of 1830.	The Second Bank of the United States held government funds and issued money.	Jackson gave government jobs to his political supporters.
One group, the Cherokee, appealed to the Supreme Court, which ruled in their favor.	Jackson opposed the bank and vetoed the renewal of its charter.	Opponents accused him of corruption.
Jackson ignored the ruling. Thousands of Indians were moved to the west, including the Cherokee.	The bank went out of business. Inflation and depression followed.	Jackson defended his system, saying it broke up one group's hold on government.

PRACTICE

CALIFORNIA CONTENT
STANDARD 8.8.1

The Jackson Years

Directions: Choose the letter of the *best* answer.

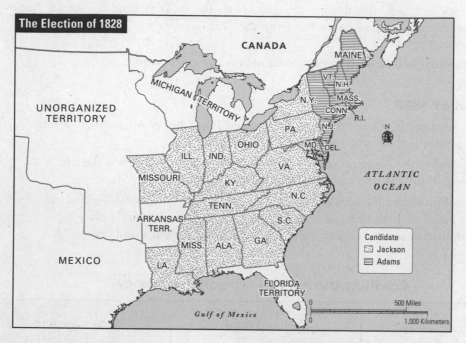

The Election of 1828

CANADA

MAINE

UNORGANIZED TERRITORY

MICHIGAN TERRITORY

VT. N.H.
N.Y. MASS.
CONN. R.I.
PA. N.J.
OHIO MD. DEL.
ILL. IND.
VA.
MISSOURI KY.
TENN. N.C.
ARKANSAS TERR.
S.C.
MISS. ALA. GA.
LA.
MEXICO
FLORIDA TERRITORY

ATLANTIC OCEAN

Gulf of Mexico

Candidate
Jackson
Adams

500 Miles
1,000 Kilometers

1 **Looking at the map, it is clear that Jackson was least popular in the**

A Midwest.

B Northeast.

C Northwest.

D Southeast.

2 **Jacksonian democracy gave political power to the**

A educated.

B wealthy.

C majority.

D minorities.

3 **Under the spoils system, jobs went to**

A factory workers in the cities.

B National Bank managers.

C Jackson's political supporters.

D people best suited for them.

4 **Jackson's solution to white settlers' hunger for land was the**

A Indian Removal Act.

B Northwest Ordinance.

C Second U.S. Bank.

D Spoils System.

5 **In the 1828 election, which party supported Jackson?**

A Democratic

B Libertarian

C Republican

D Whig

REVIEW

CALIFORNIA CONTENT
STANDARD 8.8.2

Westward Expansion

Specific Objective: Describe the purpose, challenges, and economic incentives associated with westward expansion, including the concept of Manifest Destiny (e.g., the Lewis and Clark expedition, accounts of the removal of Indians, the Cherokees' "Trail of Tears," settlement of the Great Plains) and the territorial acquisitions that spanned numerous decades.

Read the summary below to answer questions on the next page.

Lewis and Clark

Expansion westward to the Pacific Ocean began in 1803 when President Jefferson sent Meriwether Lewis and William Clark to explore the newly acquired Louisiana Territory. They were instructed to find a water route across the continent. Part of their job was to establish good relationships with Indians and describe what they saw. They traveled all the way to the Pacific Coast and back.

Indian Removal

By the 1820s, white settlers had pushed Indians westward. However, there were still many Indians in the East. The Indian Removal Act of 1830 called for the government to negotiate treaties that would force these Indians to relocate west. They would be given less valuable land in what is now Oklahoma and parts of Kansas and Nebraska.

Trail of Tears

The Cherokee refused to sign the treaties. The Supreme Court supported their right to remain on their land. In 1838, federal troops, under orders from President Jackson, made 16,000 Cherokee march along what is now known as "The Trail of Tears," from Georgia to Oklahoma. One quarter of those on the forced march died along the way.

Manifest Destiny

By the 1840s, many Americans believed it was their "manifest destiny" to stretch across the continent from the Atlantic to the Pacific oceans. Although already occupied by Indians and Mexicans, white settlers viewed this land as unoccupied. Americans also worried that the French or Spanish might establish colonies there.

Economic Incentives

The Homestead Act of 1862 gave 160 acres of land to anyone willing to live on it and farm it for five years. White settlers were not prepared for the difficult journey or harsh living conditions. Still, many rushed to the Great Plains to claim the free land. Land speculators also bought huge plots of land. They hoped to sell it later for profits. The lure of instant wealth from mining and timber rights drew others.

PRACTICE

CALIFORNIA CONTENT
STANDARD 8.8.2

Westward Expansion

Directions: Choose the letter of the *best* answer.

1 Manifest Destiny was the idea that

A Americans would establish colonies.

B it was America's fate to include Mexico and Central America.

C Americans would one day conquer England.

D it was the fate of the United States to stretch from the Atlantic Ocean to the Pacific Ocean.

2 The Homestead Act of 1862

A forced Indians to make treaties that would take away their lands and relocate them westward.

B sent Lewis and Clark to explore the Louisiana Territory.

C gave 160 acres of land on the Great Plains to anyone willing to live on it and farm it for five years.

D made it possible for the Cherokee and other Indians to stay on their lands in the Southeast.

3 Which Indian tribe had to endure the Trail of Tears?

A Cherokee

B Apache

C Sioux

D Crow

4 The chief economic incentive the government offered to settlers in the West was

A gold mines.

B free land.

C new businesses.

D timber.

5 The purpose of the Lewis and Clark expedition was to

A lead Native Americans to the West.

B look for gold and other minerals.

C find a water route to the Pacific Ocean.

D scout out land for a new railroad.

6 The Trail of Tears was a result of

A Manifest Destiny.

B the Indian Removal Act.

C the Homestead Act.

D the Lewis and Clark expedition.

REVIEW

CALIFORNIA CONTENT
STANDARD 8.8.3

Women in the West

Specific Objective: Describe the role of pioneer women and the new status that western women achieved (e.g., Laura Ingalls Wilder, Annie Bidwell; slave women gaining freedom in the West; Wyoming granting suffrage to women in 1869).

Read the summary below to answer questions on the next page.

Role of Pioneer Women
Life on the western frontier was harsh for both men and women. Women's work was vital in settling the Great Plains. In their letters home, many women recorded the harshness of pioneer life. Others talked about the loneliness. Living miles from others, women were often their family's doctors—setting broken bones and delivering babies—as well as their everyday caretakers.

Laura Ingalls Wilder
Some true-life examples of the lives that women led on the frontier can be found in the books written by Laura Ingalls Wilder. Born in a log house in 1867 in Wisconsin, Wilder lived on the frontier most of her life. She traveled by covered wagon to Minnesota, Kansas, Dakota Territory, and Missouri. Her books about her experiences as a pioneer are still read today.

Status of Western Women
Western lawmakers recognized the contributions women made by giving them more legal rights than women in the East. Women in the West could own property and control their own money. The first place women had the right to vote was in Wyoming Territory in 1869. When Wyoming sought statehood in 1890, it refused to repeal women's suffrage as a condition of entering the Union. Soon women in Colorado, Utah, and Idaho also had voting rights.

Annie Bidwell
Annie Bidwell and her husband John, married in 1868, founded the town of Chico, California. As a younger man, John became rich through mining. After he married Annie, they built a huge ranch. They employed nearly all of the native Mechoopda Maidu Indians in the area. Annie gave them religious instruction and founded a church. She also helped her husband oversee the ranch. After John died, Annie continued to run the ranch and protect the interests of the Indians under her care.

African American Women in the West
African Americans moved west for the same reasons white settlers did. Mary Ellen Pleasant moved to California during the gold rush and became wealthy working as a cook and making sound business investments. In 1860, she began working to expand the rights of blacks in California. Biddy Mason came to California with Mormon settlers as an enslaved worker. Because California was a free state, she won her freedom in the courts in 1856. She later became a wealthy landowner.

PRACTICE

CALIFORNIA CONTENT
STANDARD 8.8.3

Women in the West

Directions: Choose the letter of the *best* answer.

1 **Women in the West had harder lives than women in the East, but they also had more**

   A education.

   B free time.

   C money

   D rights.

2 **Laura Ingalls Wilder wrote about**

   A life on a riverboat.

   B slaves in the South.

   C pioneer life.

   D the gold rush.

3 **Biddy Mason won her freedom from slavery in 1856 because**

   A she earned money from the gold rush.

   B California was a free state.

   C there was no slavery in the West.

   D she escaped to Canada.

4 **Annie Bidwell and her husband founded a town in California and also a**

   A church.

   B gold mine.

   C boarding house.

   D school.

"In . . . twenty-four days, we have had murders, fearful accidents . . . whippings, a hanging . . . and a fatal duel."

—Louise Clappe, quoted in *Frontier Women*

5 **The quotation makes it clear that life on the frontier could be**

   A quiet.

   B entertaining.

   C lively.

   D dangerous.

6 **The first place in America where women had the vote was Wyoming Territory. This fact shows that in the West**

   A there were not enough men to vote.

   B sheriffs did not enforce the laws.

   C most women were unmarried.

   D many people had progressive ideas.

REVIEW

CALIFORNIA CONTENT STANDARD 8.8.4   *Western Waters*

Specific Objective: Examine the importance of the great rivers and the struggle over water rights.

Read the summary below to answer questions on the next page.

Mississippi River

When Lewis and Clark explored the Louisiana Purchase in the early 1800s, their journey showed Americans for the first time what lay to the west of the Mississippi. As settlers moved west, many chose to make their homes along the Mississippi and its tributaries (streams or rivers flowing into a larger river). It was like living near a major highway. Even after the coming of the railroads, the Mississippi was an important trade route for steamboats.

The Mississippi acts as a drain for the plains between the Rocky and Appalachian mountain ranges. It begins in Minnesota and empties into the Gulf of Mexico.

Missouri River

The Missouri River is the largest tributary of the Mississippi. It begins in Montana and empties into the Mississippi. The Lewis and Clark expedition opened this river as a travel route for American traders and settlers.

Columbia River

Lewis and Clark discovered that there was no easy passage between the Missouri River and the Columbia River. The Columbia River begins in Canada and flows into the Pacific Ocean. It forms the border between Oregon and Washington. It served as the major transportation route from the coast until the coming of the railroads.

Colorado River

This major river runs from the Rocky Mountains to the Gulf of California. Native Americans lived along this river for centuries. Some Mormons who moved west during the 1800s settled along tributaries of this river. Because the area was so dry, they had to build dams, reservoirs, and irrigation canals to supply their water needs. The river now supplies water to much of the Southwest.

Rio Grande

The Rio Grande, nearly 2000 miles long, runs from the Rocky Mountains to the Gulf of Mexico. It forms the border between modern-day Texas and Mexico. In 1845, Mexico said the boundary was the Nueces River, which was further north. The dispute over this boundary led to the Mexican-American War.

Water Rights

Settlers moving to the West found plenty of cheap land. They also found a much drier climate than in the East. Many farmers and ranchers had to bargain for the right to draw water off nearby rivers to irrigate their fields. These water rights were handed down from generation to generation. They were often the subjects of disagreements.

PRACTICE

CALIFORNIA CONTENT
STANDARD 8.8.4

Western Waters

Directions: Choose the letter of the *best* answer.

1 Lewis and Clark discovered that there was no easy passage between the

   A Colorado and Rio Grande.

   B Mississippi and Missouri.

   C Missouri and Columbia.

   D Rio Grande and Columbia.

2 In 1845, which river did Mexico claim formed the border between Mexico and Texas?

   A Colorado

   B Mississippi

   C Nueces

   D Rio Grande

3 The Mormons settled along tributaries of which river in the 1800s?

   A Colorado

   B Mississippi

   C Missouri

   D Rio Grande

4 In the 1800s, living on the Mississippi River was like living

   A in New England.

   B by the ocean.

   C on a major highway.

   D in the South.

5 When settlers in the West had to request permission to take water from a river, they were asking for

   A a river contract.

   B a fishing license.

   C water rights.

   D a right of way.

REVIEW

CALIFORNIA CONTENT
STANDARD 8.8.5

The Mexican Settlements

Specific Objective: Discuss Mexican settlements and their locations, cultural traditions, attitudes toward slavery, land-grant system, and economies.

Read the summary below to answer questions on the next page.

Mexico or United States?

In 1800, most of the southwest United States belonged to Spain. Spain had discouraged trade or contact with Americans. However, in 1821, Mexico achieved independence from Spain. As a result, the American Southwest became Mexican not Spanish. Mexico allowed American settlement and trading.

Texas

In 1821, only about 4,000 *Tejanos* lived in what was then called *Tejas*. *Tejanos* were people of Spanish origin living in Texas. Then Stephen Austin and nearly 300 American families settled there. They agreed to abide by Mexican law. By 1830, there were 30,000 people in *Tejas*. The Americans outnumbered the *Tejanos* six to one.

New Mexico

The Santa Fe Trail in New Mexico opened soon after Mexico became independent. Before this time, Pueblo Indians and Spanish descendants lived side by side and shared their cultures. Now American trading caravans crossed the plains each year.

California

Before the gold rush of 1849, 150,000 Native Americans and 6,000 *Californios* lived in California. *Californios* were people of Spanish or Mexican descent. Most lived on huge cattle ranches on former mission land. The gold rush brought great changes to California.

Vaqueros

The first cowhands were vaqueros. They were Mexicans who came to the Southwest with Spanish explorers in the 1500s. The vaqueros helped ranchers in the Southwest. The saddle, spurs, lariat, and chaps we now associate with cattle handling and ranching all came from the vaqueros.

Attitudes Toward Slavery

When Mexico won its independence from Spain, it outlawed the enslavement of people. Americans in Texas claimed they needed enslaved people to grow cotton. They convinced Mexico to let them continue the practice.

Land Grants

Many Mexican settlers in the Southwest were granted large plots of land by the Mexican government. When Mexico ceded its territories to the United States in 1853, most of these people lost their land.

Economies

California had a simple farming economy until the 1840s. However, after the discovery of gold, miners came from all over to strike it rich. Eventually, some mining camps turned into towns that gave people the chance to find jobs in fields other than farming. The same thing happened in New Mexico, when Americans discovered gold and silver there. The Santa Fe Trail brought traders and wagon trains on the way to California. Many people stayed in New Mexico and built towns.

PRACTICE

CALIFORNIA CONTENT STANDARD 8.8.5

The Mexican Settlements

Directions: Choose the letter of the *best* answer.

1 Before the gold rush, the economy of California was mainly based on

   A banking.

   B farming.

   C manufacturing.

   D mining.

2 In general, California's position on slavery in the mid-1800s was that the state

   A wanted to outlaw slavery.

   B needed slaves to mine for gold.

   C had no opinion about slavery.

   D favored gradual freedom for slaves.

3 Vaqueros were the first early-American and Mexican

   A cowhands.

   B farmers.

   C gold miners.

   D Texans.

4 In 1830, most of the Southwest belonged to

   A Mexico.

   B Spain.

   C Texas.

   D the United States.

5 Before the Santa Fe Trail opened, the people who lived in New Mexico were mainly Spanish descendants and

   A Americans.

   B Cherokee.

   C Pueblo Indians.

   D soldiers.

REVIEW

Texan Independence and the Mexican-American War

Specific Objective: Describe the Texas War for Independence and the Mexican-American War, including territorial settlements, the aftermath of the wars, and the effects the wars had on the lives of Americans, including Mexican Americans today.

Read the summary below to answer questions on the next page.

Texas War for Independence

1829   Texas belonged to Mexico. Most people living there were American.

1833   Texas asked to be a self-governing state within Mexico. Mexico refused and war broke out.

1836   Texas became an independent republic. It was called the Lone Star Republic. It had its own army and navy. Sam Houston was elected president. Texas applied for statehood.

Mexican-American War

1845   Congress admitted Texas to the Union. However, Mexico still claimed Texas and saw Congress's vote as an act of war. Mexico and the United States disagreed about the border between them.

The United States claimed that the Rio Grande was its southern border. Mexico said it was the Nueces River, which was more than 100 miles north at some points. The United States offered Mexico $25 million for Texas, California, and New Mexico. Mexico refused and war broke out in 1846 on the Rio Grande.

Territorial Settlements

1848   The Treaty of Guadalupe Hidalgo ended the Mexican-American War.

- Texas was now part of the United States.
- The Rio Grande became the border between the United States and Mexico.
- Mexico gave up an area that is now California, Nevada, Utah, most of Arizona, and parts of New Mexico, Colorado, and Wyoming.

1853   In the Gadsden Purchase, Mexico sold the United States a strip of land in what is now southern New Mexico and Arizona for $10 million.

Mexican Americans

Mexico gave up nearly half its land when it lost the war with the United States. About 80,000 Mexicans were suddenly Americans. The United States promised to protect these *Mexicanos.* But life for them changed. They became a minority in a country that spoke a different language and had a different culture. They lost economic and political power. Many also lost their land when American courts did not recognize land grants from the Mexican government.

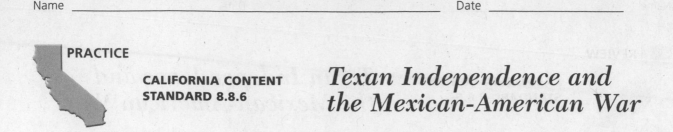

PRACTICE

CALIFORNIA CONTENT
STANDARD 8.8.6

Texan Independence and the Mexican-American War

Directions: Choose the letter of the *best* answer. Use the map to answer questions 1 and 2.

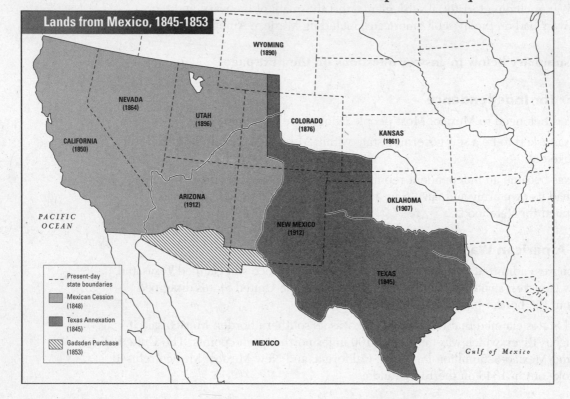

Lands from Mexico, 1845–1853

WYOMING (1890)

NEVADA (1864)

UTAH (1896)

COLORADO (1876)

KANSAS (1861)

CALIFORNIA (1850)

PACIFIC OCEAN

ARIZONA (1912)

NEW MEXICO (1912)

OKLAHOMA (1907)

TEXAS (1845)

--- Present-day state boundaries

Mexican Cession (1848)

Texas Annexation (1845)

Gadsden Purchase (1853)

MEXICO

Gulf of Mexico

1 The Texas Annexation in 1845 also included part of

A North Dakota.

B Nebraska.

C New Mexico.

D Missouri.

2 After the war with Mexico, the United States added land in which states in addition to Texas?

A Oregon, Oklahoma, and Kansas

B Oregon, New Mexico, and Colorado

C North Dakota, Oklahoma, Wyoming, Nevada, and Utah

D California, Nevada, Utah, Arizona, New Mexico, Colorado, and Wyoming

3 Which of the following events happened *last*?

A Texas became independent from Mexico.

B Texas became an American state.

C Mexico and the United States fought a war.

D Mexico became independent from Spain.

4 When Mexico ceded its land to the United States, 80,000 *Mexicanos* suddenly became

A exiled.

B homeless.

C a minority.

D wealthy.

Name _____ Date _____

Leaders of the Abolition Movement

Specific Objective: Describe the leaders of the abolition movement.

Read the summary below to answer the questions on the next page.

Benjamin Franklin

- At one time owned two slaves and accepted the common view that the black race was inferior
- After visiting a school for black children, changed his views
- Joined an abolitionist society in 1785
- Argued for educating freed slaves

Theodore Weld

- Influential abolitionist, minister, teacher, editor, beginning in 1834
- Married to Angelina Grimké, another well-known abolitionist
- Led a campaign to send antislavery petitions to Congress (1841–1843)
- Founded an interracial school (1854)

Frederick Douglass

- Formerly enslaved African American who escaped (1838) and became a well-known abolitionist, author, and ambassador
- Toured the country speaking out against slavery
- Started abolitionist newspaper, *The North Star* (1847–1860)
- Believed in abolition without violence

John Brown

- An extreme abolitionist
- Led an attack killing five proslavery neighbors when a proslavery mob destroyed offices and the governor's house in Lawrence, Kansas (1855)
- Attacked and took over U.S. weapons warehouse in Harpers Ferry, Virginia, in order to distribute the weapons for a planned slave rebellion (1859).
- Captured, convicted, and hung for murder and treason

William Lloyd Garrison

- Spoke out forcefully against slavery
- Started an important abolitionist newspaper, *The Liberator* (1831)
- Called for immediate emancipation, no payment to slaveholders

John Quincy Adams

- Presented petitions against slavery to Congress, fought the "Gag Rule" that forbade Congress to discuss or debate such petitions (1836–1844)
- Introduced a constitutional amendment to abolish slavery (1839)
- Successfully defended a group of Africans who rebelled on the slave ship *Amistad*, enabling them to return home (1841)
- Won repeal of the Gag Rule in 1844

Harriet Tubman

- Escaped from slavery in 1849
- Worked and traveled to free other slaves
- Conductor on the Underground Railroad
- Never caught, despite a reward offered for her capture

PRACTICE

CALIFORNIA CONTENT
STANDARD 8.9.1

Leaders of the Abolition Movement

Directions: Choose the letter of the *best* answer.

1 Which abolitionist preached that violence would be necessary in the fight to free slaves?

A   John Quincy Adams

B   John Brown

C   Frederick Douglass

D   Benjamin Franklin

2 Frederick Douglass said he "had been. . . dragging a heavy chain which no strength of mine could break. . . [now the] chains were broken, and the victory brought me unspeakable joy." Douglass was describing how he felt when he

A   was released from prison.

B   worked on the Underground Railroad.

C   escaped from slavery.

D   regained his sight.

3 Who introduced an amendment to end slavery?

A   John Quincy Adams

B   John Brown

C   Frederick Douglass

D   Theodore Weld

4 Which abolitionist was both an escaped slave and a famous conductor for the Underground Railroad?

A   John Brown

B   Angelina Grimké

C   William Lloyd Garrison

D   Harriet Tubman

5 What was *one* event that helped Benjamin Franklin change his mind about slavery?

A   He no longer needed help with his numerous scientific projects.

B   He read *Uncle Tom's Cabin* by Harriet Beecher Stowe.

C   He observed African-American students learning at school.

D   He became friends with the two slaves that he owned.

6 Two famous abolitionist newspapers were the *North Star* and the

A   *Abolitionist.*

B   *Agitator.*

C   *Freedom News.*

D   *Liberator.*

REVIEW

CALIFORNIA CONTENT
STANDARD 8.9.2

Early American Abolition Laws

Specific Objective: Discuss the abolition of slavery in early state constitutions.

Read the summary below to answer questions on the next page.

- The first state constitutions did not mention slavery. They said that all men were created equal. They did not mention the fact that some men (and women) were held as slaves. Over time, states changed their constitutions to limit specific practices, such as the slave trade.

- When states did vote to do away with slavery, they did not immediately free the slaves. Many passed gradual emancipation laws. These laws said a slave born after a certain date could become free at a certain age. Most of these bills paid slave owners for their loss.

- For example, in New York, a 1799 law stated that children born to slave mothers after July 4, 1799, would be freed, but only at age 25 for women, age 28 for men. Until then they would remain the property of their mother's "owner," and have to work. Slaves born before July 4, 1799 would remain slaves for life, although they would now be called "indentured servants."

1770	
1774	Connecticut and Rhode Island outlaw the slave trade.
1777	Vermont constitution forbids slavery.
1780	Massachusetts constitution forbids slavery. Pennsylvania passes gradual emancipation laws.
1784	Connecticut and Rhode Island add gradual emancipation laws.
1788	Connecticut bans the slave trade.
1799	New York passes gradual emancipation laws.
1800	

PRACTICE

CALIFORNIA CONTENT
STANDARD 8.9.2

Early American Abolition Laws

Directions: Choose the letter of the *best* answer.

1 When the Constitution was written, in 1787, there were laws banning slavery in

   A all of the states.

   B most of the states.

   C very few states.

   D none of the states.

2 The first state constitutions

   A took bold steps toward the abolition of slavery.

   B denied that slavery existed.

   C declared all men and women of all races to be equal.

   D avoided the issue of slavery.

3 Gradual emancipation laws meant that

   A slaves' rights would increase each year.

   B slavery was abolished one state at a time.

   C some slaves would be freed only at a certain age.

   D slavery would change in name only.

4 Some states allowed the ownership of slaves but banned

   A the sale of slaves.

   B slave labor.

   C mistreatment of slaves.

   D debates over slavery.

5 The first state constitution to explicitly outlaw slavery was in

   A Connecticut.

   B Massachusetts.

   C Rhode Island.

   D Vermont.

6 By making existing slaves indentured servants, New York's gradual abolition bill helped

   A slave owners.

   B slaves.

   C abolitionists.

   D state legislators.

REVIEW

CALIFORNIA CONTENT
STANDARD 8.9.3

The Northwest Ordinance

Specific Objective: Describe the significance of the Northwest Ordinance in education and in the banning of slavery in new states north of the Ohio River.

Read the summary below to answer questions on the next page.

Together, the Land Ordinance of 1785 and the Northwest Ordinance of 1787 set an orderly growth pattern for the United States. The Northwest territories did not have constitutions to protect citizens' rights. The ordinances banned slavery in the territories, setting the Ohio River as the northern boundary for the ownership of slaves. They also guaranteed freedom of religion and trial by jury, and allowed a territory to apply for state status when its population reached 60,000.

Education

- The Land Ordinance of 1785 said that land would be set aside for public schools. The territories were divided into townships. In each 36-section township, section number 16 was to be set aside for "the maintenance of public schools."

- Article III of the Northwest Ordinance of 1787 said, *"Religion, morality, and knowledge, being necessary to good government and the happiness of mankind, schools and the means of education shall forever be encouraged."* This article set up free public education for all new states.

- The idea behind supporting public education was to create informed and responsible citizens—a necessity in a democracy.

Slavery

- Article VI of the Northwest Ordinance of 1787 said:

  "There shall be neither slavery nor involuntary servitude. . . otherwise than in the punishment of crimes . . . [A]ny person . . . from whom labor or service is lawfully claimed in any one of the original State . . .may be lawfully . . .[returned] to the person claiming his or her labor."

- This meant that people could only be forced to work for someone if they had committed a crime. It also said that slaves who escaped into the territory could be returned to their owners.

- At this time all the Southern states were slave states, and some of the Northern states still allowed slavery. Article IV meant that there would be a new block of free states that would balance the voting power of the slave states. Keeping a balance between free and slave states was important so neither side could force its will on the other.

PRACTICE

CALIFORNIA CONTENT
STANDARD 8.9.3

The Northwest Ordinance

Directions: Choose the letter of the *best* answer.

TOWNSHIP, 1785					
36	30	24	18	12	6
35	29	23	17	11	5
34	28	22	16	10	4
33	27	21	15	9	3
32	26	20	14	8	2
31	25	19	13	7	1

Each township contained 36 sections.
Each section was one square mile.

1 As shown in the diagram, the Land Ordinance of 1785 set aside section 16 of every township for a school. This section was chosen because it was

  A the best piece of land.

  B one of the center sections.

  C not good for farming.

  D difficult to sell.

2 The Northwest Ordinance declared that slavery was not allowed

  A west of the Mississippi River.

  B east of the Mississippi River.

  C south of the Ohio River.

  D north of the Ohio River.

3 In 1787, people wanted to outlaw slavery in the Northwest Territories because it would

  A make slavery more profitable in the South.

  B guarantee that runaway slaves had somewhere to go.

  C keep the balance between slave and free states.

  D stop the growth of large plantations in the area.

4 For runaway slaves, crossing the Ohio River meant

  A they would surely be captured and punished.

  B slave catchers could not legally take them back across the river.

  C they had almost reached freedom in Canada.

  D they entered free territory, with no guarantee of protection.

5 The main purpose of the Northwest Ordinance was to help

  A farmers obtain free land.

  B land speculators get rich.

  C the country grow in an orderly way.

  D the abolition of slavery in the United States.

REVIEW

CALIFORNIA CONTENT
STANDARD 8.9.4

Texas and California Enter the Union

Specific Objective: Discuss the importance of the slavery issue as raised by the annexation of Texas and California's admission to the Union as a free state under the Compromise of 1850.

Read the summary below to answer questions on the next page.

Slave State: Texas

The invention of the cotton gin brought cotton farming and slavery to Texas. In 1836, Texas declared its independence from Mexico. It then asked for U.S. statehood. Growing worries over the spread of slavery kept Texas from becoming a state until 1845. At that time, Mexico still claimed its right to Texas. When Congress began debating whether to go to war with Mexico, one issue in the debate concerned slavery in Texas and other Mexican territories.

- Southern states wanted Texas in the Union because then there would be a majority of slave states in Congress.

- Anti-slavery interests in the North introduced a bill called the Wilmot Proviso. It prohibited slavery in lands taken from Mexico as a result of the war. This included Texas. The bill never became law. When the war was over, and Texas was officially on U.S. soil, it remained a slave state.

Free State: California

California asked to become a state in 1849. It had never become a territory because its population had grown so fast due to the gold rush. When California asked to enter into the Union, it caused an uproar.

- Some Southerners wanted to make California two states, with the southern half allowing slavery and the northern half outlawing it. Most Californians wanted a free state. They moved quickly in applying for statehood. They did not give slave owners a chance to move to the region.

- Letting California in as a free state would tip the balance in Congress to the anti-slavery side. Southerners were afraid Northerners might use this advantage to abolish slavery.

- Senator Henry Clay proposed the Compromise of 1850:

  —California became a free state.

  —Congress agreed not to outlaw slavery in the rest of the territories.

- The California constitution outlawed slavery. It did not grant the vote to African Americans.

PRACTICE

CALIFORNIA CONTENT
STANDARD 8.9.4

Texas and California
Enter the Union

Directions: Choose the letter of the *best* answer.

1   What issue was at stake when Texas and California tried to join the Union?

   A   Would they join as slave states or free states?

   B   Would Mexico agree to let them join the Union?

   C   How would the Spanish-speaking population learn Englilsh?

   D   Who owned the rights to gold?

2   What was Henry Clay's role in the entry of California into the Union?

   A   He tried to get California to leave the Union.

   B   He voted in favor of invading Mexico.

   C   He wanted to split California into two states.

   D   He suggested the Compromise of 1850.

3   California became a state once the Compromise of 1850 settled how the state would handle

   A   the war with Mexico.

   B   the issue of slavery.

   C   the cotton gin.

   D   the ongoing gold rush.

4   The Wilmot Proviso would have

   A   prevented war with Mexico.

   B   allowed Mexico to decide if Texas should be slave or free.

   C   admitted Texas as a slave state.

   D   kept slavery out of territories gained from Mexico.

5   Why did Mexico object to the entry of Texas into the Union?

   A   Mexico was at war with Texas.

   B   Texas owed Mexico a lot of money.

   C   Mexico, as a country, opposed slavery.

   D   Mexico claimed that it owned Texas.

6   California's constitution showed that the state

   A   agreed with the Southern states.

   B   left the question of slavery to each town.

   C   was against equality for African Americans.

   D   was the first state to allow African Americans to vote.

REVIEW

CALIFORNIA CONTENT
STANDARD 8.9.5

Slave States and Free States— Compromise and Debate

Specific Objective: Analyze the significance of the States' Rights Doctrine, the Missouri Compromise (1820), the Wilmot Proviso (1846), the Compromise of 1850, Henry Clay's role in the Missouri Compromise and the Compromise of 1850, the Kansas-Nebraska Act (1854), the *Dred Scott* v. *Sandford* decision (1857), and the Lincoln-Douglas debates (1858).

Read the chart below to answer questions on the next page.

States' Rights Doctrine	- Supported by many southerners before the Civil War - Said the U.S. Constitution was an agreement among the states; states could block the actions of the federal government they didn't like; states were free to secede from the Union - Main proponent—John C. Calhoun
Missouri Compromise, 1820	- Missouri asked for statehood as a slave state, threatening to upset the balance in Congress between slave and free states. - Henry Clay came up with the Missouri Compromise: outlawed slavery in the future anywhere north of Missouri's southern border; admitted Maine as a free state; kept the balance in Congress
Wilmot Proviso, 1846	- Proposed outlawing slavery in any territory the United States might win in the Mexican War - Slaveholders were against it; they said slaves were property and the Constitution gave equal rights to all property holders.
Compromise of 1850	- California asked to be let in as a free state. - Henry Clay suggested the compromise: California would be a free state; Congress agreed not to outlaw slavery in the rest of the territories; Congress had to promise a stronger fugitive slave law.
Kansas-Nebraska Act, 1854	- Proposed by Senator Stephen A. Douglas - Allowed popular votes in Nebraska and Kansas to decide if each would be a free or slave state (popular sovereignty) - Replaced the Missouri Compromise of 1820
Dred Scott v. *Sandford*, 1857	- Dred Scott, a slave, sued for his freedom because he had lived in a territory where slavery was illegal. - The Supreme Court ruled against him; said slaves, and all African Americans, were not citizens of the United States. - The decision increased tensions between the North and South.
Lincoln-Douglas debates, 1858	- Douglas was the Democratic Senator from Illinois; Lincoln was his Republican challenger. - In a series of debates throughout Illinois they discussed the expansion of slavery, Dred Scott, and the future of the Union. - Lincoln argued against the expansion of slavery, but not for abolishing slavery outright; Douglas argued for popular sovereignty, or allowing the population of a state to decide its own laws by voting.

PRACTICE

CALIFORNIA CONTENT
STANDARD 8.9.5

Slave States and Free States—Compromise and Debate

Directions: Choose the letter of the *best* answer.

1 The states' rights doctrine held that

  A states had fewer rights than the federal government.

  B the U.S. Constitution applied to some states but not all.

  C the federal government was useless.

  D states could choose to leave the Union.

2 Which law repealed the ban on slavery north of Missouri's southern border?

  A Compromise of 1850

  B Kansas-Nebraska Act

  C Missouri Compromise

  D Wilmot Proviso

3 In his 1858 debates with Stephen Douglas, Abraham Lincoln argued that slavery should be

  A expanded throughout the Union.

  B spread worldwide.

  C completely abolished.

  D regulated to certain states.

4 What was the aim of Henry Clay's Compromise of 1850?

  A to protect states by limiting the power of the national government

  B to resolve the issue of slavery in the territories once and for all

  C to stop the South from splitting away from the United States

  D to unite the North and South against the western territories

5 In the case of Dred Scott, the Supreme Court decided that

  A Scott should be allowed to go free.

  B Scott was not a citizen of the United States.

  C slavery was illegal north of the Missouri Compromise line.

  D slavery should not be allowed in the South.

REVIEW

CALIFORNIA CONTENT STANDARD 8.9.6

Free Blacks and the Laws that Limited Them

Specific Objective: Describe the lives of free blacks and the laws that limited their freedom and economic opportunities.

Read the summary below to answer questions on the next page.

By 1860, there were almost 500,000 free blacks in the United States. These men, women, and children had more rights than if they had been enslaved. But they were far from truly free or equal under the law. Problems of racial injustice existed in the North as well as in the South.

Segregation, Limits on Freedom, and Attacks

- In the North and in the South there was limited work for free blacks. Many freed slaves ended up working on the same farm where they had been slaves. Free blacks in the North mostly lived in cities.

- Because slaveholders feared their influence, free blacks were often segregated and kept apart, even in the North. There were laws in some states forbidding free blacks to mix with slaves, or to carry weapons.

- Free blacks were kept out of most public schools.

- There were laws in some states forbidding free blacks to travel between states. Free blacks had to carry proof of their status.

- Even by the end of the Civil War, only 5 of 24 Northern states allowed blacks to vote. No states allowed blacks to be witnesses in court when whites were a party to the case.

- Poor whites didn't like competition for jobs from blacks. Between 1829 and 1849, for example, white mobs attacked and killed free blacks in Philadelphia, Boston, Providence, New York, and Washington, D.C. White mobs also attacked and destroyed black schools, churches, businesses, and homes.

Black Codes and Exclusion

- Many Midwestern and Western states thought they would solve the "race problem" by preventing free blacks from entering. In these states, slavery had either been abolished or had never been allowed.

- Ohio had abolished slavery in its original constitution in 1802. It passed exclusionary Black Laws in 1804. Every African American entering the state had to pay a $500 bond against possible future crimes. They also had to produce court papers showing that they were free.

- Blacks were denied the right to question these laws or "for any purpose whatsoever."

- Indiana, Illinois, Michigan, Iowa, and Oregon passed similar laws, known as Black Codes. These laws went beyond trying to keep blacks from settling there. They also limited blacks' ability to own real estate, make contracts, bring lawsuits, or be a witness in court. The punishments for breaking these laws were harsh. One punishment was being sold at public auction (Illinois, 1853).

Name _____   Date _____

PRACTICE

Free Blacks and the Laws that Limited Them

Directions: Choose the letter of the *best* answer.

1 **Free African Americans who violated black codes in free states could expect to**

   A speak in court as a trial witness.

   B pay a $500 fine and go free.

   C be asked to move to a different free state.

   D be harshly punished or sold into slavery.

2 **The Black Laws of Ohio required every free black to pay a $500 bond. This law made it**

   A more difficult for free blacks to hire lawyers.

   B easier to set up schools for blacks.

   C easier to know who was legally free.

   D more difficult for free blacks to enter Ohio.

3 **Laws preventing free blacks from voting existed**

   A only in the slaveholding Southern states.

   B only in the anti-slavery Northern states.

   C only in the new states of the Midwest and West.

   D in many states throughout the Union.

4 **The movement of free blacks was limited in part because**

   A slave owners feared contact between free blacks and slaves.

   B free blacks were known to be rowdy and dangerous.

   C state governments wanted to prevent any population movements.

   D free blacks were poor and could not afford to move.

"Race prejudice seems stronger in those states that have abolished slavery than in those where it still exists . . . ."

—Alexis de Tocqueville,
Democracy in America, 1835

5 **In the quotation, French writer de Tocqueville describes race prejudice in the United States by**

   A using facts and opinions to persuade.

   B using hard facts to support an opinion.

   C stating an opinion based on observation.

   D supporting an opinion with reliable sources.

6 **What is one reason that white mobs attacked blacks in Northern cities in the 1800s?**

   A White city dwellers were afraid of slave revolts.

   B Blacks in the North published abolitionist newspapers.

   C Whites in the North feared competition for their jobs.

   D Free blacks had begun attending white schools.

REVIEW

CALIFORNIA CONTENT
STANDARD 8.10.1

The Views of Webster and Calhoun

Specific Objective: Compare the conflicting interpretations of state and federal authority as emphasized in speeches and writings of political leaders such as Daniel Webster and John C. Calhoun.

Read the summary below to answer the questions on the next page.

Daniel Webster (1782–1852)

This U.S. Senator from Massachusetts was a strong leader and powerful speaker. He supported a strong federal government. Webster believed states could not nullify federal laws. He said the people, not the states, created the Union, and only the people could dissolve it.

- **Speech at the funeral of John Adams and Thomas Jefferson (1826)**

  Underscored the uniqueness of the United States and the value of a representative democracy. Everyone must respect and preserve the Union.

- **Hayne-Webster debate (1830)**

  Webster argued that states cannot dilute the Constitution or federal authority. They must obey federal laws or call for complete revolution. There was no middle ground. Freedom and the Union go together.

- **"Constitution and the Union" (1850)**

  In this speech before the Senate, Webster supported the Compromise of 1850. He thought peaceful secession was impossible; the Union must be kept whole. The North and South should compromise, with the Constitution as a guide.

John C. Calhoun (1782–1850)

Calhoun was a South Carolina politician. He at first supported the American System and a strong national government. Calhoun served as vice president under John Quincy Adams and Andrew Jackson. He became a defender of states' rights in response to tariff policies that the South considered unfair because they favoured the North.

- **"South Carolina Exposition and Protest" (1828)**

  Anonymous essay that outlined his nullification theory. He supported the idea of a state being able to veto (nullify) a federal law within its borders. Sparked by the so called "Tariff of Abominations," Calhoun's concern was that the federal government might outlaw slavery in the future.

- **Member of the U.S. Senate (1832–43, 1845–50)**

  Calhoun supported slavery and states' rights, saying slavery was a "positive good." He favored the gag rule, which prevented discussion of the issue in Congress.

- **Opposed the Compromise of 1850**

  Calhoun opposed Webster and Henry Clay. He thought slavery should be allowed to expand into the territories. He saw this as the best way to preserve the Union because he thought that, otherwise, the South would secede from the Union.

Name _____ Date _____

The Views of Webster and Calhoun

Directions: Choose the letter of the *best* answer.

1 Daniel Webster and John C. Calhoun agreed that

   A states had more power than the federal government.

   B slavery was an evil that should be abolished.

   C the Compromise of 1850 was good for the South.

   D secession was not good for anyone.

"Liberty and Union, now and forever, one and inseparable!"

—Daniel Webster, U.S. Senate speech, January 26, 1830

---

2 When Webster made this speech, he was arguing against

   A the breakup of the Union.

   B unfair tariffs.

   C the limiting of free speech.

   D slavery.

3 John C. Calhoun first became a proponent of states' rights because

   A of his friendship with Daniel Webster.

   B he believed the South should secede.

   C of federal tariffs he considered unfair.

   D he disagreed with the Constitution.

4 Daniel Webster believed first and foremost in

   A the Union.

   B freedom of religion.

   C states' rights.

   D the two-party system.

5 Calhoun thought the best way to preserve the Union was to

   A support the Missouri Compromise.

   B encourage Northern factory owners to hire slaves.

   C allow slavery to expand into new territories.

   D strengthen the powers of the federal government.

6 John C. Calhoun believed laws could be declared unconstitutional by

   A the Congress.

   B the president.

   C individual states.

   D only the Supreme Court.

REVIEW

CALIFORNIA CONTENT STANDARD 8.10.2

North and South

Specific Objective: Trace boundaries constituting the North and the South, the geographical differences between the two regions, and the differences between agrarians and industrialists.

Study the summary and map below to answer the questions on the next page.

The Differences between North and South

The two opposing sides of the Civil War are referred to as the Union and the Confederacy, or sometimes the North and South, but their differences are more than geographic. The Midwest and the Northeast had some geographic differences but were united against slavery, and so were part of the Union. The border states had much in common, including slavery, with the South. But they chose to stay in the Union. The two western states sided with the North because they had outlawed slavery. They were less involved in the conflict.

In addition, differences in soil and climate affected Northern and Southern economies.

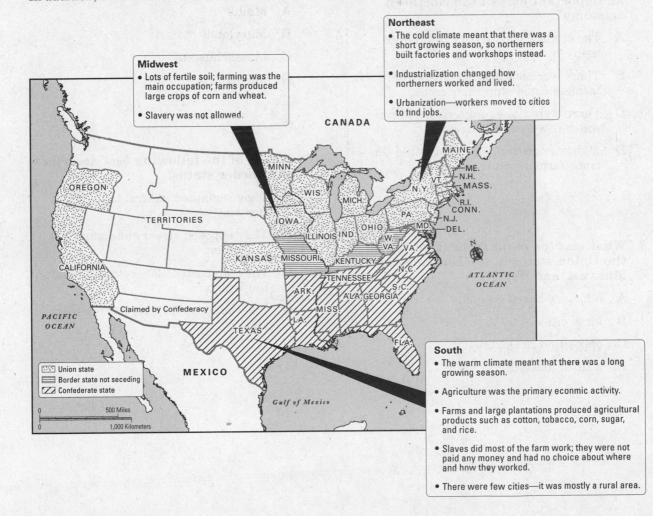

Midwest
- Lots of fertile soil; farming was the main occupation; farms produced large crops of corn and wheat.
- Slavery was not allowed.

Northeast
- The cold climate meant that there was a short growing season, so northerners built factories and workshops instead.
- Industrialization changed how northerners worked and lived.
- Urbanization—workers moved to cities to find jobs.

South
- The warm climate meant that there was a long growing season.
- Agriculture was the primary economic activity.
- Farms and large plantations produced agricultural products such as cotton, tobacco, corn, sugar, and rice.
- Slaves did most of the farm work; they were not paid any money and had no choice about where and how they worked.
- There were few cities—it was mostly a rural area.

Union state
Border state not seceding
Confederate state

500 Miles
1,000 Kilometers

PRACTICE

CALIFORNIA CONTENT
STANDARD 8.10.2

North and South

Directions: Choose the letter of the *best* answer.

1 What was the *major* characteristic of the Southern economy in the mid-1800s?

  A commerce

  B farming

  C industry

  D ranching

2 Why did manufacturing become an important part of the Northern economy?

  A The climate was too dry to produce many crops.

  B There were not enough cities where farmers could ship their crops.

  C There were not enough rivers to run water-powered factories.

  D A shorter growing season limited the crops farmers could produce.

3 What was the *main* factor that linked the Union states in the Northeast, Midwest, and West?

  A a factory-based economy

  B large cities

  C opposition to slavery

  D a rural lifestyle

4 What was a similarity between the South and the Midwest in the mid-1800s?

  A farming economy

  B large cities

  C use of slave labor

  D warm climate

5 Which state was a border state?

  A Maine

  B Maryland

  C Massachusetts

  D Michigan

6 Which of the following *best* describes the border states?

  A They remained neutral throughout the war.

  B They opposed slavery and stayed in the Union.

  C They supported slavery and stayed in the Union.

  D They supported slavery and left the Union.

REVIEW

CALIFORNIA CONTENT STANDARD 8.10.3 *The Doctrine of Nullification*

Specific Objective: Identify the constitutional issues posed by the doctrine of nullification and secession and the earliest origins of that doctrine.

Read the summary below to answer the questions on the next page.

Federal Government versus State Government

When the United States was new, there was much disagreement about the balance of power between the federal and state governments. The Constitution was designed to put those issues to rest. It defined the powers of each branch and level of government. But not everyone agreed about how to interpret the Constitution with regard to how much power the federal government should have over the individual states.

Virginia and Kentucky Resolutions

An early crisis occurred with the passage of the Alien and Sedition Acts of 1798. These four laws limited the rights of recent immigrants to the United States and upset citizens in many states, particularly Thomas Jefferson and James Madison. Jefferson and Madison favored the theory of states' rights. According to this theory, a state could nullify, or declare "not binding," any federal law within its borders believed to be unconstitutional. Jefferson and Madison wrote resolutions passed by Virginia and Kentucky stating that the Alien and Sedition Acts violated the Constitution. No other states at the time took this position.

The Alien and Sedition Acts eventually were repealed or expired, but the issue of nullification had been introduced.

Tariff of Abominations

In 1828, Congress passed a bill raising tariffs on raw materials and manufactured goods. Southerners thought the new tariffs gave Northerners an unfair advantage. They called the law the Tariff of Abominations.

Doctrine of Nullification

South Carolina was especially affected by the tariff. The vice president in 1828 was John C. Calhoun a native of that state. He returned to the doctrine of nullification. He said that a state could nullify a federal law that it found unconstitutional. The state would make the law void within its own borders.

Like Jefferson and Madison before them, those who favored the doctrine of nullification said that the Union was a league of self-governing states. They thought that each state had the right to limit the influence of the federal government. One of a state's rights was to judge whether federal laws were unconstitutional. If a state decided a law was unconstitutional it was not bound to obey it. Calhoun and his supporters also thought a state could withdraw from the Union at any time.

Opponents said that the Constitution was the supreme law of the land. In addition, they agreed that the Supreme Court alone could decide if laws were constitutional. They also pointed out that the Constitution specifically gave Congress the right to levy tariffs.

Name _____   Date _____

The Doctrine of Nullification

Directions: Choose the letter of the *best* answer.

1 John C. Calhoun was vice president in 1828. When he proposed the doctrine of nullification, he was acting in the interests of

 A   Congress.

 B   the Democratic Party.

 C   South Carolina.

 D   the president.

2 The doctrine of nullification came in response to

 A   Civil War.

 B   the Tariff of Abominations.

 C   Kentucky Resolution.

 D   Missouri Compromise.

3 The issue of nullification was *first* raised by

 A   John Quincy Adams.

 B   John C. Calhoun.

 C   Andrew Jackson.

 D   Thomas Jefferson.

4 The doctrine of nullification was based on the theory of

 A   checks and balances.

 B   federalism.

 C   separation of powers.

 D   states' rights.

5 Southern states said they would nullify laws they felt were unfair. What *else* did they do to protest unfair tariffs?

 A   declared war

 B   boycotted goods from the North

 C   asked Britain for help

 D   threatened to secede

6 Opponents of Calhoun's doctrine of nullification pointed out that Congress had the constitutional right to

 A   favor certain states.

 B   levy tariffs.

 C   rewrite the Constitution.

 D   nullify state laws.

REVIEW

CALIFORNIA CONTENT
STANDARD 8.10.4

Lincoln's Policies and Speeches

Specific Objective: Discuss Abraham Lincoln's presidency and his significant writings and speeches and their relationship to the Declaration of Independence, such as his "House Divided" speech (1858), Gettysburg Address (1863), Emancipation Proclamation (1863), and inaugural addresses (1861 and 1865).

Read the summary below to answer the questions on the next page.

Abraham Lincoln was not only a great leader, but a gifted writer and public speaker as well. His speeches and writings reveal his ideas about liberty, equality, union, and government, ideas he said sprung from "the sentiments embodied in the Declaration of independence."

Lincoln became president in 1861, shortly before the attack on Fort Sumter. During the Civil War, Lincoln's ideas about liberty for enslaved African Americans changed and more directly reflected the ideals of the Declaration of Independence. His hopes for leading the nation towards reunification ended when he was assassinated in 1865, shortly after beginning his second term as president.

"House Divided" speech (1858)

- In his Senate campaign debates against Stephen Douglas, Lincoln stated that "A house divided against itself cannot stand;" the nation would have to be all free states or all slave states.
- Slavery was "a moral, a social and a political wrong;" Argued against the expansion of slavery
- The Declaration proclaimed that the 13 colonies were now a new nation; Lincoln was urging the divided country to think of itself as one nation.

First Inaugural Address (1861)

- Said the North would not invade the South, but it would defend federal property in the South; Southerners and Northerners were friends and brothers, not enemies.
- Did not want to abolish slavery
- The Declaration united the colonies in a common struggle against Great Britain; Lincoln asked that Northerners and Southerners remember what they have in common.

Emancipation Proclamation (January 1863)

- Freed slaves living in states controlled by the Confederacy
- Extended the Declaration's belief that "all men ... are endowed ... with certain unalienable Rights ... Life, Liberty and the pursuit of Happiness"
- The Declaration began a war of liberation; the Emancipation Proclamation changed the Civil War to a war of liberation.

Gettysburg Address (November 1863) (Commemorated Union soldiers who died at Gettysburg)

- The country was founded on the ideals of freedom and equality, ideals the Union was fighting to preserve.
- The ideals of freedom and equality are the foundation of the Declaration of Independence.
- Mentions the founding fathers' dedication "to the proposition that all men are created equal."

Second Inaugural Address (1865)

- Said the war was about slavery
- Looked toward the end of the war and a healing of the split between North and South
- Once again, Lincoln reminded a divided country that it was one nation, united in the struggle for freedom.

PRACTICE

CALIFORNIA CONTENT
STANDARD 8.10.4

*Lincoln's Policies
and Speeches*

Directions: Choose the letter of the *best* answer.

1 What statement *best* describes Lincoln's sentiment as expressed in his "House Divided" speech?

   A There would be a civil war between North and South.

   B Congress would continue to compromise about slavery.

   C The issue of slavery was weakening the United States.

   D Slavery would be outlawed in Illinois.

2 In the Gettysburg Address, Lincoln said that the country was based on the idea that "all men are created equal." He was echoing the words of

   A the Bill of Rights.

   B the Declaration of Independence.

   C the Constitution.

   D the Emancipation Proclamation.

3 During the Gettysburg Address, Lincoln spoke of "the great task remaining before us." This task was to

   A preserve freedom and democracy.

   B clean up the battlefield.

   C win a second term as president.

   D rebuild the South.

4 Which of the following showed a change in Lincoln's ideas about slavery?

   A House Divided Speech

   B First Inaugural Address

   C Emancipation Proclamation

   D Gettysburg Address

5 How did the Emancipation Proclamation reflect the ideas of the Declaration of Independence?

   A It supported Southern independence.

   B It gave slaves the right to vote.

   C It freed Southern prisoners of war.

   D It supported freedom for slaves.

"With malice toward none, with charity for all . . . let us bind up the nation's wounds."

—Abraham Lincoln,
Second Inaugural Address, 1865

6 What *best* summarizes Lincoln's sentiment as expressed in this excerpt from his Second Inaugural Address?

   A We must have a commitment to hospitals for veterans.

   B We must have an attitude of forgiveness toward the South.

   C We must have a plan to raise money for the war.

   D We must have a plan to abolish slavery in border states.

Name _____ Date _____

CALIFORNIA CONTENT
STANDARD 8.10.5

Civil War Leaders and Soldiers

Specific Objective: Study the views and lives of leaders (e.g., Ulysses S. Grant, Jefferson Davis, Robert E. Lee) and soldiers on both sides of the war, including those of black soldiers and regiments.

Read the summary below to answer the questions on the next page.

Ulysses S. Grant—Union General	
"Find out where your enemy is, get at him as soon as you can, strike at him as hard as you can, and keep moving on." Grant's war strategy	• Won first major victories for the Union in Tennessee • Became commanding general of all the Union armies in 1864 • Solid strategy and persistence in going after Lee's army led to victory • Accepted Lee's surrender at Appomattox Court House in 1865

Jefferson Davis—President of the Confederate States	
"All we ask is to be let alone." Davis describes the South's position	• Former senator from Mississippi • Did not want to be president of the Confederacy; he was not good at compromise and didn't like anyone to criticize him • Had a difficult job: form a new government and wage war at the same time • Jailed for two years after the war, never tried for treason

Robert E. Lee—Confederate General	
"Save in defense of my native State, I never desire again to draw my sword." Lee declines to lead the Union Army, 1861	• Respected by Northerners and loved by white Southerners • A strong unionist; considered slavery "a political and moral evil" • Refused to fight against fellow Virginians • Won early victories in 1862; forced Union troops out of Virginia; held out against great odds for almost two more years after defeat at Gettysburg

White Soldiers	Black Soldiers
• At first, most were volunteers; both sides later instituted drafts. Draftees could pay substitutes to fight in their place. • Soldiers on both sides suffered from poor food and unhealthy living conditions. • As the war dragged on, the South had fewer men to replace those who were killed and wounded. It also had fewer resources to take care of the soldiers.	• Able to serve after the Emancipation Proclamation; 180,000 African Americans in the Union Army by the end of the Civil War • Fought in all-black regiments, usually led by white officers • Had to fight for equal pay; given the worst jobs • Faced harsh treatment and death if captured by Confederates

Copyright © McDougal Littell/Houghton Mifflin Company

PRACTICE

CALIFORNIA CONTENT
STANDARD 8.10.5

Civil War Leaders and Soldiers

Directions: Choose the letter of the *best* answer.

1 Ulysses S. Grant's *major* role in the Civil War was to

  A lead a regiment of black soldiers.

  B be vice president of the Confederacy.

  C defeat Robert E. Lee at Gettysburg.

  D lead the Union army to final victory.

2 *One* reason Robert E. Lee declined command of the Union army is because he

  A did not support the idea of the Union.

  B served in the Confederate government instead.

  C refused to fight people from his home state.

  D was too busy running his plantation.

3 Jefferson Davis became president of the Confederacy even though he

  A lived in the North.

  B preferred to serve as a general.

  C had never held an elected office.

  D owned no slaves.

4 Which is *true* about African-American soldiers in the Civil War?

  A They fought only for the Confederacy.

  B They had to be drafted in order to fight.

  C They were paid the same as white soldiers.

  D They were usually given the worst jobs.

5 Why did soldiers from the South have a disadvantage compared to those from the North?

  A They were drafted rather than choosing to fight.

  B The South had fewer resources to support the troops.

  C Their generals were not willing to keep fighting.

  D They did most of their fighting on Northern soil.

6 How did General Robert E. Lee feel about slavery?

  A He was willing to defend it to his "last drop of blood."

  B He became a general so he could "eradicate this injustice."

  C He considered it "a political and moral evil."

  D He believed it was "necessary to the greatness of the South."

REVIEW

CALIFORNIA CONTENT STANDARD 8.10.6

Critical Events in the Civil War

Specific Objective: Describe critical developments and events in the war, including the major battles, geographical advantages and obstacles, technological advances, and General Lee's surrender at Appomattox.

Read the summary below to answer the questions on the next page.

Strengths, Weaknesses, and Strategies

- **North:** huge advantages in manpower and resources, including factories, railroads, and shipyards; strong leader in Lincoln; strategy to blockade the Southern coast and control the Mississippi River to cut the Confederacy in two; most fighting was in the South, far from Union supply lines
- **South:** main advantage was good leaders like Lee; fought a defensive war, close to supply lines and motivated to defend their homes. Hoped to use cotton to get France and Britain to support the Confederacy.

Advances in Military Technology

- Rifles that shot minié balls much farther and more accurately than muskets could. Direct assaults by infantry and cavalry were less effective. Higher casualty rates, more severe injuries.
- Ironclads were warships covered with iron. They could withstand attack better than wooden ships. First used in 1862, especially helped Grant on the Mississippi.

Important Civil War Events

1861
- April 12: War begins when Confederates attack Fort Sumter in South Carolina.
- July 12: Union defeated at First Battle of Bull Run.

1862
- Grant wins important victories in Tennessee.
- Union captures New Orleans; gains control of most of the Mississippi River.
- Lee takes over the Army of Northern Virginia; ends Union threat in the state.
- Lee invades Maryland, defeated at Antietam.

1863
- January—Lincoln issues the Emancipation Proclamation.
- Focus of the war shifts to ending slavery.
- African Americans join the Union army in large numbers.
- July: Confederates defeated at Vicksburg, Mississippi and Gettysburg, Pennsylvania.
- Confederacy split in two; tide turns in the Union favor.

1864
- March: Grant takes control of all Union forces.
- June: Grant begins 10-month siege at Petersburg, Virginia.
- Sherman wages total war across Georgia.

1865
- Lee's troops are forced to flee Richmond.
- April 9: Lee surrenders to Grant at Appomattox Court House, ending the war.
- Grant offers generous terms of surrender.

PRACTICE

CALIFORNIA CONTENT
STANDARD 8.10.6

Critical Events in the Civil War

Directions: Choose the letter of the *best* answer.

1   The Civil War began at

A   Fort Sumter.

B   Gettysburg.

C   New Orleans.

D   Vicksburg.

2   The North had an advantage over the South from the start of the Civil War because it had

A   better military leaders.

B   more farms that could produce food.

C   stronger ties with England.

D   more people and other resources.

3   The siege of Vicksburg ended with

A   General Lee's surrender.

B   Grant taking control of the whole Union army.

C   the Confederacy split in two.

D   Union troops withdrawing from Virginia.

4   The Emancipation Proclamation came after the Union victory at

A   Antietam.

B   Gettysburg.

C   Petersburg.

D   Vicksburg.

5   A new military technology that led to increased casualties was the use of

A   blockades.

B   ironclad warships.

C   minié balls.

D   sieges.

6   What critical event in the Civil War happened at Appomattox?

A   Lee surrendered to Grant.

B   The South broke through the Northern blockade.

C   Lee won a battle in the North.

D   The first battle of ironclads was fought.

REVIEW

CALIFORNIA CONTENT STANDARD 8.10.7

Effects of the Civil War

Specific Objective: Explain how the war affected combatants, civilians, the physical environment, and future warfare.

Read the summary below to answer the questions on the next page.

Soldiers

Food and Clothing— Rations in the camps were plentiful at the beginning of the war. Yet many soldiers in the field went hungry because supply trains could not reach them. At the beginning of the war, Union soldiers were given shoddy clothing and shoes. Some Confederate soldiers didn't even receive shoes, because the states didn't cooperate and share supplies.

Health—Soldiers in the field were often wet, muddy, or cold. Their camps were unsanitary and unhealthy.

Soldiers might go weeks without bathing. People didn't know then that germs caused disease and so sanitary conditions were not a priority.

Casualties—About 620,000 soldiers died in the Civil War, 360,000 for the Union, and 260,000 for the Confederacy. It was the deadliest war in American history. More than twice as many men died of disease as died from battle. About 50,000 men died in Northern and Southern prison camps where the conditions were terrible. An additional 535,000 soldiers were wounded, and many had limbs amputated.

Civilians

Women—Women on both sides took over jobs on farms and in cities that had previously been done only by men. They also worked as volunteers and nurses on the battlefields.

Slaves—As the war progressed, many slaves refused to work or ran away from the farms and plantations where they worked. Eventually the Thirteenth Amendment ended slavery completely.

The Environment

North—The North became more industrialized as a result of the demands of war.

South—Union general William Sherman had a strategy that called for destroying nearly everything in his path, including the lives of ordinary civilians. He moved through the South tearing up rail lines, burning crops and burning and looting towns. In the course of the war, farms and plantations were destroyed, including much of the livestock and machinery. Factories were demolished.

Future Warfare

The Civil War was the first modern war, using recent inventions like the telegraph, trains, and steam power. New military technology, like the rifle, Gatling gun (an early machine gun), and ironclad ships changed the way armies and navies fought. Direct assaults by soldiers on foot or on horseback were less effective. Warfare became more efficient and deadly.

PRACTICE

CALIFORNIA CONTENT
STANDARD 8.10.7   *Effects of the Civil War*

Directions: Choose the letter of the *best* answer.

1 *Most* Civil War soldiers died of

   A disease

   B food poisoning.

   C gunshot wounds.

   D land mines.

2 How did the Civil War affect the lives of women?

   A They were forced to spend the war in hiding.

   B They were forbidden to do factory work.

   C They had to do jobs they had not done before.

   D They refused to support the war effort.

> "Since we left Chester—solitude. Nothing but tall blackened chimneys to show that any man has ever trod this road before us. This is Sherman's track. It is hard not to curse him."
>
> —Mary Chesnut, *A Diary from Dixie*

3 This passage from Mary Chesnut's diary shows

   A the results of a fire in a weapons factory.

   B the results of a major slave uprising.

   C the effects of the war on Southern civilians.

   D the effects of the Confederate retreat.

4 Which of these statements *best* summarizes how the war changed life in the North and South?

   A Both regions suffered equal damage.

   B The South's way of life was almost destroyed.

   C Life in the North was not changed by the war.

   D Slavery still supported the Southern economy

5 How did warfare change after the Civil War?

   A Warfare became more deadly.

   B Direct assaults by foot soldiers became more common.

   C The use of the navy decreased.

   D The horrors of the war made people decide not to fight again.

6 How did actions by slaves during the war affect life in the South?

   A Slaves kept the economy going until after the war.

   B Slave resistance made it harder to grow enough food.

   C Slaves made up for losses in the Confederate army.

   D Slaves did nothing differently during the war.

REVIEW

CALIFORNIA CONTENT
STANDARD 8.11.1

Reconstruction

Specific Objective: List the original aims of Reconstruction and describe its effects on the political and social structures of different regions.

Read the summary below to answer the questions on the next page.

Goal of Reconstruction (1865)

- To readmit Confederate states into the Union and rebuild Southern society.

Conflicts over Reconstruction (1865–1867)

- Congress started the Freedmen's Bureau to help both black and white Southerners and to set up schools for blacks in the South.
- Lincoln favored a charitable plan, including pardoning Southern officials and allowing Southern states to send representatives to Congress.
- President Andrew Johnson, a Democrat, continued Lincoln's policies.
- Southern states passed black codes that kept blacks from enjoying the same rights as whites.
- Republicans in Congress took control of Reconstruction and pushed for a more extreme, or radical, plan to control the South and help blacks.

Effects of Reconstruction

- Congress said that each state must agree to three Amendments—the Thirteenth, Fourteenth, and Fifteenth. These ended slavery, extended citizenship to African Americans, and gave African American men the right to vote.
- Political alliances were formed between Northerners who came South to help Reconstruction (carpetbaggers), poor white farmers who supported the Republicans (scalawags), and African Americans.
- New progressive state constitutions were written.

Changes to the South

- African Americans gained the right to move from place to place, attend schools, and to organize churches.
- African Americans were elected to state and federal legislatures.
- Planters replaced the slave plantation system with sharecropping.
- Democrats regained power in the South.

Compromise of 1877 Ends Reconstruction

- Federal troops removed from the South.
- Federal funds helped to rebuild the South.
- Democrats promised to respect African Americans' rights, but Reconstruction governments in the South collapsed.

PRACTICE

CALIFORNIA CONTENT
STANDARD 8.11.1

Reconstruction

Directions: Choose the letter of the *best* answer.

1 **What was the *main* purpose of Reconstruction?**

A to unite the states and rebuild the South

B to give African Americans equal rights

C to pardon former Confederate generals

D to take land away from plantation owners

2 **Why were "carpetbaggers" distrusted in the South during Reconstruction?**

A As Northerners who came to the South, they represented a recent enemy.

B As poor whites and African Americans, they competed for jobs.

C As African Americans who went north after emancipation, they were considered spies.

D As traveling salespeople, they were making a profit from the war.

3 **In response to the black codes passed by Southern states, Congress**

A decided to end the process of Reconstruction.

B passed laws to give African Americans more rights.

C helped re-elect President Andrew Johnson.

D allowed the black codes to stand without challenging them.

4 **Whose plan for Reconstruction did President Andrew Johnson follow?**

A Abraham Lincoln

B radical Republicans

C former Confederate soldiers

D the majority of plantation owners

5 **The Radical Republicans thought that Reconstruction should be controlled by the**

A Congress.

B president.

C states.

D Supreme Court.

6 **How did the Compromise of 1877 help the South?**

A It allowed use of federal troops to keep order.

B It allowed northern politicians to run the southern states.

C It provided funds for rebuilding the South.

D It helped support a railroad company to link the North and South.

REVIEW

CALIFORNIA CONTENT
STANDARD 8.11.2

The Migration of African Americans

Specific Objective: Identify factors in the movement of former slaves to the cities in the North and to the West and their differing experiences in those regions.

Read the summary below to answer the questions on the next page.

Reasons African Americans Left the South

- African Americans in the South were now free but had no land or money.
- In 1866, a secret group called The **Ku Klux Klan** began violently attacking African Americans in the South.
- **Sharecropping** (a system in which workers farmed land for landowners) made it difficult for poor white and black families to survive.
- White Southerners restricted the rights of African Americans by instituting literacy tests and poll taxes that kept blacks from voting.
- In the 1890s, **Jim Crow laws** made segregation official in a number of areas of Southern life.

NOTE: Economists refer to "push factors" driving people away from an area.

Reasons African Americans Moved to the North

- The North was experiencing a boom in industry, and jobs were plentiful.
- The North was not as segregated as the South.
- As African Americans settled in the North and found jobs, they sent for their extended families and friends.

Reasons African Americans Moved to the West

- **The Homestead Act** of 1862 offered 160 acres of free land on the Plains to anyone who would farm it and live on it for five years.
- There were jobs on ranches, in mining towns, and in rapidly growing western towns and cities.
- Railroads made it easier to move west.
- Many people went west in the hope of finding gold.

NOTE: Economists refer to "pull factors" drawing people toward an area.

Differing Experiences of African Americans

- African Americans who migrated north often faced discrimination and segregation, as well as some violence directed against them.
- Some African Americans in the West were forced to borrow money and work for the lender to pay off the debt.
- Others, like the Exodusters (named after the flight of the Hebrews from slavery in the Old Testament), who moved west as part of the Homestead Act, were relieved

PRACTICE

CALIFORNIA CONTENT
STANDARD 8.11.2

The Migration of African Americans

Directions: Choose the letter of the *best* answer.

1 **A factor that pulled African Americans toward the West was the**

   A sharecropping system.

   B Ku Klux Klan.

   C industrial boom.

   D Homestead Act.

2 *One* **factor that drove African Americans to leave the South was**

   A cheap land.

   B the Ku Klux Klan.

   C an industrial boom.

   D the gold rush.

3 **The Exodusters moved west to**

   A own their own land.

   B join the U.S. Army.

   C mine for gold.

   D work in factories.

4 **Opportunities that drew African Americans to the Midwest and Northeast during the late 1800s, included**

   A mining and ranching.

   B jobs in industry.

   C free land.

   D the chance to find gold.

5 **For African Americans in the 1860s, the North was a place where**

   A an economic recession made many people return south.

   B literacy tests and poll taxes prevented voting rights.

   C discrimination and segregation still made life difficult.

   D the Homestead Act provided 160 acres of free land.

6 **In Western states in the mid- to late-1800s, opportunities for African Americans were often negated or overshadowed by**

   A literacy tests.

   B working off debts.

   C Jim Crow laws.

   D poll taxes.

REVIEW

CALIFORNIA CONTENT
STANDARD 8.11.3

African Americans after the Civil War

Specific Objective: Understand the effects of the Freedmen's Bureau and the restrictions placed on the rights and opportunities of freedmen, including racial segregation and "Jim Crow" laws.

Read the summary below to answer the questions on the next page.

Freedmen's Bureau of 1865 set up to help African Americans.

- Established schools and hospitals and distributed clothes, food, and fuel for African Americans.
- Helped African Americans gain economic independence by teaching them skills to find jobs and vote.

Black codes passed to limit rights of African Americans.

- Required written proof of employment or a person could be forced to work on a plantation.
- Barred African Americans from meeting in unsupervised groups.

Contract System kept African Americans bound to the land.

- African Americans returned to work on plantations, not as enslaved people, but as wage earners.
- Laws punished workers for breaking contracts, even if workers were being mistreated.
- Workers could not leave plantations without permission.

Sharecropping kept African Americans in poverty.

- A worker rented a plot of land, promised a share of his crops to the landowner.
- The landowner sold food and clothing to the sharecropper on credit.
- Often the sharecropper ended the season owing money to the landowner.
- Sharecroppers wanted to grow food for their families; landowners forced them to grow cash crops.

Voting Laws and Poll Taxes kept African Americans from voting.

- Reading test required in order to vote.
- People charged a **poll tax**—a fee for registering or voting that African Americans could not pay.
- To allow poor whites to vote, grandfather clause said if you or your ancestor had been eligible to vote before 1867, you didn't have to pass a test or pay a tax.

Jim Crow laws made segregation official in the South.

- Supreme Court decision in *Plessy* v. *Ferguson* (1896) ruled that segregation was lawful provided that blacks and whites had access to equal facilities.
- End result of Jim Crow and *Plessy* v. *Ferguson* was that whites and blacks had separate schools, separate public facilities, and separate entrances to stores and public building.

PRACTICE

CALIFORNIA CONTENT
STANDARD 8.11.3

African Americans after the Civil War

Directions: Choose the letter of the *best* answer.

1 Black codes were designed to

A help African Americans get jobs.

B get cheap laborers for landowners.

C make voting easier for African Americans.

D limit the rights of African Americans.

2 The Freedmen's Bureau helped African Americans

A buy land in the West.

B get an education.

C buy old plantations.

D move to the North.

3 Reading tests and poll taxes made it harder for

A people to cheat at the polls.

B whites to take advantage of blacks.

C African Americans to vote.

D politicians to trick voters.

4 Although the end of the Civil War signaled an end of slavery, the South continued segregation due to

A the Freedmen's Bureau.

B the plantation system.

C Jim Crow laws.

D grandfather clauses.

5 The sharecropper system kept many African-American families

A in debt to landowners.

B away from the polls.

C from reuniting after the war.

D from attending school.

6 The Supreme Court decision in *Plessy* v. *Ferguson* (1896) supported

A Reconstruction.

B the Freedmen's Bureau.

C Jim Crow Laws.

D the Ku Klux Klan.

REVIEW

CALIFORNIA CONTENT
STANDARD 8.11.4

The Rise of the Ku Klux Klan

Specific Objective: Trace the rise of the Ku Klux Klan and describe the Klan's effects.

Read the summary below to answer the questions on the next page.

Origins and Goals

- Founded in 1866 in Tennessee as a secret social fraternity
- First Grand Wizard was a former Confederate general, Nathan Bedford Forrest, who turned the Klan into an instrument of terror in 1867
- Initial Goals—remove radical Republicans (who wanted to help African Americans) from control of South, restore Democratic control, and keep African Americans from gaining power

Methods

- Targeted African Americans and some white Republicans, mostly in rural areas of South
- Came at night, dragging people from their homes
- Used beatings, house burnings, lynchings
- Dressed in white robes with hoods to hide their faces

Success

- No protection for victims; no help from law officials
- Supported by racist Southerners; frightened those who wanted to help
- President Andrew Johnson had appointed many of the military authorities in the South. They were against Reconstruction and would not help victims of the Klan.
- By scaring African Americans and white Republicans away from the polls, the Klan successfully increased its power.

President Grant and the Klan

- In 1868, African Americans in the South helped Republican Ulysses S. Grant become president, despite attacks by the Klan.
- To ensure that African Americans would be able to vote in future elections, Republicans passed the 15th Amendment, which guaranteed the right to vote to African-American men.
- The 15th amendment, ratified in 1870, was not enough to stop Klan intimidation and violence.
- With the backing of President Grant, Congress passed a tough anti-Klan law in 1871.
- Federal marshals then arrested thousands of Klansmen.
- With the Klan held in check, the elections of 1872 were free, fair, and peaceful across the South. Grant won a second term.
- Unfortunately, the Klan would rise again in future years.

PRACTICE

CALIFORNIA CONTENT
STANDARD 8.11.4

The Rise of the Ku Klux Klan

Directions: Choose the letter of the *best* answer.

1 *One* of the goals of the Klan was to

 A convince African Americans to leave the South.

 B encourage the South to secede from the Union again.

 C keep African Americans from voting.

 D improve living conditions for everyone in the South.

2 How did President Andrew Johnson's actions affect the power of the Klan?

 A The military authorities he appointed did nothing to stop Klan violence.

 B Johnson had federal marshals arrest thousands of Klan leaders.

 C The president was a former Klansman and helped them gain power.

 D Johnson urged Congress to pass anti-Klan laws.

3 In the 1800s to early 1900s, what legal justice could people attacked by the Klan obtain?

 A a hearing with fines and penalties for the attackers

 B charges brought by local police against the attackers

 C a lawsuit for damages filed against the attackers

 D absolute injustice, as the law sided with attackers

4 The anti-Klan bill Congress passed in 1871

 A had little or no effect on the Klan.

 B was enforced in the North but not the South.

 C was strongly protested by President Grant.

 D helped ensure a fair election in 1872.

5 How was President Grant's anti-Klan bill of 1871 enforced?

 A by local police officers

 B by groups of local militias

 C by the U. S. Army

 D by federal marshals

6 The Ku Klux Klan supported the Democratic Party because Democrats

 A had supported Reconstruction.

 B wanted whites to control the South.

 C controlled the House and the Senate.

 D had more power in the North.

REVIEW

CALIFORNIA CONTENT
STANDARD 8.11.5

The Constitution and Reconstruction

Specific Objective: Understand the Thirteenth, Fourteenth, and Fifteenth Amendments to the Constitution and analyze their connection to Reconstruction.

Read the summary below to answer the questions on the next page.

Changing the Constitution

Sometimes it is necessary to amend, or formally change, the Constitution to adapt to social change and historical trends, such as the end of slavery. That was the case with the Thirteenth, Fourteenth, and Fifteenth amendments. These amendments were an important part of Reconstruction. The Republicans wanted equality to be protected by the Constitution itself.

Thirteenth Amendment (1865)

- It ended slavery in the United States.
- Lincoln's Emancipation Proclamation applied to enslaved people in the Confederacy. Many African Americans in the border states were still enslaved. The Thirteenth Amendment banned slavery in every part of the country.

Fourteenth Amendment (1868)

- It stated that all people born in the United States were citizens and had the same rights.
- All citizens, including African Americans, were to be granted "equal protection of the laws."

Fifteenth Amendment (1870)

- Citizens could not be stopped from voting "on account of race, color, or previous condition of servitude."
- The Fifteenth Amendment was not aimed only at the South. African-American men had not been allowed to vote in 16 states. With this amendment, the nation turned more toward democracy.

Outcome of the Amendments

- In most cases, the success of these amendments was limited. White Southerners could not bring back slavery. However, they did everything in their power to make sure that the new amendments were not enforced in the South. They intimidated former enslaved people and prevented them from voting, and they violated the civil rights of black Southerners in other ways.
- The amendments did not apply to women or Native Americans living on tribal lands.
- It would be almost 100 years before African Americans would truly gain civil rights. It would not be until 1920 that women would gain the right to vote.

PRACTICE

CALIFORNIA CONTENT
STANDARD 8.11.5

The Constitution and Reconstruction

Directions: Choose the letter of the *best* answer.

1 Congress passed the Thirteenth Amendment because

A The Emancipation Proclamation only applied to the Confederate states.

B President Johnson had repealed the Emancipation Proclamation.

C The Emancipation Proclamation had been declared unconstitutional.

D President Lincoln had rescinded the Emancipation Proclamation before he died.

2 In the aftermath of the Thirteenth, Fourteenth, and Fifteenth Amendments, African Americans living in the South were

A welcomed into Southern society.

B still discriminated against, sometimes violently.

C without legal voting rights.

D doing well economically, and able to vote.

3 What was a consequence, or outcome, of the Fifteenth Amendment?

A All former enslaved people became citizens.

B White Southerners found ways of preventing African Americans from voting.

C Women finally acquired the same political rights as men.

D Slavery finally came to an end.

4. The Fourteenth Amendment states that anyone born in the United States is a citizen who is

A entitled to the right to vote.

B guaranteed equal protection under the law.

C responsible for performing military service.

D eligible to run for president.

5 During what period in the history of the United States were the Thirteenth, Fourteenth, and Fifteenth amendments passed?

A during the Civil War.

B during Reconstruction

C during the period leading up to the Civil War

D when the Founding Fathers were writing the Constitution

6 What do the Thirteenth, Fourteenth, and Fifteenth amendments all have in common?

A They ended the Civil War.

B They increased the power of the Southern states.

C They granted civil rights to soldiers who had fought for the Confederacy.

D They were intended to correct injustices created by slavery in the United States.

REVIEW

CALIFORNIA CONTENT
STANDARD 8.12.1

Agricultural and Industrial Development

Specific Objective: Trace the patterns of agricultural and industrial development as they relate to climate, use of natural resources, markets, and trade and locate such developments on a map.

Read the summary below to answer the questions on the next page.

After the Civil War, which ended in 1865, agricultural and industrial development soared in the United States. In particular, the period 1878 to 1898 was one of tremendous growth. Industry and agriculture expanded together. Some are the factors that influenced growth and innovation:

- Abundant natural resources, such as lumber, water, and minerals, were used to manufacture a variety of goods. Deposits of coal, iron, and oil fueled the growth of industry. Settlement and mining in the West created a demand for better transportation.

- Gold and silver, from mines in the West, provided money that could be invested in industry in the East.

- Population growth created demand. The U.S. population grew from 31.5 million in 1860 to 76 million in 1900. This growth created a huge market.

- Improvements in transportation meant raw materials and manufactured goods could be moved from one part of the country to another. In 1869 the first transcontinental railroad line was completed, stretching across North America. From 1880 to 1890, the miles of railroad track more than double in the West and South.

- Many of the lines went through Chicago where meat packing could grow as an industry. As a result, Chicago became a transportation center.

- The high demand for steel rails led to the growth of the steel industry.

- A wide variety of agricultural products could be grown thanks to different climate zones. Cotton, rice, sugar cane and tobacco were grown in the South; corn and wheat in the Midwest; beef cattle and sheep in the Southwest; and fruit, wine, and wheat in the West.

- Industries developed regionally to take advantage of nearby agricultural products. For example, textile mills were built in the South, where cotton was produced. Flour mills were built in the Midwest, where wheat was grown. Railroads brought cattle from the West to meatpacking plants in the Midwest.

- Technological advances and inventions meant improved manufacturing and farming techniques, leading to further increased production.

Name _____ Date _____

Agricultural and Industrial Development

Directions: Choose the letter of the *best* answer.

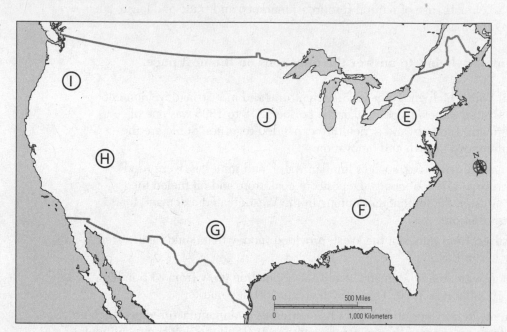

Use the map to answer questions 1 and 2.

1 By the 1890s, region *F* on the map had

A no industry but produced cotton, sugar cane, rice, and tobacco.

B a growing textile industry.

C a large number of flour mills and meatpacking plants.

D an economy based on enslaved labor.

2 Beef cattle, raised on ranches, were most likely to be found in which area on the map?

A area *E*

B area *F*

C area *G*

D area *J*

3 What *direct* impact did the development of the railroads have on the Midwest?

A Chicago became an important transportation hub.

B Southern states sent their cotton to textile mills in Chicago.

C New kinds of crops could now be grown in the Midwest.

D The Midwest was slower to develop than the West.

4 How did settlement of the West affect industrial development in the East?

A Businesses in the East began to fail because of greater competition.

B Gold and silver from Western mines provided money for Eastern industry.

C Many people moved west and created a labor shortage in the East.

D Eastern industry slowed down to allow the West time to catch up.

REVIEW

CALIFORNIA CONTENT
STANDARD 8.12.2

Federal Indian Policy

Specific Objective: Identify reasons for the development of federal Indian policy and the relationship of Native Americans to agricultural development and industrialization.

Read the summary and map to answer questions on the next page.

Federal Indian policy after the Civil War was driven by the continuing demand for land. American Indians of the Southeast were moved west in the 1830s. New agricultural inventions helped settlers farm this land.

The Indian Wars In the 1850s, gold and silver were discovered in the West. By the 1870s, much of Indian Territory had been invaded by settlers and miners. The government frequently broke treaties and promises. A series of wars lasted from 1864 through 1890. By the 1880's, most Plains Indians had been forced onto reservations.

"Americanizing" Some reformers believed that the best way to help the Indians survive was to make Native Americans like whites—to "Americanize" them. In 1887, the **Dawes Act** encouraged American Indians to give up their traditional ways and become farmers. In the end, the act only harmed Indian interests. Over time, many sold their land for a fraction of its real value.

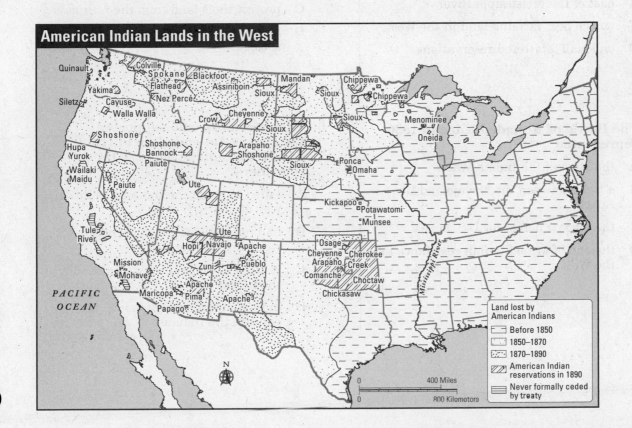

American Indian Lands in the West

PRACTICE

CALIFORNIA CONTENT
STANDARD 8.12.2

Federal Indian Policy

Directions: Choose the letter of the *best* answer.

Use the map on page 181 to answer
questions 1–3.

1 **Most American Indian land in the
West was lost**

   A before 1850.

   B between 1850 and 1870.

   C between 1870 and 1890.

   D after 1890.

2 **By 1890, most American Indian tribes
were living**

   A close to the U.S. border with Canada.

   B east of the Mississippi River.

   C on the best farming land in the West.

   D on small, scattered reservations.

3 **The Battle of Wounded Knee in 1890
represented**

   A the start of the Indian Wars.

   B a fight between the Navajo and the
Apache.

   C the biggest defeat for U.S. forces.

   D the end of armed Indian resistance in
the West.

4 **The *main* reason behind federal
Indian policy of the late 1800s was
the desire**

   A to educate whites about Indians.

   B to gain access to Indian land.

   C to protect the Indians from whites.

   D to prevent intertribal warfare.

5 **Reformers hoped that the Dawes Act
of 1887 would help American Indians**

   A preserve their traditional way of life.

   B make more profit from selling their
land.

   C protect their land from the railroads.

   D become part of mainstream American
society.

6 **The reformers who supported
the Dawes Act ended up hurting
American Indians because the
reformers**

   A failed to value the Indians' traditional
way of life.

   B had not realized that the Indians
were city dwellers.

   C refused to allow the Indians to sell
their land.

   D did not spend enough money to
educate the Indians.

REVIEW

CALIFORNIA CONTENT
STANDARD 8.12.3

Government Support of Business

Specific Objective: Explain how states and the federal government encouraged business expansion through tariffs, banking, land grants, and subsidies.

Read the summary to answer the questions on the next page.

The Growth of Government Power

Government played an active role in the rapid expansion of industry after the Civil War. In order to deal with the demands of the war, the national government had grown larger and more powerful. Its strength continued to grow after the war was over. The government used its increased power and resources to encourage business expansion.

Federal Banking System

Andrew Jackson vetoed the charter of the Second National Bank in 1832. As a result, by 1860 there were more than 10,000 different types of bank notes in the country. Many banks failed. People wanted a single national currency. A national currency would be acceptable anywhere in the country without risk. Congress responded in 1863 and 1864 with the **National Currency Act** and the **National Bank Act.** These acts established a new system of national banks. The system was safer, simpler, and more secure. Having a national banking system helped businesses and industry to grow. It especially helped those, like railroads, that operated in many states.

Tariffs

Tariffs on imported materials and goods protected U.S. producers from foreign competition. Such tariffs meant that imported goods cost more. They made it easier for U.S. industries to expand and prosper. Tariffs generally favored industry over agriculture. There was ongoing debate over these policies.

Land grants and Subsidies

The government used land grants to encourage settlement and business development in the West. The industry that the government helped the most was the railroads. The railroads received land grants, loans, and subsidies (financial aid). The **Bureau of Land Management** estimated that 80 railroads received title to federal land about twice the size of Colorado. In 1862 Congress passed a bill calling for two companies to build a **transcontinental railroad** that would join the Central Pacific in the West and the Union Pacific in the East and stretch across North America. The line was completed in 1869 in Utah.

PRACTICE

CALIFORNIA CONTENT
STANDARD 8.12.3

Government Support of Business

Directions: Choose the letter of the *best* answer.

1 **After the Civil War, the federal government was**

A too weak to get involved in expanding business.

B careful not to give any Western land away for free.

C willing to play a strong role in supporting industry.

D against giving subsidies (aid) to particular companies.

2 **A national banking system was better for business because it**

A explained clearly the value of all the different local currencies.

B gave more power to the local governments.

C made banking less risky and kept banks from failing.

D allowed each state to have its own currency.

3 **Tariffs in the late 1800s helped to**

A protect American industries from foreign competition.

B make imports more affordable.

C make it easier for farmers to export their harvests.

D ease negotiations between workers and owners of industry.

4 **The U.S. government encouraged the building of a transcontinental railroad, knowing the completed line would**

A be the longest rail line in the world.

B keep the South from winning the Civil War.

C encourage settlement and development of the West.

D stop American Indian attacks on settlers.

5 **The U.S. government gave the Union and Central Pacific railroads monetary aid for each mile of track they built, in order to encourage them to**

A choose the shortest route.

B build as quickly as possible.

C fight with each other.

D head for Utah.

6 **The U.S. government gave land grants to railroad companies so that**

A tracks could pass through government-owned land.

B the government would not have to give the companies loans.

C the companies would be motivated to work harder.

D the companies would know where to put the railroad lines.

REVIEW

CALIFORNIA CONTENT
STANDARD 8.12.4

Leaders in Industry

Specific Objective: Discuss entrepreneurs, industrialists, and bankers in politics, commerce, and industry.

Read the summary and table below to answer questions on the next page.

Magnates and Philanthropists

The end of the 18th century and beginning of the 19th century saw the age of the magnate. A magnate is a powerful leader in industry. Some of these men used questionable business practices and were known as robber barons. At the same time, most were also philanthropists, people who give large sums of money to charities.

Early Life	Business Dealings	Philanthropy
Andrew Carnegie (1835–1919)		
• From Scotland; worked in textile mill at 13	• 1873 the Carnegie Company • Controlled steel industry; made best and cheapest product. • Cuts in workers wages led to violent Homestead strike of 1892	• Gospel of Wealth: duty to use money to help others • Donated about $350 million, especially to universities and libraries
John D. Rockefeller (1839–1937)		
• Born to poor family in upstate New York	• Built his first oil refinery in 1863 • Formed monopoly, Standard Oil Trust in 1882; controlled 95% of oil refining in U.S. • Reputation as a robber baron	• Gave away $500 million to worthy causes
Leland Stanford (1824–1893)		
• Born to wealthy family New York • Trained as lawyer	• One of Big Four entrepreneurs (a person who assumes risk for questionable business deals); built the Central Pacific Railroad • Eighth governor of California	• Founded Stanford University in honor of his young son, who had died of typhoid fever
John Pierpont Morgan (1837–1913)		
• Born to wealth in Connecticut	• J. P. Morgan & Co. powerful banking house • Financed U.S. Steel, which bought out Carnegie Steel; worlds first billion-dollar company	• Gave money to museums and Harvard University

Copyright © McDougal Littell/Houghton Mifflin Company

Name _____   Date _____

Leaders in Industry

Directions: Choose the letter of the *best* answer.

Cartoon appearing in *Puck* magazine, January 23, 1889

1 **According to the cartoon, people like John D. Rockefeller**

A have too much influence on government.

B should only work in the oil industry.

C should run for Congress.

D have too much interest in business.

2 **Andrew Carnegie, John D. Rockefeller, Leland Stanford, and J.P. Morgan were all**

A successful politicians.

B involved in the banking industry.

C powerful magnates.

D military officers.

3 **John D. Rockefeller formed the Standard Oil Trust. The purpose of a trust was to**

A control a particular industry.

B avoid paying taxes.

C promote small businesses.

D earn money for lawyers.

4 **Leland Stanford was one of the "Big Four" who built**

A Standard Oil Trust.

B the California state capitol.

C Hearst Castle.

D the Central Pacific Railroad.

Name _____ Date _____

Specific Objective: Examine the location and effects of urbanization, renewed immigration, and industrialization.

Read the summary below to answer the questions on the next page.

Industrialization

- **Plentiful natural resources:** forests, large water supplies, coal, iron, silver and gold increased factory production, which spread beyond Northeast
- **Corporations:** larger and more impersonal
- **Industrialization:** led to **urbanization** as people moved to cities for jobs

Urbanization

- **Industries:** drawn to cities because of good transportation and plentiful workers
- **High immigration:** newcomers from other lands settled in cities
- **New technology:** skyscraper, elevator, and electric street cars helped cities absorb millions
- **Streetcars and railroads:** spread outward from city's center, creating suburbs

Immigration

- **New wave of immigrants (after 1890):** from Southern and Eastern Europe
- **Eastern-European and Italian Immigrants:** settled near where they landed—Ellis Island, New York City
- **Asian immigrants:** settled in northern California near where they arrived at Angel Island, San Francisco, California
- **Jobs:** took low-paying jobs in cities

Effects of Urbanization

- **Overcrowding:** caused disasters, such as fires
- **Political machines** (organizations that control local governments): seized control of major cities, broke rules, accepted bribes, stole money; also built parks and schools and helped immigrants
- **City slums:** garbage in streets, no running water, open sewage
- **Mass culture:** World's Fairs, amusement parks, and baseball

The Conservation Movement

- **Environment:** threatened by growth of industry and cities
- **President Theodore Roosevelt:** loved the out-of-doors; crusaded for conservation and preservation
- **Public lands:** preserved more than 200 million acres
- **Wildlife refuge:** established first refuge for wildlife conservation and protection
- **National parks:** doubled number of parks

Name _____ Date _____

Urbanization and Industrialization

Directions: Choose the letter of the *best* answer.

Use the graph to answer questions 1 and 2.

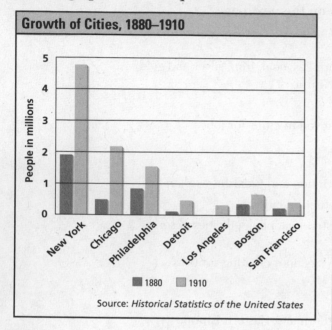

Growth of Cities, 1880–1910

People in millions

New York · Chicago · Philadelphia · Detroit · Los Angeles · Boston · San Francisco

■ 1880   ■ 1910

Source: *Historical Statistics of the United States*

Use the graph to answer questions 3 and 4.

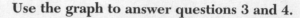

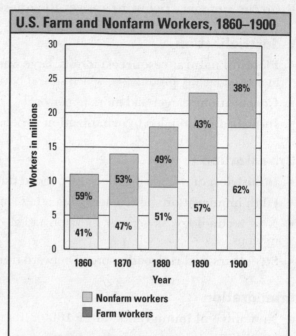

U.S. Farm and Nonfarm Workers, 1860–1900

Workers in millions

1860: 59% / 41%
1870: 53% / 47%
1880: 49% / 51%
1890: 43% / 57%
1900: 38% / 62%

Year

□ Nonfarm workers
■ Farm workers

1 Which *two* cities show the greatest population increase between 1880 and 1910?

  A New York and San Francisco

  B Philadelphia and New York

  C Chicago and New York

  D Philadelphia and San Francisco

2 Based on the graph, which city's population increased by the greatest amount between 1880 and 1910?

  A Chicago

  B New York

  C Boston

  D Philadelphia

3 Which statement describes the trend shown on the graph?

  A The number of cities declined.

  B There was less factory employment.

  C There were fewer farm workers.

  D Factory workers' wages declined.

4 How did immigration affect California during the period shown on the graph?

  A Immigrants from Southern Europe often traveled to California.

  B Many Asian immigrants settled in northern California.

  C Most immigrants to California settled elsewhere.

  D Few immigrants came to California during this period.

Name _____ Date _____

REVIEW

CALIFORNIA CONTENT
STANDARD 8.12.6

The Labor Movement

Specific Objective: Discuss child labor, working conditions, and laissez-faire policies toward big business. Examine the labor movement, including its leaders, its demand for collective bargaining, and its strikes and protests over labor conditions.

Read the chart below to answer the questions on the next page.

Child Labor	Working Conditions
• 1.5 million children (10–15 years old) working in 1890 • Children paid very little; half of what adults made	• Crowded factories and sweatshops; no safety equipment • Long hours; hard work; low wages; no sick leave; no health insurance • 2,000 railroad workers killed every year

Laissez-Faire Policies	The Labor Movement
• **Laissez-faire (French for "allow to do"):** government "hands-off" approach toward businesses • **Beliefs of Laissez-Faire:** business, if unregulated, would benefit nation • **Government and labor:** did not help labor, even when practices were unfair or dangerous • **Government and business:** used tariffs, land grants, and subsidies to help businesses • **Corporations:** not regulated • **Existing laws:** not well enforced	• **Unions formed:** only a union of all workers in an industry had collective bargaining power to force a company to listen • **Strikes and boycotts:** used to get attention of business owners

Leaders	Strikes and Protests
• **Mary Harris "Mother" Jones:** dedicated labor leader; worked especially for coal miners and against child labor • **Samuel Gompers:** founded the American Federation of Labor (AFL) in 1886; improved working conditions; had 1.7 million members by 1904 • **Eugene V. Debs:** president of American Railway Union; jailed when he called a strike after the Pullman Company refused to negotiate	• **Railroad strike 1877:** begun by workers rather than a union; disrupted entire country; did not prevent a pay cut but showed workers' anger • **Union Pacific railroad 1884:** strike organized and won by Knights of Labor; inspired hundreds of thousands of workers to join the union • **Haymarket Affair 1886:** strike in Chicago turned violent; police and striking workers killed • **Homestead strike 1892:** against a Carnegie-owned steel mill in Pennsylvania; union members locked out; violent battle; state militia escorted nonunion members to work for four months; broke the union • **Pullman strike 1894:** started with Pullman workers being cheated; spread to entire rail industry; brought rail traffic to a halt; President Cleveland stepped in; jailed Eugene V. Debs

Copyright © McDougal Littell/Houghton Mifflin Company

Name _____   Date _____

The Labor Movement

Directions: Choose the letter of the *best* answer.

1 Labor unions give workers the power of

  A collective bargaining.

  B regulations.

  C factory ownership

  D *laissez-faire* policies.

2 When government adopts *laissez-faire* policies toward big business, it

  A uses the courts to limit the size of corporations.

  B employs union leaders.

  C uses tariffs to limit competition.

  D adopts a hands-off attitude toward business regulation.

"The workers asked only for bread and a shortening of long hours of toil. The agitators gave them visions. The police gave them clubs."

—*The Autobiography of Mother Jones* (1925)

---

3 It is clear from her words that Mother Jones believed the demands of the workers were

  A within reason.

  B met with concern.

  C presented falsely.

  D inviting danger.

4 Which statement about working conditions in the late 1800s is *true*?

  A Workers received basic health insurance.

  B Factories were small and had few workers.

  C Only men could work in factories.

  D Factory work was hard and dangerous.

5 Which statement is *true* of strikes in the late 1800s?

  A They were frequently held over minor issues.

  B They could turn violent.

  C Workers gave up too quickly.

  D Workers demands were usually met.

6 The American Federation of Labor was founded by

  A Andrew Carnegie.

  B Eugene V. Debs.

  C Samuel Gompers.

  D Mother Jones.

Name _____   Date _____

REVIEW

CALIFORNIA CONTENT
STANDARD 8.12.7

Immigrants in the Industrial Age

Specific Objective: Identify the new sources of large-scale immigration and the contributions of immigrants to the building of cities and the economy. Explain the ways in which new social and economic patterns encouraged assimilation of newcomers into the mainstream amidst growing cultural diversity. Discuss the new wave of nativism.

Read the summary below to answer the questions on the next page.

The New Immigrants

The new wave of immigrants after 1890 did not come from Northern and Western Europe as previous immigrants had.

- Southern Italians, Jews from Eastern Europe, and Slavic people from Poland and Russia came through Ellis Island in New York City.
- Asians came through Angel Island in San Francisco, California.
- Mexicans came across the U.S. border into Texas.

Immigrant Contributions

- Helped New York, Boston, Philadelphia, Pittsburgh, and Chicago grow
- About half settled in Massachusetts, New York, Pennsylvania, and Illinois
- Pooled money to open houses of worship and publish newspapers
- Supported politicians from their native country who helped them find jobs
- **Japanese and Chinese:** settled in West; many Chinese helped build railroads; others opened restaurants and stores in Western cities
- **Mexicans:** came north, especially after the Mexican Revolution in 1910; took jobs on farms, ranches, and in mines in Texas and California

New Patterns

- Immigrants quickly settled into low-paying jobs in cities.
- Employers and labor unions helped them learn to speak and read English, and taught them how to be Americans.
- In turn, the immigrants' native cultures rubbed off on America, e.g., ethnic food, music, and language.

Nativism

- Many native-born Americans were afraid immigrants would take their jobs.
- They also distrusted political machines controlled by immigrants.
- Many wanted the borders closed, especially to non-white immigrants.
- The Chinese Exclusion Act of 1882 banned Chinese immigration for ten years.

PRACTICE

CALIFORNIA CONTENT
STANDARD 8.12.7

Immigrants in the Industrial Age

Directions: Choose the letter of the *best* answer.

1 Immigrants to the United States from Southern and Eastern Europe during the Industrial Age tended to settle in the

A Midwest.

B Northeast.

C South.

D West.

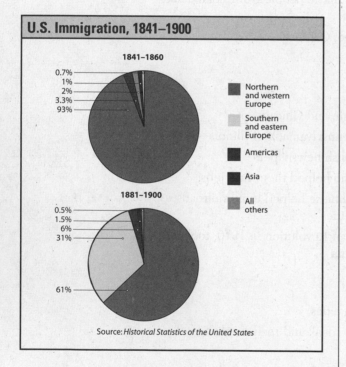

U.S. Immigration, 1841–1900

1841–1860

0.7%
1%
2%
3.3%
93%

■ Northern and western Europe
■ Southern and eastern Europe
■ Americas
■ Asia
■ All others

1881–1900

0.5%
1.5%
6%
31%
61%

Source: *Historical Statistics of the United States*

2 From the circle graphs, it is clear that the immigrant group that *increased* the most after 1881 was from

A the Americas.

B Asia.

C Northern and Western Europe.

D Southern and Eastern Europe.

3 One sign of a rise in nativism in the late 19th and early 20th centuries was

A hiring Chinese laborers to build the railroads.

B the opening of Ellis and Angel Islands.

C the passage of the Chinese Exclusion Act.

D teaching English to immigrants.

4 Which statement *best* describes the kinds of jobs new immigrants took?

A They transfered skills into a variety of professional jobs.

B They tended to obtain small land parcels and become farmers.

C They took whatever low-paying jobs they could find.

D Most immigrants ran their own businesses.

5 Immigrants have added their food, music, and words to American culture. This shows that

A there is no common culture in America.

B immigrants to America abandoned their native cultures.

C immigrants have enriched American culture.

D Americans had no prejudice against immigrants.

REVIEW

CALIFORNIA CONTENT
STANDARD 8.12.8

Grangerism and Populism

Specific Objective: Identify the characteristics and impact of Grangerism and Populism.

Read the summary below to answer the questions on the next page.

Grangerism

- **The Grange:** officially known as Patrons of Husbandry; formed in 1867
- **Original purpose:** social group for farm families
- **Formed cooperatives:** group-owned organizations that bought grain elevators and sold directly to merchants; allowed farmers to keep profits
- **Demands:** wanted states to regulate railroad rates; argument went to Supreme Court
- **Victory for Grange:** *Munn* v. *Illinois* (1877); court ruled that government could regulate businesses that serve public interest; paved way for other limits on big business

Populism

- **Farm productivity:** led to surplus of food, driving prices down; farmers needed money to pay back loans for new machinery
- **Populist Party (or Pcoplc's Party):** formed by farmers in 1890; backed free silver
- **Free silver policy:** called for unlimited coining of silver; leading to inflation; meant higher prices for crops
- **Gold standard policy:** against free silver; government backs every dollar with gold; gold supply limited so fewer dollars in circulation; keeps prices down; backed by bankers, and business leaders
- **Election of 1892:** John B. Weaver—Populist Party candidate; got more than one million votes; showed strength of movement
- **Election of 1896:** Populists joined Democrats in supporting William Jennings Bryan (free silver) versus Republican William McKinley (gold standard)
- **William Jennings Bryan:** argued for free silver; fought for reforms that later became law—8-hour workday and suffrage for women
- **Winner of 1896 election:** William McKinley; beginning of end of Populists Party

Name _____   Date _____

Directions: Choose the letter of the *best* answer.

1 The Populist Party was organized by

A bankers.

B communists.

C farmers.

D women.

2 Populists favored free silver because

A it would decrease the money supply.

B they supported bankers.

C they invested in silver mines.

D it would mean higher prices.

3 The efforts of the Grange in the late 1800s led to

A regulation of railroad prices.

B state-owned grain elevators.

C the dismantling of the rail industry.

D cooperatively owned railroads.

4 William Jennings Bryan had an impact on American history because he

A was backed by wealthy bankers.

B supported the gold standard.

C was a Populist president.

D spoke for Populist reforms.

5 The Grange formed cooperatives. These were organizations

A that supported William McKinley.

B owned and run by farmers.

C that supported big business.

D dedicated to the gold standard.

6 The Supreme Court decision in *Munn* v. *Illinois* most benefited

A bankers.

B factory owners.

C farmers.

D railroads.

Name _____   Date _____

REVIEW

CALIFORNIA CONTENT
STANDARD 8.12.9

Important Inventors and Inventions

Specific Objective: Name the significant inventors and their inventions and identify how they improved the quality of life.

Read the chart below to answer the questions on the next page.

Late Nineteenth-Century Inventions

There were thousands of inventions in the late 19th century. Some made life easier or more pleasant in small ways (cold cereal, golf tee, fountain pen, paper cup, player piano, the zipper, desk-top pencil sharpener, dishwasher, vacuum cleaner, double-edge safety razor, dust pan) and some changed our way of life forever.

Inventor	Invention	Improvement in Quality of Life
Thomas Edison	• Usable light bulb (1880) • Way to deliver electricity to buildings	• Safe, practical electricity for homes and businesses • Electric power for machines and streetcars • Opened world to electrical inventions • Beginning of recorded entertainment
Alexander Graham Bell	• Phonograph • Motion pictures • Telephone (1876)	• People could communicate from a distance using speech • Switchboards allowed businesses to connect many phones • Created new jobs for women
Orville and Wilbur Wright	• First flight by a powered aircraft (1903)	• Shortened travel times • Airmail transported goods more quickly
Christopher Latham Sholes	• Typewriter (1867)	• Improved business communication • Opened new jobs for women
Henry Bessemer and William Kelly	• Bessemer steel process (c. 1850)	• Increased steel output • Made steel stronger and more durable than iron; made many products better • Allowed new forms of building, such as skyscrapers
George Eastman	• Kodak camera (1888)	• Enabled ordinary people to take photographs • Helped create photojournalism
Elias Howe	• Sewing machine (1846)	• Mass production of shoes and clothes • More people could afford store-bought clothes

Name _____   Date _____

Important Inventors and Inventions

Directions: Choose the letter of the *best* answer.

"The first message of the telephone
was: 'Mr. Watson, please come here,
I want you.'"

—the words of Alexander Graham Bell's assistant,
Thomas A. Watson

1 This brief message from Bell to his assistant was important because it

A was the first sound recording.

B showed that people could send speech over a distance.

C led to the invention of electricity.

D signaled a new way that people could use the telegraph.

2 Which invention quickly opened more jobs for women?

A airplane

B camera

C light bulb

D typewriter

3 The inventor responsible for changing the kind of power used in factories was

A George Eastman

B Thomas Edison

C Christopher Latham Scholes

D Orville Wright

4 How did Elias Howe's invention of the sewing machine transform American life in the late 19th and early 20th centuries?

A Clothing styles became limited to basic colors and simple patterns.

B Fewer people were needed in factories to produce the same amount of clothing.

C Clothes from stores and catalogs became widely available and affordable.

D More people made their own clothes instead of buying them.

5 An important effect of the Bessemer steel process was

A the growth of skyscrapers.

B improvement in communication.

C the invention of electricity.

D growth of the clothing industry.